This book is dedicated to the memory of Oscar Pease, fisherman of Edgartown,
and to that of his wife, Nellie.

Published by Devereux Books
PO Box 503
Marblehead, MA 01945

Internet address: www.devereuxbooks.com

Library of Congress Cataloging in Publication Data

Grayson, Stan, 1945 –
Cape Cod Catboats
ISBN 0-928862-05-5
1. Cape Cod Catboats — History.   I. Title
VM311.C3373 2002
623.8'22   83-26440

Book design by Alyssa Morris
Printed in Singapore

TABLE OF CONTENTS

— •◆• —

ACKNOWLEDGEMENTS

——— •◆• ———

QUITE A NUMBER OF PEOPLE shared with me their memories, experience, and the occasional photograph. They are listed alphabetically and include: Jon and Roxane Agne, Dave Biddle, Wayne Blake, Arthur Bloomer, Philip Carling, Thalia Cartwright, William Coleman, John and Tally Garfield, Merv Hammat, Doug Goldhirsch, Mark Harper, Dave Jenney, Robert Luckraft, Bill Menger, Paul Morris, Joe Nickerson, Mike O'Brien, Charles O'Donnell, Adrian Offinger, Bob Reddington, Bill Sayle, Al Terry, Jr., and Alan Vaitses. A special thanks to Townsend Hornor and Lewie Howland who read and commented on the manuscript and to Paul O'Pecko at the Mystic Seaport Museum Library.

Organizations that were of special assistance include, in Massachusetts: the Bourne Archives, Chatham Historical Society, Martha's Vineyard Historical Society, Quincy Historical Society, Marie Henke at the Nantucket Historical Society, Cindy Nickerson at the Cahoon Museum of American Art in Cotuit, the Society for the Preservation of New England Antiquities, the Osterville Historical Society, and the Hart Nautical Collections at the MIT Museum. The library staff at the Peabody Essex Museum was always helpful. In Rhode Island, thanks to the Herreshoff Marine Museum, Jill Ridell at the Museum of Yachting, and Clark Poston at the International Yacht Restoration School.

Finally, a special thanks to all those boat owners who participated in the survey for the chapters on production daysailers and cabin catboats, and those whose stories appear in Chapter 10.

Photo Credits

Courtesy of the Bourne Archives: 64-65, 70

Courtesy of the Cahoon Museum of American Art: 176-177

Courtesy of The Catboat Association: x, 8, 19, 112, 179 top

Courtesy of the Hart Nautical Collections at the MIT Museum: 47

Courtesy of the Martha's Vineyard Historical Society: 20, 25, 31, 33, 36

Courtesy of the Museum of Yachting: 119

Courtesy of Mystic Seaport Museum, Mystic, CT, Edward W. Smith Collection: 12, 38

Courtesy of the Nantucket Historical Society: 16, 23, 27, 30, 94, 158, 178

Courtesy of the Osterville Historical Society: 2-3, 49, 54, 124-125, 182-183

Courtesy of the Quincy Historical Society: 187

Courtesy of the Smithsonian Institution: 17

Courtesy of the Society for the Preservation of New England Antiquities: 61, 67, 100

Courtesy of Compass Classic Yachts: 131, 132

Courtesy of Ed Crabbe: 105

Courtesy of William Coleman: 167

Photographs by Tally Garfield: 121, 136, 150, 152

Courtesy of Douglas Goldhirsch: 169, 170

Photographs by Stan Grayson: 37, 106, 110, 134, 144, 179 bottom, 180, 181, 184-185, 186, 188, 189 (top left and bottom) 190

Photograph by Mark Harper: 161, 189 top right

Courtesy of Hutchins Co. Inc.: 145, 146

Courtesy of Lewie Howland: 114

Courtesy of Jimmy Kittredge: 128

Courtesy of Bill Menger: 133, 153, 155

Courtesy of Al Terry: 72, 73, 74, 75

Author's Collection: 4, 10, 29, 34, 50, 58, 62, 68, 69, 80-81, 84

A NOTE ON SOURCES

IN LATE 1982, as I was completing work on the first edition of *Catboats,* a chance remark resulted in my briefly meeting with a man who had once been an active part of the busy catboat scene at the Quincy Yacht Club in the years before and after World War One. He had even known the great boatbuilder, Charles C. Hanley. Within a few months of that meeting, C. Willis Garey, then in his 90s, passed away. In the years that I have spent researching catboats and their era, actually meeting a primary source such as Mr. Garey has been an extraordinary experience for me. One is fortunate, in fact, to occasionally track down a descendant of a 19th century catboat builder or sailor, and even more fortunate if surviving memories are reliable. Still, it occasionally happens and the fruits of such interviews are reflected in these pages as appropriate.

The biggest single source of research material exists in the pages of the boating magazines, principally *The Rudder,* but *Yachting, Motor Boating,* and others also have an important place. I have focused as much attention as possible on the work of key figures who wrote during the period of the mid-1890s to the mid-1930s. Generally, they were still close enough in time to the beginnings of the catboat's story to be worth the closest scrutiny.

Besides the magazines, the *Catboat Association Bulletin* was invaluable. In particular, the early issues were most useful. In them, John Leavens shared his research and discussions with the fast-dwindling number of old-timers who could speak with first-hand experience about the time when catboats were an everyday sight. Perhaps no one man did so much to preserve such knowledge as did John. Books that will be of special interest to researchers of yachting history, including the role of the catboat, include *Traditions and Memories of American Yachting* by William Picard

Stephens, and *Their Last Letters,* which presents important correspondence between Nathanael Greene Herreshoff and William Picard Stephens, annotated by John W. Streeter.

Plans sources: Those interested in plans for Fenwick Williams catboats should contact: Murray G. Peterson Associates, Inc., 48 Jones Point Road, South Bristol, ME 04568 (peterson@lincoln.midcoast.com). *WoodenBoat* offers plans for several catboats including designs by Charles Wittholz, Fenwick Williams, and Joel White. Plans for Phil Bolger's 12' 3" plywood catboat are available from Harold H. Payson & Co., Pleasant Beach Road, South Thomaston, ME 04858. www.instantboats.com. Brewer Yacht Designs (www.tedbrewer.com) offers plans for a hard-chine, 22-foot plywood catboat and a 25-foot model for traditional construction.

INTRODUCTION

—◆—

TODAY, ON CAPE COD, the image of the region's indigenous boat appears seemingly everywhere. It can be seen carved and then gilded in gold leaf on signs for everything from real estate agencies to insurance businesses, from antique shops to health clinics. Sometimes, even people who aren't sailors learn that these evocative little images represent the Cape Cod catboat, a vessel that, in some sense, has come to remind people of the uniqueness of their natural environment while recalling a past that has long since ceased to exist.

Only a relatively few boat types have ever become as closely associated with a specific geographical location as has the catboat with Cape Cod. Here, and at the islands of Martha's Vineyard and Nantucket, the catboat was once the boat of choice for fishermen. Later, when adapted as a racing and cruising yacht, the catboat's popularity quickly spread up and down the coast and, in fact, throughout the country.

The story of the catboat is long and wonderful. Here is a uniquely American boat whose design has seriously been ascribed to a 19th-century medium and a spiritualist's séance! Here is a boat that was the favorite for fishing of an American president, Grover Cleveland. Here is a boat that for well over half a century performed ably in a wide variety of different and difficult fisheries. In its most artful form, the catboat also provided racing sport for some of the country's wealthiest yachtsmen. At the same time, it made sailing accessible to people who might otherwise never have owned their own boat. So-called party boats, meanwhile, operated from New England to New Jersey. What's more, catboats possessed such inherent charm and appealing shapes that they became favorite subjects of photographers and artists. Among the latter, Edward Hopper's work stands out in particular.

Although examples of other important traditional American small craft exist in limited numbers, the catboat has been something of a phenomenon. Not only are a surprising number of wooden versions still sailing, but thousands of fiberglass models have been built. Today, new boats continue to be sold on a regular basis. That suggests something quite special about a boat type that dates back to the mid-19th century.

Why, when, and how did all this develop? What is the relationship both in time frame and substance of the Cape Cod catboat and catboats developed in the New York area and Rhode Island? Why do a surprising number of people still sail catboats today? This book presents the results of my ongoing search for the knowledge that would provide answers to those and many other questions.

A comment is in order regarding this book's title. Although the primary focus here is on the Cape Cod catboat, substantial attention is paid to the catboat as developed in the New York area and in Rhode Island. Why? The reason simply is that the Cape Cod catboat never existed in geographic isolation. Inspiration for key features of the type almost certainly came from elsewhere and, while distinct, the Cape Cod catboat was certainly influenced by important, earlier developments in the other locales. That said, a comparison of the classic Cape Cod cat to designs from other regions does much to explain why it is this version of the genre that has maintained the greatest popularity. In its overall blending of form and features, the Cape Cod catboat offers a timeless appeal that most other types do not.

Finally, I should add that while this book represents my latest research on the subject, I do not believe that it necessarily represents the final word. There almost certainly exists undiscovered material, a painting, letters, photographs, scrapbooks, or very old magazines, which will further add to our understanding of this magical subject.

Stan Grayson
Marblehead, Massachusetts
June 2002

A CATBOAT TIMELINE

— ◆ —

Circa 1830 - 1835 — Centerboard fishing boats emerge in the New York area that are at some point equipped with interchangeable rigs: jib and mainsail or mainsail only. It is likely that Andrew Crosby sees one of these boats during a voyage from his Cape Cod home to New York.

1833 — Charles Frederick Herreshoff designs and builds *Julia,* a mainsail-only, keel-type, small yacht of a pre-existing type known in Rhode Island as a "Point Boat."

1837 — Death of Andrew Crosby at Osterville, Massachusetts

Circa later 1840s — Mainsail-only centerboard boats are built for racing in the New York area.

1851 - 1852 — Bob Fish builds a mainsail-only racing boat with a centerboard that is named *Una* by her owner and is sent to England.

1859 — Charles Frederick Herreshoff and his sons John B. and Nathanael G. build the mainsail-only, centerboarder *Sprite* as a family yacht. The racing of such boats is extant in Narragansett Bay by this period.

Circa 1857 - 1860 — After an unknown period of development subsequent to their father's death, Charles W. and Horace S. Crosby refine a model that becomes the first commercially sold Crosby mainsail-only, centerboard boat. It is bought by a Chatham fisherman.

Circa 1860 — The name "catboat" is applied to the Crosbys' boat.

1865 — The Herreshoffs build at least two 16-foot mainsail-only centerboarders for racing.

1870 — The post-Civil War era of yachting witnesses an increasing variety of designs for boats that are now known more generally as "catboats." They are raced by professionals and some amateur sailors.

1872 — Founding of Beverly Yacht Club in Massachusetts to promote interest in the racing of small boats by amateur ("Corinthian") yachtsmen. Catboats predominate.

1873 — First Crosby catboat built as a yacht.

1875 — The racing of sloop and cat-rigged sandbaggers with shiftable ballast has become established as a popular sport.

1876 — Gil Smith establishes a boatshop at Patchogue, New York, with hope of selling his catboats to the increasing numbers of wealthy summer visitors to Long Island.

1878 — Catboat racing emerges as a regular feature of summertime activity at Mattapoisett, Massachusetts and other villages on Buzzards Bay. The name "catboat" now appears to be widely used to describe centerboard, mainsail-only boats.

1884 — Charles C. Hanley builds his first catboat, *Surprise,* at Monument Beach.

1889 — In a race sponsored by the Eastern Yacht Club in Marblehead, the C. C. Hanley-built *Harbinger* defeats two famous cutters and attracts new interest and enthusiasm for catboats and catboat racing.

1895 — Crosby Catboat and Yacht Building Company established in Brooklyn to build racing catboats for the New York market.

1897 — James W. Lathrop establishes J.W. Lathrop & Company, marine engine builders, at Mystic, Connecticut. Lathrop engines become a favorite of many catboat fishermen and yachtsmen.

1900 — Crosby shops are flourishing in what locals call "Crosby Town" or "Crosby Circle" in Osterville.

1904 — Cape Catboat Association of Massachusetts Bay founded to encourage catboat racing. D Class catboats are the mainstay and are actively raced for over a decade.

1918 — Post-World War One pleasure sailing sees the introduction of new one-designs and these, together with motorboats, signal a dramatic decline of general interest in catboats.

1920 — Beetle cat introduced by Carl and John Beetle in New Bedford.

1931 — Designer Fenwick Williams introduces an 18-foot catboat, the first in a series of enduring designs that would help stimulate renewed interest in the type.

1935-'36 — The last Crosby catboat is built.

1946 — Carl Beetle launches a commercially unsuccessful effort to build fiberglass boats with the BB Swan, a marconi-rigged catboat.

1963 — Breckenridge Marshall develops the fiberglass, 18-foot Marshall Sanderling, igniting renewed interest in catboats.

THE HARBOR IN TIME

———— ·◆· ————

THE SIGHT of a Cape Cod catboat going about her daily business, shouldering unperturbed through the steep chop that sweeps across the extensive shoals of Nantucket Sound, is among those many once-common scenes that have altogether vanished. Once, hundreds of such boats worked these waters under sail alone, their canvas neatly patched here and there, the several rows of reefing pennants rattling on the sail as the boatman luffed up to haul a lobsterpot over the coaming and into what was then called the "standing room." Later, with the day's catch secure in the clear seawater inside the live well, the fisherman would turn for home.

Suppose he's on a broad reach; perfect, for he will make his best time and may even get to bed before it is quite dark. The smooth, manilla mainsheet is eased off now, running through big, single-sheave wooden blocks that are not quite in need of a coat of varnish. He does not notice the smell of his wooden barrel of baitfish as he moves forward to lower the centerboard so it is just where he likes it when the wind is abeam as it is just now. There is a pleasant, muffled sort of burble as the wooden boat moves through the sea, and the wake left behind is smooth. Seen from dead ahead, the boat's bow is upswept to breast the seas. The stem is mostly plumb, vertical except for a bit of a curve down near the waterline, which has a pleas-

ing hollow shape that the fisherman has always liked. It is a bow shaped by wisdom and experience. It is just like the bows on other boats built by the same builder back in the early 1880s, and it gives the boat a purposeful look as steadily, steadily, she plows right ahead through the endless succession of gray-green, quartering seas.

The wheel is only pleasantly firm in his hand, for he had put two reefs in his big sail just before noon when the southwest breeze came on. He did this quickly and methodically and almost without thinking about it, working the topping lift and halyards and sheet and pennants in a kind of practiced rhythm so that the procedure was completed efficiently, without any apparent hurry. When this was done, he let the boat drift off for a time, his gaff not yet peaked back up and the topping lift supporting the boom while he ate a big ham sandwich made on thick slices of the bread that his wife had baked. With his lunch, he drank cold water from a clay jug that was nestled into a neat coil of anchor warp right forward inside the little cabin. He had plenty of anchor rode in the boat and it was in perfect condition. There were times when the fisherman had ridden out terrible storms to his anchor, pumping with the big pump that fed into the centerboard case, and praying hard, but these times had been rare.

Only when he nears home does the breeze begin to slacken. Without thinking twice, he heads the boat higher up into the fading breeze, works his halyards and lift and sheet again, and nimbly shakes out the day's reef. He is not a big man, but his slenderness is all muscle and sinew and he can work alertly for hours, day after day, with surprisingly little rest. By the time he enters the harbor, the boat is ghosting through smooth water in a breeze so light that the summer visitors watch in wonder that a boat can move at all. He sees that most of the other catboats are now back from their day's work. The sail of one latecomer hangs from the gaff, which has been slacked to a horizontal position so that the remains of the breeze will dry the sailcloth and help prevent mildew. Standing now, he can see a fisherman kneeling in the cockpit of one of the catboats, the first in the harbor to have a gasoline engine. He knows that this machine is made primarily out of iron, is painted dark red and has a shiny brass plaque that identifies its maker and its place of manufacture. Such an engine is an interesting idea, the fisherman thinks, and maybe he will have one himself. But not yet, somehow, he thinks. Not yet.

It is hard to imagine that the sight of these boats as they dot the harbor's moorings and docks, will not be here always, as they have since the fisherman was a boy. No, this is not something he thinks about very much. In fact, the harbor is even more full of catboats now than he can ever remember. Not only are the fishing boats here, but so are a dozen or more yachts. Most of these are owned by people who have a summer cottage in the town. Two others are laying over on their way to Boston where they will sail in a big race that he has heard about. He has looked at these other catboats with a curious yet appraising eye. He knows that big cash money is bet on the outcome of their races,

more sometimes than he will earn in a whole year. Their white paint glistens and their varnished spars sparkle like amber-colored glass in the last yellow-orange sunlight of the day. He has seen the cotton sails with their impossibly long, vertical panels, and knows them to be works of art that look as white as frost against the sky.

So, as the fisherman coasts alongside the lobster shack near the head of the harbor and tosses his lines to the boy who has come out to meet him, he has no thought that a scene like this will begin to fade before too many more years have passed. He won't be alive to see the day when his boat and the others like it, and the fine catboats built to race and to cruise, and all the men who built them, are gone altogether. Even though he knows most things must pass, he would not believe how close this world would come to being lost.

Believed to be one of at least two craft named Volante *owned by Nantucket's John "Junior" Fisher, this island-built catboat has the overhanging stern preferred by most Nantucket fishermen. The boat's squared-off cabin, round ports, low freeboard and somewhat ungainly coaming distinguish it from more refined Crosby models. This* Volante's *general appearance suggests she may have been built in the 1880s, but her high-peaked sail is a more "modern" touch. The block for the throat halyard is suspended from an unusual "crane-type" mount. Here, the boat's sail seems to be setting well although the gaff has apparently been raised on the wrong side of the topping lift.*

PART ONE

THE OLD DAYS

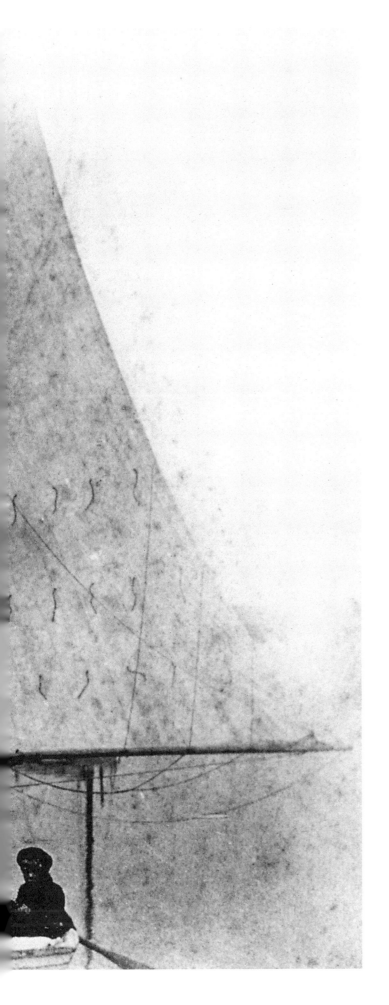

CHAPTER ONE

A SAIL IN THE MIST

———— •◆• ————

*"If there is truly an American vessel — mind you I
don't say rig — that deserves being described as the
National type, it is the catboat.*
—THOMAS FLEMING DAY, *The Rudder,* 1896

*"A peculiar type is rarely of native birth; it is generally
a form brought from some other locality and modified
by the slow process of elimination and addition."*
— F. E. NEWELL, *The Rudder,* 1901

I T IS WELL OVER A CENTURY since Thomas
Fleming Day, founder of one of America's
first magazines devoted entirely to pleasure
boating, took up his pen to consider a subject that
continues to beguile and even puzzle historically
minded sailors today — the catboat and its origins. How was it — the curious can only wonder
— that the catboat, and the Cape Cod catboat in
particular, ever came into being? What forces of
nature conspired to produce a vessel so perfectly
adapted to work some of New England's most
challenging waters? How was it that a boat type
was created and then reigned supreme for its
many intended tasks for over half a century?

*Osterville, Massachusetts, circa 1888. Herbert Crosby stands beside a buoy-
ant-looking, half-decked catboat. The boat is rigged with permanent reefing pennants and its sail has three sets of reef points. The mainsheet feeds
to the cockpit from a block mounted midway on the boom, rather unusual
but no doubt practical. The boom is mounted on a pedestal just abaft the
mast. The blocks for the halyards and topping lift are deck-mounted so the
rigging won't obstruct the mast hoops. With its big centerboard and ample
sail, this Crosby catboat must have been a wonderful sailer.*

Thomas Fleming Day was not immune to fascination with the catboat's history. After all, when *The Rudder* was begun in the early 1890s, harbors from Cape Ann, Massachusetts, to New Jersey were full of a fascinating variety of catboats. These distinctive boats were, by the mid-1880s, immediately recognizable by their shallow-draft hull equipped with a centerboard. The beam represented approximately half of the boat's load waterline. As size increased above 25 feet or so, though, the beam did not increase in proportion. The boats had a single, gaff-rigged sail set on a mast mounted in the bow.

Those were the basics, but regional differences regarding hull lines, freeboard, cabins, and other details abounded. To cite but one example, catboats designed for shallow but protected water, such as Long Island's Great South Bay were typically more narrow than the Cape Cod models, the general rule being a beam one third of the boat's length. The principal locales for the boat's development included New York, New Jersey, Rhode Island, and Cape Cod. In fact, however, regional varieties of the general type could be found from Maine to Florida and the Gulf Coast, from San Diego to San Francisco, and elsewhere.

The Rudder in its formative years under Day was a wonderful blend of elegantly written articles, boat plans and commentary, how-to tips, news items, and even poetry submitted by sailors capable of expressing their love for the sport in what was often surprisingly evocative 19th-century language. The magazine chronicled a vibrant world of sailing. While it paid occasional homage to the grand yachts of Gilded Age millionaires, *The Rudder's* heart and soul involved boats for the emerging middle class that had begun to have the time and income to take up the sailing of canoes, small craft, and later, in the early 1900s, motorboats.

In fact, catboats were raced by wealthy "yachtsmen," but they also served as cruising boats for well-to-do professionals, and men of more modest means, and they were the craft of choice for inshore fishermen along much of the northeast coast. So it was that catboats had a place in *The Rudder's* pages for many years and, thanks to Day and his writers, our knowledge of the catboat's origins, and its role in yachting, is much enriched. When their work is considered together with that of the great historian of American yachting, William P. Stephens, and a few boating journalists whose work is credible, one can piece together a reasonably satisfying story about the origins of the catboat and its development. One can even find some marginally satisfactory answers to that other inevitable question: "Why is it called a *catboat?*"

No doubt with tongue in cheek, Thomas Day once noted that the "early history of the catboat is involved in mystery.... It is said that at one time there dwelt in New York no less than eight men who publicly claimed to have invented the centerboard, and one even went so far as to have the claim worded on the surface of his tombstone...."

Thomas Fleming Day, founding editor of The Rudder. *A superb editor and yachtsman whose enthusiasm for boats of all kinds ignited the interest of thousands of readers, Day was long fascinated by catboats. In the late 1890s, he published enough catboat material that some readers "growled" and he reduced the percentage of such stories and plans.*

A score or more of years ago it was no uncommon thing to meet the man who built the first catboat, and today you frequently find yourself in company of his son or grandson."

The Theory of Evolution

Although theories about the catboat's origins have generated occasionally charming legends — in particular, the one relating to the Crosby family's development of its distinctive boats — the suggestion that any one man *invented* the catboat is difficult to accept. If one diligently sorts through the work of Day, Stephens, and the best efforts of Howard I. Chapelle, one can only emerge believing in what, for want of any better term, we may call the "theory of evolution." That is, what came to be known as the catboat and, in its ultimate state of development, the Cape Cod catboat, was the result of a gradual selection process spurred by the very specific sailing conditions in certain waters and the fisheries in which the boats were involved. There was a step-by-step adaptation by different individuals of a type of rig, a type of hull, and the centerboard, until a sort of boat emerged that proved itself ideal for use in a specific area.

It occurred to Thomas Fleming Day, as it has to others right down to the present, that an examination of small boats depicted in paintings or engravings might help the historian determine when and where the catboat's evolution began. Day focused on pre-1800 pictures of the Hudson River and the East River and found that, although quite a variety of ships, sloops, and schooners were present, the only craft with a single mainsail were rowing boats. He saw nothing resembling a catboat. Also prevalent in the late 18th and early 19th centuries were heavily built ship's boats. These were entirely open craft with a mast that could be stepped through a thwart located at the boat's greatest beam. Sprit or gaff rigs were used. Day, Stephens, and Chapelle all believed that such rigs and boats were the basis for an evolution into what eventually became popularly known as catboats, and that the New York area was the primary locale for the evolution, which spread both up and down the coast.

Day tried to imagine the result of an early 19th-century, undecked craft being modified to meet the needs of a New York waterman beginning around 1816.

Frequently sailing in rough water, he decides that some covering forward is necessary, and laying his craft ashore proceeds to deck in the fore portion. Along comes a man who is building a boat somewhat similar. Taking cue from this he places and extends the deck, and cutting a hole in the king plank steps his mast through it. Then gradually as boat after boat is built, the mast is placed further forward and the deck carried further aft until at last it covers all the hull with the exception of the standing room [cockpit]. As the mast goes forward the sail increases, and consequently stability is sought for and found in increased beam. As the beam increases, the comparative draft is diminished, and a wide, shallow boat is produced.

Howard Chapelle, at different times, advanced somewhat conflicting suggestions about the catboat's origins. But his basic conclusion was that although the catboat's history before 1850 was a matter of conjecture, it was "likely that the cat is a modification of the old centerboard sloops of the '40s, so common in New York waters in those days. These sloops were designed to work under mainsail alone, when desirable, so it was natural that a type should evolve that would require no headsail." As they evolved, such boats actually sprouted two rigs, a sloop rig ("jib and mainsail") for summer and a more easily handled cat rig ("mainsail") for winter.

Whether Day's or Chapelle's theory was correct, they both share the theme of evolution from one sort of boat to another that better suited the manner in which it was to be used and the waters in which it was sailed. The key point, perhaps, is simply the recognition that what is familiar now as the classic Cape Cod catboat form was the result of gradual change and refinement that had other boat types or features, the centerboard in particular, as a starting point.

New York and New Jersey

Thomas Fleming Day concluded that the basic shape of the catboat was in place between 1830 and 1840, although he admitted that he had no proof or record of such a boat. Neither did anybody else: Day was simply making an educated guess. By the early 1850s, however, there was a record. That's because, in 1852, a boat that would be generally recognizable to anyone today as a catboat — a bit narrow, to be sure, and dainty — was sent to England where, according to W. P. Stephens, it was "at once recognized as an

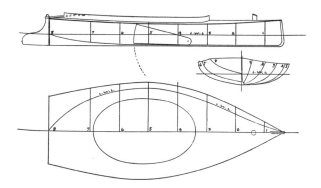

Here are the lines of Bob Fish's Una, *probably built in 1851 or 1852. These are the earliest drawings of a boat that would be recognizable as a "catboat." Although the "ram-style" bow would give way to a plumb stem as catboats evolved,* Una's *outboard rudder would characterize many such boats for decades.*

American novelty." This boat was a 16 1/2' x 6 1/2' x 9" "racing" catboat with a centerboard, and single sail set on a mast in the bow. Simply rigged with a single halyard for throat and peak, the boat had been designed and built in a shore-side area of tidal mudflats known variously as Saltersville, Pamrapo, and then Bayonne, New Jersey. Its creator was "Cap'n" Bob Fish.

Bob Fish fits rather neatly into the theory that the New York area was where the catboat had its genesis. Fish, who had grown up with boats as a fisherman and oysterman became well-known for his diverse skills as a professional skipper of big yachts, both in the U.S. and abroad, and for his handling of racing sandbaggers. Thomas Day described Fish as

> a remarkable man, uneducated, with no knowledge of naval architecture, and handicapped by a belief in many of the absurd fallacies of his class, but nevertheless an observer and thinker, a good boat sailor in both small and large craft, and a capable mechanic. . . . He had the gift of sailing, plenty of hard common sense, and much practical experience, and with greater natural advantages he would have made a successful yacht designer.

What Day was describing here was an entire class of boat designer that existed before formal, university training in the field became common. Instinct, experience, and eye were the chief tools of designers like Fish, who would be labeled "rule of thumb" men by Day and others. One such rule as stated by Fish: "The more sail a boat has, the more board she wants." A. Cary Smith, who learned his craft under Fish's tutelage but augmented it with somewhat more formal studies, recalled the rule-of-thumb method like this: "The whole business was purely eye work, and the element of chance entered largely into the result." But when the eye possessed a natural talent, like that of Fish, Smith, and a number of others, the result could be extraordinary boats.

When Fish turned to designing and building small craft, he opened a South Brooklyn boat shop, first on Front Street in 1840 and later on Water Street. In 1850, he moved his shop across New York Bay to New Jersey and it was there that the first meaningful record of catboats seems to have been generated. The details are somewhat contradictory, although the overall story is the same. In one scenario, recorded by W. P. Stephens, the British earl Mount Charles paid a visit to Bob Fish in 1852. The earl could afford as many boats as he wanted and, in fact, then owned 18 yachts. He was reportedly so smitten by Fish's little 16 1/2-footer that he purchased her.

But did the Earl really visit Bob Fish and purchase a boat? In a 1906 article on "Men Who Have Made Yachting," *The Rudder* focused on one of the country's earliest and most influential yachtsmen, a Scottish-born New York businessman named William Butler Duncan. Although he retired from active sailing in 1863, in part because the activity seemed to him to conflict with the fact that a civil war was going on, Duncan had owned a number of boats before his retirement. One was a sloop named *Una*. Another was a Bob Fish catboat of the same name, which *The Rudder*'s story says, was "13 feet long, 7 feet beam, and five inches draft, with a three-foot centerboard. . . . She had a plumb stem and a square stern, and on the stern in large letters was painted the name *Una*." (Una was a not-uncommon 19th-century woman's name. The author Nathaniel Hawthorne's eldest daughter was named Una.)

In *The Rudder* story of 1906, *Una* was taken by Butler to England as a gift to his friend, the earl Mount Charles. The other version says that the earl himself shipped the boat home. However, both versions agree that the boat was launched in London on Hyde Park's Serpentine pond. There, Butler skippered *Una* in a race against a sloop-rigged boat. "The course was to be five times up and down the Serpentine. . . . When the *Una*, sailed by Mr. Duncan, finished the fifth round, the other boat was beginning the third round. The Park was thronged with spectators, prominent among whom were Prince Albert and his suite."

In 1854, the boat was shipped to Cowes. There, recalled, Stephens, "she represented the extreme of simplicity and maneuverability as compared with the local craft her size and larger . . . her speed and handiness in smooth water and moderate breezes made her popular and gave the name to the type . . . 'una boat'." The British writer Dixon Kemp recorded that the sailors at Cowes

Almost regarded the *Una* as a little too marvelous to be real . . . and no wonder in less than a year there was a whole fleet of Unas at Cowes, and about the Solent. . . . The earl's sailing master, John Hollis, was very perfect in the management of the *Una,* and waltzed her about as cleverly as a Rhode Island fisherman in many sailing matches.

Una was apparently well cared for. The boat was reportedly still sailing in the 1890s by which time she had the company of the other una boats to which Kemp referred. The fact that lines drawings of *Una* were made from her half model is what enabled Stephens, Day, and others to focus on 1852 as a certain date by which time a boat that embodied the basics of a catboat — a shallow draft centerboarder with a single sail and mast in the bow — was in existence. Back in his shop by the New Jersey mudflats, Bob Fish found a ready market for boats like *Una*, and for centerboard-equipped sandbaggers that could be sailed either with sloop or mainsail-only rigs. Stephens reported that fleets of Fish's catboats (by the time Stephens wrote of this subject in the mid-1890s, "catboat" was the long-accepted name for such craft) went to numerous locales from New Orleans and Savannah to Boston, not to mention inland lakes. He also reported that "every water-side estate or farm on the Hudson, the Delaware and the Connecticut rivers had a catboat of the type of *Una* and up to 25 feet in length made fast to a little pier or anchored nearby, and used for the double purpose of a vehicle for transportation and for pleasure sailing."

Due south of Bob Fish's boat shop lay New Jersey's great coastal bays. Long expanses of shoal water separated from the Atlantic by low-lying barrier islands fringed with sea grass, Barnegat Bay and the waters south to Atlantic City and Cape May were then a natural wonder, tailor-made for shallow-draft sailing craft. It may well be that boats similar to *Una*, whether developed independently or influenced by events around New York, were plying Barnegat Bay at the same time that they began appearing just to the north.

The form of the Barnegat Bay catboats and, later, Atlantic City catboats as they subsequently developed, was that of a comparatively low-sided, open boat. Cabins were typically removable "summer cabins" with roll-up canvas curtains that

The summer cabin, its sides rolled up for ventilation, is plainly evident in this photograph of a New Jersey catboat. The boat is well-rigged and is sailing here with a reef in her sail. The boom is mounted to the mast with jaws, eliminating any hardware. Big single blocks are used for the mainsheet, which would appear in some danger of chafing on the edge of the box housing the steering gear.

would permit ventilation as appropriate. Rather boxy looking, permanent cabins also existed that must, at least, have afforded comfortable sitting head room. Eventually, very large catboats, over 32 feet long, became common as party boats in Atlantic City. Boats of generally similar form were built by the hardy Jersey baymen of the wonderful white cedar and oak that then abounded in the area. These were used for fishing, freighting, and commercial bird hunting as well as to carry sportsmen during duck season, a time when the big catboats might have in tow a distinctive Barnegat Bay sneakbox loaded with decoys.

Both small and large catboats that shared the Jersey boats' low-sided hulls, plumb ends and, eventually, summer cabins were also built for use on Long Island's Great South Bay. Thomas Fleming Day never forgot the impression that one of the larger of such boats made on him: "I gazed upon her boom, a spar which in comparison with that on my boat appeared an enormous stick . . . this boat found no difficulty in sailing away from anything on the Sound in her day . . ."

Rhode Island

Writing a series on American working craft in *Boating* magazine in 1907, William Lambert Barnard reported the name of one of the individuals who claimed to have invented the catboat. "There is also the claim of an ingenious old man in Tiverton, R.I., named Babbett, who died some years ago at an advanced age and who ever claimed to have built the first cat boat, to have invented the type there in Rhode Island." But Lambert did not give any details of Mr. Babbett's old boat, such as whether it had a centerboard or what were its general proportions. Nor did he advance a date. He did acknowledge that it was certainly possible for Mr. Babbett, among others,

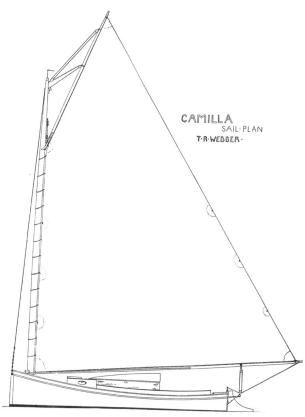

Designed and built by T. R. Webber in New Rochelle, New York, in 1876, Camilla had a nearly vertical stem and stern although the stem's slight rake aft gave her a 27' 7" waterline that was two inches longer than her length on deck. The beam was 12 1/2' and the board up draft was three feet. The squared off corners on the little cabin were typical until the mid-1880s. The permanent cabin contained two berths while the summer cabin offered a pair of larger berths. The boom is located on the mast by jaws. The wheel drove the rudder by "tiller ropes." Camilla had an 800 square-foot sail.

to have developed a catboat, or something like a catboat, independently and at the same time as a similar boat was created elsewhere. This is not particularly far-fetched given the realities of travel and communication in the 19th century. Of course, it begs the question — just what *did* Mr. Babbett define as the features that made a catboat?

While we have no information about Mr. Babbett's invention, whatever it was, it does not seem likely to have been equipped with a centerboard. In July 1887, historian W. P. Stephens received a letter from one Mr. Morton Toulmin. As a schoolboy in 1836–38, Toulmin reported that he had "spent a good deal of time in Newport,

This drawing of a "Newport Boat" shows the rather tall, narrow sail, and full-keel hull of a boat type in use during and after the early 1830s.

centerboard) lapstrake hulls. Boats like this were in common use in Rhode Island then. We know this because the abandoned hull of one of them was converted into a painting studio by artist Sydney Burleigh in 1906. This "Newport fish and lobster boat" was referred to as "old," according to Burleigh, in the 1870s. The boat had served for years as a ferry at Sakonnet Passage. Preserved by the Little Compton Historical Society, a sign in front of Burleigh's *Peggotty* reads: "Catboat of 1850. Artist's studio 1906." A similar but later boat built in 1875, according to Howard Chapelle, is the *Button Swan,* which is preserved at the Mystic Seaport Museum. In his American Small Sailing Craft published in 1951, Chapelle labeled this a Providence River Boat.

An article about *Button Swan*'s builder, William Munroe, but known by the name Button Swan because of his small size and the fact that he was raised by a Newport fisherman named John Swan, was published in *Scribner's Magazine* in 1921. The author of this article, Christopher Grant La Farge,

R. I., and at that period, the boats in general use were deep keels, and I cannot remember to have seen a single centerboard boat in Newport Harbor." The mainsail-only keel boats then predominant in Newport were widely known as "Newport boats" or "Point boats," after the part of town (now Long Wharf) where most of the builders were located. A boat of this type appears to have been the model for the first of four cat-rigged boats built by Charles Frederick Herreshoff (Nathanael's father) beginning in 1833. *Julia,* a 23-foot keel model, was followed by *Julia II* and *Julia III* before 1860.

The Newport boats are one part of the Rhode Island story. Another began at some point in the early 1840s — perhaps earlier but no later than the early 1850s. The boats were 16- to 18-foot mainsail-only craft with shallow-draft (but not

Peggotty was a replica of a Newport fish and lobster boat built by the gifted Bob Baker, who is shown here at the tiller. Simple, stable, and well up to dealing with conditions in their immediate locale, boats like this had a live well located amidships. They were not equipped with a centerboard.

described such boats as follows: "Sixteen feet, sometimes eighteen was the standard length; rather broad, and with a low free-board. Lap straked and no part decked over; fairly deep keel and inside ballast under the floor. . . . The mast stepped clean in the bows . . . single halyard and a mainsheet." Here was a sort of catboat. It lacked a deck and a centerboard, nor was it called a catboat at the time, but, like the Point Boat, it had what would come to be called a cat rig.

It is clear that mainsail-only, gaff-rigged boats without centerboards existed at Newport at a comparatively early date. But what about centerboards? Was a boat that bore the hallmarks of the classic centerboard catboat developed in Rhode Island independently and more or less at the same time as those in the New York area, and possibly, Cape Cod? This seems to be a real possibility.

At some point, Newport's undecked, single-sail boats evolved further or, perhaps more accurately, faded as quite a new species was born. The "real" Newport or Narragansett Bay catboat, with a comparatively beamy, carvel planked hull and a centerboard may have emerged by the early- to mid-1850s. In the 1970s, Catboat Association

members John and Laura Saunders wrote an article about the Saunders family of Rhode Island. They believed that John Gould Saunders built an 18-foot catboat named *Bloomer,* probably at South Kingstown between 1851 and 1855. They also suggest this boat was equipped with a centerboard, a device that actually had been patented in 1811 by Joshua Henry and Jacocks Swain of Seaville, New Jersey (near Cape May). The oldest surviving example of a centerboard, Rhode Island catboat — although not authentically preserved — is the yacht *Sprite,* designed by Charles F. Herreshoff, assisted by his son John and 11 1/2-year old Nathanael G. Herreshoff. Launched in 1859, this was the first of a number of centerboard Herreshoff catboats, all designed by Nathanael as yachts. In 1885, when the Hull Yacht Club printed a detailed roster of its members' boats, the oldest one was named *Clio,* a catboat built in 1860 by the Herreshoffs.

As time passed, Newport's wharves, such as Bannister Wharf and Long Wharf, became a center for the building of a variety of catboat types, including both pleasure and working models, the latter operated by the Yankee, Irish, and Greek fishermen

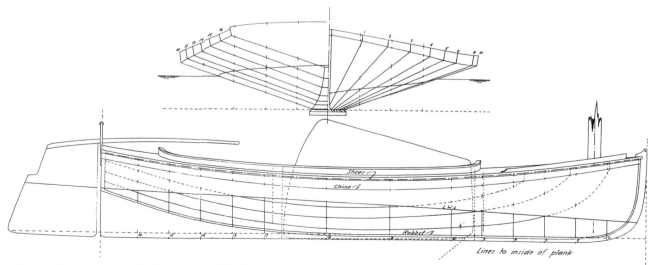

While vee-bottoms were typical of a generation of Rhode Island catboats, this boat's configuration was so extreme that Howard Chapelle called it a "diamond bottom catboat." Perhaps built as early as 1870, the boat was said to have "never been beaten" prior to 1882. Dimensions: 17 1/2' x 9' 8" by 1' 6".

of the area. William Lambert Barnard described a typical Newport centerboard catboat, in comparison to those of Cape Cod, as having a more vee-shaped bottom, a straighter sheer with less freeboard forward, and a gaff that was not as highly peaked. While some had raking transoms with underhung rudders, barndoor rudders with an elliptical cutout on the top side were more common. The aft cabin bulkheads were generally narrower than the width of the cockpit, which

required the cockpit coamings to curve in to meet the bulkhead. Such boats were popularly ordered in lengths of about 26 feet with beams of about 10 feet and usually had a draft of about three feet. Some, reportedly, were half-decked (lacked a cabin house) but managed to squeeze a bunk and small stove into the space available beneath the deck.

Other types were also developed. These included boats of some 30 feet in length, intended to fish the banks well off Block Island. They carried tall

This photograph of the 23-foot keel catboat Falcon *was shot off Goat Island in 1886 when the boat was two years old.* Falcon, *probably built in Newport by Thomas Stoddard, shows the style of coaming typical of Rhode Island catboats, whose cabin bulkhead was narrower than the cockpit so that the coamings curved in to meet it. The boat's plumb stem and flat-topped cabin are typical of catboats of this period. At the wheel is W.W. Smith who, with his brother Edward, was an avid photographer and photographed some wonderful images of Rhode Island sailing. In 1893, W.W. Smith was lost when* Falcon *hit a reef off Aquidneck Island in a squall. His brother made it to shore aboard the boat's removable bowsprit, which was not fitted when this photograph was taken.*

masts but shorter gaffs and booms than other types. Such rigs would have been better suited to sailing in bigger seas that could build offshore, and the taller sail would not lose the wind so readily when down in the ocean's swells. In addition, keel catboats were built in a variety of sizes, although boats of around 20 feet proved most popular. One such boat was *Falcon*, a 23-footer built in 1884 at the Point, probably by Thomas Stoddard. This boat had a removable bowsprit on which to set a small jib to improve balance, if desired. *Falcon* proved a capable cruiser but was lost, together with her owner William W. Smith, in an 1893 storm in Narragansett Bay when she struck a reef. This ended the life of a fine sailor and fine photographer who had chronicled many aspects of the Rhode Island boating scene. There were also much larger Newport catboats similar to *Falcon* but built as party boats. They had enlarged cabins and generous beam and freeboard for the comfort of guests.

Cape Cod

While Bob Fish was busily developing his popular boats in New York and the Newporters were creating their own types, two young boatbuilders in Osterville, Massachusetts, embarked on designing what would become the most famous and long-lived of all the vessels that would bear the name "catboat." Their names were Charles W. (born in 1823) and Horace S. (born in 1826) Crosby. The small craft then in use for fishing around Cape Cod were primarily double-ended pinkies and Block Island boats. They were not particularly fast boats, not particularly shallow draft, and they did not possess the ability to carry heavy loads of fish. Developing a more able and efficient boat for Cape fishermen was a problem that Andrew Crosby, father of Charles and Horace, had hoped

to address with a new type of boat. But Andrew Crosby, who built coasters of different types, died at age 42 in 1837 before his conception, whatever it was, could become a reality. Andrew's death delayed, but did not end, the development by the Crosby family of a new style of boat.

At some point in their lives, both Andrew Crosby and his wife Tirza had come to believe in spiritualism, a curious but important religious movement in 19th-century America. Spiritualism prompted the establishment of dozens of religious sects (the Shakers among them), and the emergence of a number of self-proclaimed prophets of new religions. A cornerstone of many spiritualists' beliefs was that it was possible to communicate with the dead through a medium. This notion had such appeal that, by 1854, according to Ruth Brandon's book, *The Spiritualists,* an Illinois senator "presented a petition signed by fifteen thousand of his constituents, all of them spiritualists, demanding that Congress finance an official commission which would investigate the apparent attempt on the part of beings from another world to communicate with this one."

Crosby family legend — repeated by every historian and journalist who has examined the subject — was that Andrew's widow Tirza held a séance that resulted in a medium named "Mrs. Manley" describing Andrew's idea for a wide, shallow-draft boat with a plumb stem and stern and the mast stepped in the bow. Although the whole idea of the spiritualist séance would come to be exposed as a matter of self-deception or, in the case of professional mediums, an elaborately staged ruse, there is no doubt that believers were sincere.

There is another version of the Crosby story, however, that, while still containing a spiritual theme, also buttresses the notion that New York was, ultimately, the locale where the catboat originated. In 1928, the oldest Crosby alive was Herbert F. Crosby. Herbert had been born in 1853 and was the eldest son of Horace S. The 75-year-old Herbert was then a widower, living peacefully but actively in Osterville where he rented his house in the summer to "city people." He spent his days in his boat shop and slept aboard a little power cruiser of some 18 feet in length that was tied up amidst a variety of catboats. There in Osterville, Herbert Crosby was amused by his grandchildren and received what was reported to be a steady stream of visitors, many of whom were distinguished men from on and off the Cape who came to talk catboats. In the summer of 1928, one of those visitors was a journalist named Gregory Mason, whose family owned a 20-foot Crosby catboat named *Sheldrake* that had been built around 1898.

Mason visited Crosby on a drizzly day during what was apparently a summer of such poor weather that Herbert had not made his annual cruise to the Vineyard. The purpose of the visit was for Mason to gather material for an article for *Motor Boating*. Herbert greeted him in a rather high-pitched voice saying: "So, Cap'n, you want to hear about the building of the first Cape Cod cat?" And he prefaced his story about the first catboat with the statement: "My father and uncle invented her, that is, Horace Crosby and Worthington Crosby. That must have been a good 80 years ago, long before Cape Cod had concrete highways and gift shops along 'em enough for a man to spend a fortune in a couple of miles."

Reading Mason's article today, one gets the impression that Herbert Crosby probably had a well-rehearsed answer to questions about the catboat and its origins. Even so, his version as given to Mason is different from some and even dispenses with the famous séance, replacing that spiritual legend with another one that involves a bewitched sewing table. But Herbert began his tale to Mason by noting that Andrew Crosby's coasting vessels had to be shoal draft enough to beat out of Cotuit and that this was accomplished by the use of leeboards. Then, he told Mason that on one of his grandfather's voyages, "he saw the first centerboard he'd ever seen. I think it was up New York way, an' he probably mentioned it to his sons." So, for the centerboard, at least, we have Herbert F. Crosby reporting that Andrew had first seen one at New York.

But how did the centerboard get translated to the Cape Cod catboat? That is where the Crosby legend according to Herbert comes in. Herbert claimed that in the winter of 1837, within only a few months of Andrew Crosby's death, 11-year-old Horace and 14-year old Worthington, neither of whom had ever built a boat, decided to do so. He said they began going into the swampy areas around Osterville seeking oak trees with the right bends.

"They knew just about the kind of boat they wanted," Herbert Crosby told Mason, "something about 18 feet long, staunch to go offshore, and quick in the eye of the wind. Naturally she had to be shoal draft and they thought they'd try to build one of those centerboards they'd heard their father speak about. But they didn't know how to do it."

The answers to their questions, Herbert F. Crosby believed with what to Mason was total sincerity, came from their dead father through their mother, the medium. "They went to her and asked her if she thought a centerboard would work in the kind of boat they were planning. She didn't say a thing at first, but just looked at her little sewing stand. When the stand began to rock and to shake, she said 'Yes, boys, a centerboard would be all right.'" Even this seemingly peculiar tale has its basis in an aspect of spiritualism. That is, according to author Brandon, "the acme of strangeness was reached in the extraordinary story of the 'new motive power,' by which a woman imparted energy to a machine."

Subsequently, said Herbert, any questions were posed to their mother and answered as "yes" if the sewing stand rocked and "no" if it didn't. What this story has in common with the séance in which Mrs. Manley was a medium who provided Andrew's answers, is that Andrew Crosby is credited as the man who really "invented" the Cape Cod catboat, even though he was dead at the time.

Mason wrote: "There was no mistaking the sincerity of Captain Crosby's ringing voice and his slightly moist eye as he enunciated the Crosby creed that the first catboat was really designed not by Worthington and Horace Crosby but by their dead father, the sea captain who had first dreamed of centerboards for Cape Cod waters."

It is very much worth noting that a third version of the birth of the first Crosby catboat was told by Herbert's younger brother, Horace Manley Crosby. ("Manley" became a rather popular name in the Crosby family.) Horace Manley was born in 1871 when his father Horace S. was 45 years old. His version of the story was that Horace S. had little patience for the séance story. Instead, Horace Manley reported that his father had seen and been impressed by the cat-rigged boats built in Newport, Rhode Island, and that these were a primary inspiration.

In 1902, after F. E. Newell went to Osterville for The Rudder, he was led to a similar conclusion and wrote that "we may suppose that the Cape boats are descended of a vessel built in Rhode Island and brought years ago to ply in Cotuit waters." This is worth pondering, for Newell appears to have been a serious scholar of the subject. But he provided no details about this supposed vessel, or its date.

The End of the Beginning

The precise year of the launching of the mysterious ancestor of all the Crosby catboats is unlikely ever to be determined. Herbert was no more specific about the date this boat was launched than to say, in 1928, that it "must have been a good 80 years ago." But what, exactly, "a good" meant was not pursued by Mason. If one takes the 80 years literally, the date for would have been 1848, 11 years after Andrew's death. Other family claims, though also vague, put the date at about 1850, but both dates are probably optimistic. The writer William Lambert Barnard, presumably after some discussion with the Crosbys in 1907, placed the date as "about 1857." That's the same year suggested in F. E. Newell's article in The Rudder in 1902. In 1932, after detailed discussions with H. Manley Crosby, who provided him several half models for study, Howard Chapelle gave 1860 as the date for the first Crosby catboat.

The first Crosby catboat is said to have been named Little Eva. It's worth noting that Little Eva was a character in Harriet Beecher Stowe's widely read Uncle Tom's Cabin, first published in 1852, calling into further question 1848 or 1850 as a reliable date. W. P. Stephens recorded that Little Eva was followed by bigger boats and that 1860 was a crucial year. That's when a Chatham fisherman "placed an order on the promise of Horace that he need not pay for her if she was not successful." According to Stephens, this catboat proved burdensome, seaworthy [able to negotiate Chatham Bar], and fast. Rather quickly, the Crosby brothers received orders that soon totaled

100 boats. Thus began the evolution of the Cape Cod catboat by the men who would always remain most closely associated with the type. Lines taken from Crosby half-models by Howard Chapelle show a progression in the boat's form. The comparatively flat sheer, steep deadrise and slack bilge of a model carved in 1870 gradually changed. When the lines were taken from a model built a quarter century later, they showed a hull with a gracefully curved sheer, reduced deadrise and fuller lines that would improve the boat's initial stability and the ability to carry sail.

In conclusion, the best information available suggests that the first Crosby catboat appeared between 1857 and 1860 and was the end result of at least a decade of development influenced by centerboard-equipped, jib-and-mainsail boats in New York and centerboard boats in Rhode Island. Now, in a replay of nature's survival of the fittest, the days of the pinkie and Block Island boats began to draw to a close. By the eve of the American Civil War, the great heyday of the catboat — and the most long-lived type that would become famous as the Cape Cod cat — had begun.

The Name

Whatever the inspiration, the launching at Osterville of *Little Eva* — a boat that Herbert Crosby reported was half as wide as it was long — was said to have attracted fishermen from several

Here, catboats are clustered at the north side of Nantucket's Steamboat Wharf, circa 1904.

The Evolution of Crosby Catboats (1870 - 1895)

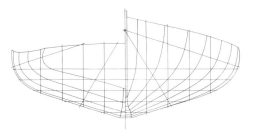 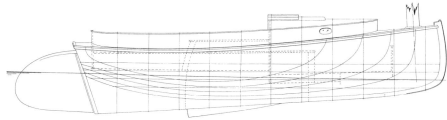

23' 10" Catboat of 1870 by Horace S. Crosby

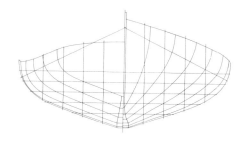 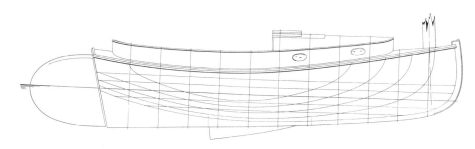

24' 6" Catboat of 1883 by Horace S. Crosby

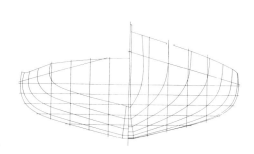 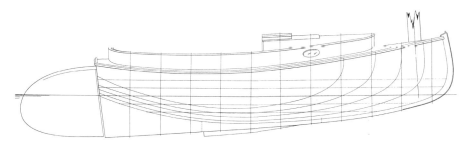

23' 4" Catboat of 1895 by H. Manley Crosby

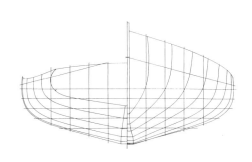 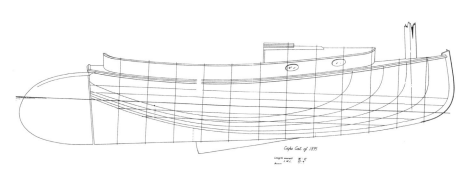

26' Catboat of 1895 by H. Manley Crosby

The lines of these four Crosby boats, as taken by Howard Chapelle from half models, show an evolution that spanned a quarter century. Deadrise and bilge shapes evolved to yield a more powerful hull on the later models, which possessed more sweeping sheerlines that improved appearance.

parts of the Cape. Some of these men showed up in their pinkies, which were reportedly outsailed by Horace S. in his new creation that was, legend has it, either "quick as a cat" or that came about "as quick as a cat." Hence the name "catboat." Herbert Crosby told Gregory Mason that the boat was "quick and nimble as a cat so they called her a cat-boat an' that's how the name started." Who was the "they?" We don't know.

While it begs too many questions, this version of how the catboat got its name could be accurate. Occasionally, one's man's flash of inspiration sticks and enters the language. It is said, for example, that a friend of Cameron Waterman took one look at Waterman's little "rowboat" or "detachable" motor sometime around 1906 and concluded that, as it was not mounted inside the boat, it should be called an "outboard." Thus did a type of motor, created by a law student at Yale, enter the language with a label coined by a now-forgotten acquaintance.

Assuming one accepts the idea that, sometime around 1860, somebody in Osterville began call-ing the Crosby sailboats "catboats," one must ask the question, "What about all the other 'cat-boats'?" When and how, for example, did people begin calling Bob Fish's boats "catboats?" It seems likely that if Bob Fish sold a boat known as a "cat-boat" in 1852, it would not have been named a "Una boat," by the English. Or, was the situation in England as *The Rudder* described it: "The *Una*'s vic-tory brought the cat rig into fashion in England, and the funny part of the outcome was that the name of the boat was mistaken for the name of the type." But was there even a rig then referred to as a "cat" rig? We don't know.

The fact is that boats with a single, gaff-rigged sail are depicted in 16th-century Dutch paintings and engravings, but these weren't called catboats, or referred to as being "cat rigged," either. Neither were the early single-sail boats at Newport called catboats. In their day, they were known as "Point Boats," "Pointers," "Newport boats," "Newport-rigged," or even "sloop boats." They came to be called catboats at *a later time*. Boats with a similar rig were popular in many locales in America by the mid-to-late 19th century. But although it is natural now to see a picture of one of these boats and say "Look, a catboat!," there is little, if any, documentation to support that they were called catboats in their own time. Instead, one finds ref-erences simply to "boats" or "yachts."

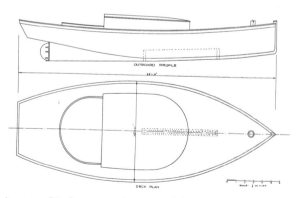

These drawings of Violet *were made as part of the Works Progress Administration's "Historic American Merchant Marine Survey" in the 1930s. Built at Cedar Key, Florida, in 1885, apparently for commercial use, the boat had a plumb stem and general appearance reminiscent of New Jersey catboats of the era. Her rudder looks comparatively tiny. The sail is peaked low, suggesting* Violet's *best performance would have been when off the wind. The sail may have been loose-footed. The boat's dimensions were: 29' 4" x 10' 11" x 2' 8 1/2".*

An explanation for all this is simply that, eventually, the name catboat gradually spread, perhaps from Cape Cod, and was then used to describe any boat that had a single gaff-rigged sail. So, what Bob Fish may have known as a "boat," "sailboat," "mainsail boat," or "yacht," later became termed a "catboat." In a letter written to W. P. Stephens on August 11, 1935, Nathanael G. Herreshoff recalled "I certainly did not know our boats as 'cat boats,' in my early days and not till after the '60s." This means that America's most famous yacht designer and a student of the subject who was acquainted with dozens of designers and builders could not recall hearing the term "cat boat" until the 1870s.

It is also clear that, even years after Fish built *Una* and others like her, an effort was made by some to distinguish (whether correctly or incorrectly) between a "cat-rigged" boat and a "catboat." This suggests that the term "cat" may have been applied to the rig before it came to denote an entire boat. But there is even less explanation for why a rig came to be called a cat rig than there is for why the boat came by its name.

In 1884, when the *Report on the Ship-building Industry of the United States* was published, it referred to Barnegat Bay's "light-draught sailboat" as "an American invention and goes by the name of the cat-rigged boat." That's awkward! A year later, when the Hull (Massachusetts) Yacht Club published its extensive roster of boats, what anyone today would call catboats were referred to instead as "cat-rigged" boats. Clearly, the *cat* portion of the name had somehow become common but not necessarily the term *catboat*. It does seem likely, however, that, during or before the golden age period of 1885 – 1895, people eventually wearied of trying to make distinctions regarding a predominant but specialized style of boat. By 1890 or so, the name "catboat" was pretty well settled, a name that may, indeed, have spread from Cape Cod.

By 1905, when this party of 10 was photographed at Onset, Massachusetts, at the head of Buzzard's Bay, the Cape Cod catboat had become a common sight in New England waters.

A freshly caught swordfish rests in the cockpit of Anna W. *Owned by Captain Everett Poole of Menemsha,* Anna W *carried a long, wide bowsprit when rigged for swordfishing. The photograph is believed to have been taken in the 1930s.*

CHAPTER TWO

WORKBOAT

—◆—

*"I am the only one of my generation from my village [Chatham, Mass.] who took to the sea, or even went fishing —
I was called 'Cap'n' when I was only 14 and sailing a boat. The engines, the big cats, and the men who went
to sea fishing in them, are a thing of the past, and live only in the memory of a few of us."*

—AVERY SMALL, ex-fisherman, 1965 (born 1894)

THE LONG-VANISHED WORLD of the 19th and early 20th-century working Cape Cod catboat exists now only in the yellowed and brittle pages of some old magazines, in a few precious reminiscences, and as images preserved in a frustratingly limited number of photographs. It was a world peopled by several generations of extraordinarily tough and resourceful men and boys who sailed for decades without engines or marine weather forecasts, who worked long days and longer nights, and who braved fogs and steamer lanes and storms. That said, they viewed their labor as relatively easy in comparison to the work of the Grand Banks fishermen and whalers, some of whom eventually took to fishing alongshore in catboats themselves.

It was a hard life and not to be romanticized, but it gave a man independence. The catboat fishermen lived, as fishermen always have, according to the tides and the seasons, beginning with mackerel in early spring, lobsters and swordfish in sum-

mer, and scallops, mackerel, and cod in the fall. When going for mackerel, the boat's usual crew of man and boy would often be supplemented by an additional fisherman or two. Then, the catboat would have in tow a 16-foot dory, perhaps built by Lowell's Boatshop in Amesbury, Massachusetts. The dory was loaded with gear and nets that were set by anchors or rigged with floats, the catboat being made fast to the net's downwind end. Then, the nets and boats would drift through the sea and, at night, twinkling lanterns atop six-foot bamboo poles would attract the fish. The dories were used to pluck the fish from the net.

When seeking seasonal species like bluefish, mackerel, or cod, the catboat men worked every day that they could and would be gone for days at a time. The largest boats ventured to Georges Bank, a three-day sail. "That would seem to me," said Martha's Vineyard fisherman Oscar Pease, "to be pretty hairy. But then again, that was their livelihood. It was pretty risky, a hard way to live."

During shell fishing season, the fishermen typically worked a six-day week. Often, their day began before dawn and ended after dark. No matter what the time of year, the labor was hard. The fishermen got their livelihood from the sea by dint of wiry muscles, smart boat handling, and a seemingly inborn knowledge of what to do and when that was, in reality, passed along from man to boy.

"My grandfather and one of his friends taught me to box a compass," reported Joseph Chase Allen of Martha's Vineyard. "Before I could read, I could pick out the position of the points on the compass but I didn't know what the letters were. They taught me to splice a line and how to tie most of the working bends when my fingers were so small that they had to use a piece of worn-out clothesline. They taught me the sails of a square-rigged ship. . . . They used to cuss me blue when I forgot the differences between the main royal and the forestaysail. They were stiff-necked, self-sufficient, and they detested anyone who was inquisitive."

But they were great sailors. The catboat fishermen, it might be stressed, did not navigate the difficult waters of Nantucket and Vineyard Sound and Buzzards Bay from one buoy to the next with the aid of depth sounders and electronic instruments. Rather, they scoured every rip and shoal relying on their knowledge and instinct, the set of the currents, the color of the water, the sounding lead and, one must assume, their centerboards to indicate depth. Joseph Chase Allen, who, as a boy, actually sailed with the generation of fishermen born between about 1845 and 1875, never quite got over their skill at finding their way. "They smelled their way through fog and snowstorms," he recalled. "There was no other explanation for it. We always carried a compass on the boat that I sailed with but nobody ever took it out of the

cabin. . . . I don't know how they did it."

Workboat Evolution

The working catboat sailed by the men who taught Allen went through three general design evolutions. First, beginning around the late 1850s and ending around 1900, there were the boats designed purely as sailing craft to meet the needs of fishermen. The second phase involved the coming of power and the almost immediate adoption — beginning around 1903 — of the internal combustion engine. Finally came the third phase in which the internal combustion engine was not viewed merely as auxiliary power but as the primary motive force for the boat. When that happened, rigs were dispensed with altogether and the catboat was converted to a powerboat. Later, with a bigger engine installed, hull revisions, sometimes with a wheelhouse planted on their deck aft, such vessels bore little resemblance to the perfectly adapted boats that had once emerged from so many harbors to fish the shallow waters for which they had been bred, and sometimes the Atlantic ocean as well.

Details of working Cape Cod catboats built between 1860 and the early 1880s are relatively scarce. Only a few photographs, descriptions, and lines plans survive. The earlier models, in particular, tended to be low-sided, open boats. When cabins began to be added, they were flat-roofed and had, until the 1870s, squared-off corners that required less labor than steam-bent coamings and cabin sides. Chapelle drawings exist of a Crosby model said to be of 1870 vintage (see Chapter One). Although the date may be early, the boat has the graceful, steam-bent sides and cockpit coamings that began to predominate at some point, perhaps, during that decade, and which stand out now as a signature feature of the catboat.

Iced in: The catboat Bobby *of Nantucket has been fitted with a "wheelhouse" that permitted the boat to be steered while affording some protection from the weather. Circa 1930s.*

Subsequent to the appearance of such cabins, reference to any boat with a squared-off cabin almost always included the word "old" or "old-fashioned."

Because a large cockpit was of chief importance to fishermen, the cabins of the working boats were only large enough for the necessities. These included space for a cooking stove and a pair of berths ("transoms") on either side. The little cabin had a door on one or both sides of the centerboard trunk but, on the earlier models, a sliding hatch for the companionway was not always fitted, resulting in awkward access. The cabin was usually divided by the centerboard trunk, which also extended back into the cockpit. These catboats had *big* centerboards. Until the high-peaked gaff came into vogue on Cape Cod catboats around 1880, the centerboard trunk was set well aft in order to better balance the low-peaked rigs. In some of those boats, in fact, the board was entirely in the cockpit. But, with high-peaked gaffs, the board's location moved forward together with the center-of-effort of the sail.

There was a rule of thumb for the placement of the board in a typical boat, as reported by William Lambert Barnard in 1907: "The centerboard, which is usually one-third the boat's length, is placed with its forward end approximately two-sevenths of her [the boat's] length aft of the stem."

In the cockpit, a seat might be installed on either side that ran for half the cockpit's length. Seats were not by any means universal, however, and many working catboats were built without them, or else with only a small seat in each corner of the cockpit beside the tiller or wheel. If the latter, the helmsman could straddle the wheelbox but the rest of the big cockpit was often left open to facilitate the handling of lines and other gear. Among the many unanswered questions regarding these catboats is why so many boats up to about 22 or perhaps 23 feet in length were tiller steered —

sometimes with a tiller that looks impossibly short. Although it is possible that these boats were better balanced than we might imagine, they were also fitted with tackle that could be attached to the tiller and take some of the load off the helmsman.

Hulls of the boats built before 1870 had overhanging "counter" sterns with underhung rudders. However, this style was almost entirely replaced on working boats by the advent of the "squared-off stern" and outboard rudder ("barndoor" rudder because of its size). This design was extant at least by 1870 and was generally preferred by fishermen because, among other things, a squared-off hull was less expensive to build than the alternative model. But fishermen also believed that such rudders added steering leverage and that their boats could carry on to windward longer as the winds increased if equipped with a big, barndoor rudder. Despite this general preference, working catboats ordered by Nantucket fishermen, or built there, typically had overhanging sterns, a feature so prevalent that they were sometimes referred to as the "Nantucket model."

The boats built before the mid-1870s generally lacked the graceful sheer and more cohesive forms that were finally achieved by the early to mid-1880s. By then, the best Crosby designs and those of a few other designers had achieved a more attractive appearance, whether built with squared-off or overhanging sterns. The counter-stern designs were said to provide some after-deck on which to step, which could simplify furling the sail and reaching the reef points on the long booms. But the booms still extended several feet beyond the transom and photographs of nearly every boat from the period show that they were rigged with permanent reefing pennants for the first two reef points. This permitted the clew to be hauled in from the safety of the cockpit.

Once it had achieved its highest form in the mid-1880s, the working Cape Cod catboat was not further evolved, unlike catboats designed as racing yachts, some of which did assume peculiar proportions (relating to measurement rules) and over-sized rigs. Still, particularly by today's standards, the pre-internal combustion working catboat had an imposing sail. The accompanying box has the figures that tell the story of *Goldenrod,* a 22-foot fishing boat built for Everett A. Poole of Menemsha, Massachusetts. *Goldenrod* had a boom that was at least seven feet longer than the boat itself and spread a 525-square foot sail, roughly a quarter larger than that of a modern Marshall 22. The *Goldenrod* was said to have been the fastest catboat in Menemsha, and Poole used her in various ways. He pursued lobsters in summer and during the rest of the year he went out handlining, trawling, and codfishing.

Portrait of *Goldenrod,* a 22-foot Working Catboat of 1897

Builder: Herbert F. Crosby, Osterville, Mass.

Fisherman: Everett A. Poole, Menemsha, Mass.

Length Overall: 22'

Extreme Beam: 11'

Draft: 24"

Cabin Dimensions: 12' long by 9' wide (comparatively large)

Steering: Tiller

Kinds of Stock: Oak keel, cypress planks, oak cabin trunk

Fastenings: Copper (sic) and galvanized iron

Sail foot x hoist: 29' x 18'

Finish: White paint, copper bottom paint, painted canvas cabin top, varnished spars

Price: with anchor, rode, and boat hook: $450.

Underway with her boom crutch in place and her anchor propped against the bulkhead is Thelma. *Here we see Charles B. Cleveland on the bow pulpit, which was rigged for swordfishing. Rodney Cleveland (son) handles the wheel. Atop the cabin is the keg that would be used as a float once the fish was harpooned.*

How much did *Goldenrod*'s $450 price represent in the economy of that time, when a modest house on Cape Cod may have cost $600 - $700. One can safely suggest that *Goldenrod*'s price, like that of her predecessors and successors represented a meaningful sum, perhaps equivalent to about a year's earnings for a fisherman like Poole. To put that in some perspective, a skilled joiner of that era might earn about $2.50 per day and work 56 hours per week. However, it is unlikely that such a man was employed for every possible day. One can guess that a reasonable wage for a skilled workman might have ranged from some $550 – $800 per year. It is quite possible that a hard-working fisherman could have earned more. Nantucket's George Andrews remembered that, during the summer, a catboat skipper could earn eight dollars a day from the summer party clientele, and many boats were kept quite busy with such work.

In 1902, a few years after *Goldenrod* was built, Charles Crosby built a 27-foot catboat for Andrews's father, a Nantucket fisherman. The *Wonoma* cost Mr. Andrews $681. Built of cypress planking over oak frames, and fastened with the usual galvanized-iron boat nails, *Wonoma* had extra equipment that included an additional shelf in the cabin, more varnish work than usual, and outrigger sockets. A wide transom berth was built on each side of the centerboard trunk, which supported a hinged table. The boat had a kerosene stove, lamps, and running lights. Some workboats had a marine toilet, although most made do with a wooden box that enclosed a bucket. Boats like the Crosby-built *Goldenrod* and *Wonoma* were highly regarded and known to provide good value. Perhaps their biggest weak point (in terms of ultimate longevity) was their galvanized iron fastenings.

Size

In general, the smaller boats — 17 to 20 feet — were used principally for scalloping. Boats intended for lobstering, swordfishing, mackerel and cod fishing, and for the occasional freighting of fish typically ranged from 22 to 28 feet. Many also served in summer as party boats taking "sports" bluefishing or vacationing families for afternoon sails and picnics. Catboats primarily intended for offshore work such as netting mackerel or dragging, or as packets that carried barrels of salted fish, live fish, grain, livestock, or general merchandise were the biggest. These boats ranged from 32 to 40 feet (the size of many party boats to the south at Atlantic City, New Jersey) or, in the case of the Crosby-built *Nickerson,* aka "the Big Nick,* 45' 9". This, the largest catboat of which there is any record, was built for Rufus F. Nickerson of Chatham in 1900/1901, probably by Wilton Crosby. The boat was painted black to be more visible in fog.

Today, Rufus's grandson, Joe, recalls that the *Nickerson* was really a family endeavor and that the investment in the vessel was shared by Rufus's sons: Joe, Rufus A., and George. What manner of men were these? "Powerful as hell," said Joe Nickerson. "My grandfather and father stood about 5' 9" and weighed 190 pounds. This was good. It took two men to hoist the sail."

Although he does not remember all of the boat's specifications, Joe Nickerson recalled in the fall of 2001 that the sail had four sets of reef points, and that the beam was about 17 feet (it was listed officially in 1931 as 15' 5"). These numbers only begin to give an impression of the boat, however, because the *Nickerson,* as delivered from the builder, was tiller-steered and had no engine. After one season, the Nickersons installed wheel

Built in 1876, Lillian *served for years to ferry passengers from Nantucket up harbor to Wauwinet. It cost passengers 35 cents each way to make the trip. Seated on* Lillian's *long, cushioned cockpit seats or perched atop the cabin, visitors must have stored away pleasant recollections of their cruise aboard what would have been a steady, stable boat.*

steering and a fine Murray & Tregurtha engine, which nearly killed Joseph as he slept on one of the bunkbed-style transom berths. "It was either an exhaust leak or it was sucking all the air out of the cabin," said his son. "He was lucky that they were able to revive him."

The *Nickerson* ranged widely, fishing on Georges Bank, at Block Island, Nomans Land, and elsewhere in Cape waters, trolling for codfish and seining for mackerel. This continued until the deaths of Rufus F. and his son George. Although the surviving Nickersons ran the boat for a time with two hired fishermen, they sold the boat in 1910. "My father took a job on a big estate in Marion running the boats," said Joe Nickerson, "and my uncle concentrated mostly on the Old Harbor Inn, which he had built in 1900." The big *Nickerson* was sold to Nantucket and later was owned in Vineyard Haven before she was acquired by a New York salvage company.

The *Nickerson*'s size was unusual. "I think there were more 23-foot cats than anything else," remembered Joseph Chase Allen. "Usually they had a man and a boy or two men living aboard and sometimes they didn't get home for several weeks at a time."

If 23-footers were most popular on the Vineyard, it was reported that most boats at Chatham were 24 to 26 feet, while those built for use as Nantucket party boats ranged from 36 to 40 feet. When asked why these boats for Nantucket were so large, one of the Crosbys reportedly noted it must have been a fad. Most, if not all, were reportedly converted to carry a jib. Chapelle wrote that these big party boats sailed only in fair weather.

Power

When the *Goldenrod* was built, marine engine development on the East Coast was in its early stages. In 1897, the same year that *Goldenrod* was launched into the water at Osterville, two brothers down the coast in Connecticut began selling the first of the two-cycle engines that would make them famous. Their names were Frank and Ray Palmer, and they had by then been tinkering with a succession of rather cranky little motors in little boats on Long Island Sound. In Boston, a well-known steam engine and marine equipment maker named Murray & Tregurtha introduced an elegantly polished but more cumbersome four-cycle engine. Then, within just a few years of these pioneering efforts, dozens of marine engine companies were established, and commercial fishermen were a primary market for their wares. In New England, the primary makers whose engines would find their way into the catboats included Lathrop (Mystic, Connecticut), Bridgeport, (Bridgeport, Connecticut), Mianus (Mianus, Connecticut) and Palmer Brothers (Cos Cob, Connecticut). All built similar two-cycle engines, although each had its specific selling points.

The likely impact of internal combustion on sail-only boats that had by then been refined over a period of some 40 years was not lost on the more philosophical of the catboat skippers. On the Vineyard, Joseph Chase Allen reported that Captain Ellis Luce saw his first marine engine and predicted that "The catboat is doomed!" It was a prediction that took the wind out of Allen's sails "partly because it scuttled our long-range hopes and dreams, for we couldn't envision a waterfront without catboats berthed at the bollards."

But Ellis was correct. With the adoption of engines and their promise of labor savings and increased earning power, there came working catboats designed from the outset to have an auxiliary. Generally these engines were a single-cylinder "one-lunger" but sometimes a two-cylin-

der was ordered. At the outset, it was not uncommon for a fisherman to order an engine that was too small to drive the boat in anything except a near calm. This was either a simple mistake or, and perhaps more likely, the relatively low-powered motors first installed actually seemed to the fishermen to be something of a miracle. After all, they offered the wondrous ability of actually motoring directly home instead of waiting for hours for a breeze or trimming one's big sail in an effort to catch the slightest zephyr. After the initial wonder had subsided, it probably occurred to people that more powerful engines meant the boat could be driven home even against a good breeze from the wrong direction, and the true sailing auxiliary emerged.

Even if an engine was not ordered for a new boat, it was typical, by the early 1900s, for a shaft log to be bored and then filled with an easily removed wooden plug. The assumption was that the owner would eventually purchase an engine, an assumption that was almost universally correct. The accompanying chart gives the principal dimensions of an auxiliary catboat as recorded in 1907 by William Lambert Barnard.

A Crosby catboat circa 1906 designed for fishing at Chatham, Mass.

Length Overall: 23' 4"

Length of Waterline: 22' 6 1/2"

Beam: 11'

Draft: 2' 4"/6' 6"

Bow freeboard: 4' 4"

Least freeboard: 1' 9"

Sail area: 650 sq. ft.

Inside ballast: 2,500 lbs.

Price: $650 (add $300 - $400 for engine)

The 1906 boat's dimensions are worthy of some note. First, the beam was in accordance with the rule of thumb — about one-half the length of the boat's load waterline. Second, the draft with board up was typical for boats of 23 to 25 feet. Two-feet, six inches was then considered as the appropriate maximum board-up draft, and that only on boats of 30 feet in length. This shallow draft was one of the Cape Cod catboat's most distinctive and reassuring features, for Nantucket and Vineyard Sounds were areas aptly defined by the writer William Lambert Barnard as "a large number of shoals separated by shallow water."

This 23-footer's imposing sail is also worth a remark. It has commonly been assumed that the availability of internal combustion engines led to the catboat's big sail being reduced in size, making it easier to handle and to reduce the necessity for reefing. But, clearly, this was not always the case with new boats during the early days of power. Soon, however, the retrofitting of a one-lunger into an older boat would inevitably be accompanied by a reduced rig.

"That's what they always did when they got power," Vineyard fisherman Leonard Vanderhoop told John Leavens, the visionary who, with Paul Birdsall, founded the Catboat Association in 1962. "They cut the sails and the booms down. I don't know how they carried all the sail and mast they put on catboats before power." Mr. Vanderhoop's question is one that echoes down to the present day!

Photographs of early (1905 – 1910) engine installations in catboats appear to be nonexistent. The one reproduced here, taken at a somewhat later date, shows an engine in a Newport catboat. The installation looks a bit awkward because the

Photographs of engine installations are exceedingly rare. This one, made in 1918, shows a two-cycle "one-lunger" installed in a Newport catboat. Here, the cylinder head appears to have been removed.

engine is angled steeply, although this would not have been a problem for the two-cycle machine was lubricated by an oil/gas mixture. Of course, the engine's weight was well aft of where a boat's ballast was normally placed, and one assumes some compensation was made for this. The location did mean, however, that the centerboard and live wells could probably be left intact. As things developed, the machinery was moved forward in the cockpit, and the engine was installed at a much-reduced angle. That did affect the board and rig.

Like apparently every catboatman on the Cape or islands — except for one — Everett Poole was impressed by the potential of the internal combustion engine. To Poole, who fished out Menemsha, the engine offered the greatest possibility of getting in and out of Menemsha Creek on one tide, taking full advantage of his catboat's shallow draft. That is why, in 1903, Poole had a five-horsepower engine installed in *Goldenrod*. The

installation required that *Goldenrod*'s centerboard be shortened. The boom and, perhaps, the mast and gaff as well were cut down. The T & W engine that Poole had selected — locally manufactured in New Bedford — proved itself unreliable. Eventually, while lobstering off Gay Head, the engine stalled and couldn't be started. Poole's son Donald, who was along that day, remembered that when his father gave up trying to get the engine going, he disappeared into the cabin only to emerge with a variety of tools. Methodically, Everett Poole disconnected the engine from the exhaust pipe, shaft coupling, and engine mounts. Then he threw it overboard. "There, boy," he told his son, "that won't bother us any more. Let's put the sail to her."

But the damage had been done. Once, when Joseph Chase Allen was crewing for Poole after a new engine had been installed, they had the misfortune of picking up a lobster pot buoy in

The name of this pipe-smoking African-American scalloper and his catboat — photographed at Nantucket — are presently unknown. Frequented by the diverse crews of whaleships and politically influenced by Quakers, Nantucket abolished slavery in 1773. African-American fishermen had long since become an integral part of island life when this photograph was taken, perhaps in the 1920s.

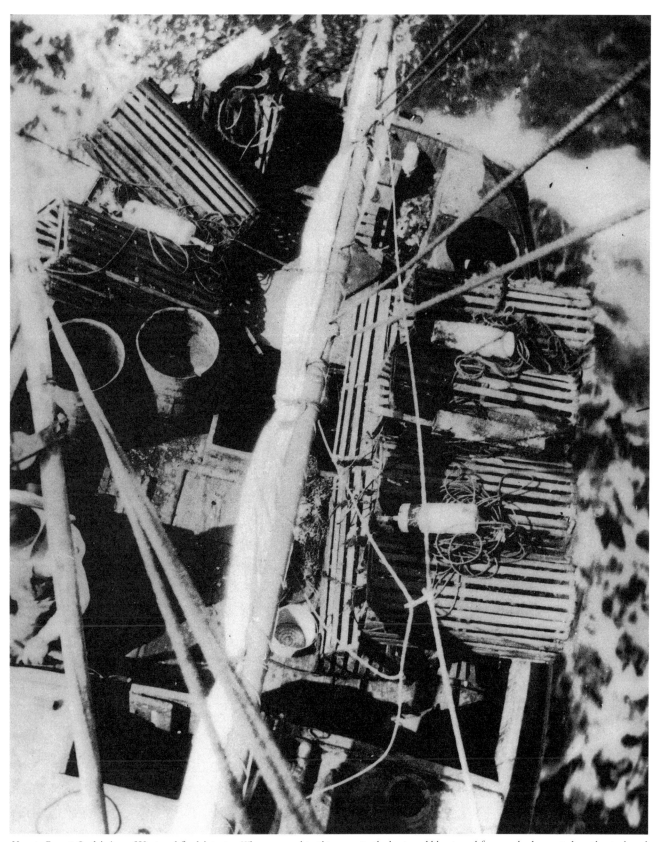

Here is Everett Poole's Anna W *rigged for lobstering When engaged in this pursuit, the boat could be steered from a wheel mounted on the starboard cabin bulkhead.*

Goldenrod's propeller. This pulled the stern bearing out of the boat, resulting in a nasty situation with water flooding in around the shaft and the buoy jammed between the sternpost and rudder. That was removed by Allen. Everett Poole held the boy — holding an axe in one hand — by his ankles over the stern. With the water flow largely halted with rags and the ability to steer restored, they had, said Allen, to beat their "way home against a head wind in a boat that had a very poor setting sail and half her centerboard had been taken out when they put the engine in. You can imagine how she handled. That was the *Goldenrod,* once the fastest boat that ever sailed out of Menemsha Bight, but in those days, she wasn't fast anymore. . . . [The engine] raised hell with everything. . . . [it] did her in." Poole sold the *Goldenrod* in 1913 after owning her for 16 years, and bought a larger catboat.

In the summer of 1941, a writer and catboat sailor named James S. Pitkin arranged to spend two weeks near Chatham and see what he could learn from a man who "enjoyed the undisputed reputation of being the most skillful catboat skipper on Cape Cod." This man was Captain Carol Nickerson and he owned an engineless, 24-foot Crosby catboat that he moored below his house overlooking Pleasant Bay. All his working life, Captain Nickerson had arisen an hour before dawn and, so long as Pleasant Bay wasn't frozen over, he had sailed southeast from Chatham to fish. "He was," said his descendant Joe Nickerson only half jokingly, "the only one who could sail up Chatham Harbor with a head tide and no wind. He had a white beard and mustache and wore a Sou'Wester hat and looked exactly like one of those old sea captains in pictures."

In the summer of 1941, Carol Nickerson shared some of his experiences with James Pitkin and,

over a decade later, in a wonderful article in *Yachting* in 1953, Pitkin described some of what he had learned. According to Pitkin, Captain Nickerson had never installed a motor because he had never felt the need for one, since "he had been able to come and go pretty much as he pleased." But these comings and going were recognized by all who could appreciate such things, as remarkable displays of skill by an intelligent and expert boat handler. Pitkin reported that Nickerson's sail

was remarkably large even for a boat that had no motor. He had had the sail recut three times before obtaining precisely the shape he desired. It was full in an arc from peak to tack and flat in the triangle area extending from the clew. As he headed into the channel, he eased his sheet and trimmed it experimentally until the only portion of the sail that was drawing, however fitfully, was the triangular area extending from the clew. The pressure on this after area, extending inboard from the end of his long boom, tended to produce a weather helm. And since the whiffs of a listless offshore breeze vary in direction, his experience enabled him to maintain a constant steerage way and glide steadily to windward.

In this matter of sail trimming, Captain Nickerson always kept his boom well outboard and never trimmed it over the counter. It was amazing to see him work to windward through a fleet of racing sloops with booms amidships while his boom was well outboard and his luff was fluttering merrily. But he was travelling to windward faster than the racing fleet.

How long Captain Nickerson continued to demonstrate his sailing skills and work his catboat is no longer known. He died in the late '40s or early '50s and his old catboat spent some 50 years slowly deteriorating in a field. Certainly, by the

Menemsha Basin, early 1920s. The catboats are (l. to r.) Anna W, Helen, *and* Beatrice. Helen *has one of the high-sided, able skiffs typical of Martha's Vineyard tied up astern.*

end of World War Two, working catboats of any sort around Cape Cod had pretty much given way to more modern types. On Martha's Vineyard, however, one man returned from overseas, put his catboat back in shape, and returned to fishing in the same manner as he had done before the war. His name was Oscar Pease and he eventually became the last of all the catboat fishermen.

The End of the Line

What would ultimately prove to be the last of all the working catboats was constructed beginning in the winter of 1928 by the most famous boatbuilder on Martha's Vineyard. His name was Manuel Swartz (he sometimes appended Roberts — his wife's maiden name — to the end of his name, thus becoming Manuel Swartz Roberts) and his

boat shop stood on Edgartown Harbor close by the Chappaquiddick ferry landing. (It still stands but as an art gallery.) By 1928, Manuel had built some 140 boats that dotted the island's harbors. The new boat was built for Thomas Pease, who had previously fished and sailed parties aboard a 23-foot Crosby-built catboat and then a 17-footer. As was the custom in those days, Mr. Pease gave Manuel a general idea of what he had in mind and also suggested a similar boat that embodied the shape he wanted. In this case, the boat he referred to was moored in Chilmark, a full-bowed 20-footer that Manuel had built in 1914.

Thomas's son, Oscar, reported the order for the boat in this fashion. "Father said, 'Well, Manuel, I've got a thousand dollars of interest money and I think I'd like you to build me a 20-

Manuel Swartz Roberts, Edgartown's famous boatbuilder, was nicknamed the "Old Sculpin" by the island's gifted chronicler, Joseph Chase Allen. Roberts built Vanity *for Thomas Pease in 1928.*

foot boat. I want a centerboard, a fish well, a six-horsepower Lathrop engine, and will you do it?'"

Manuel agreed to the price, which was by then probably somewhat on the low side. By 1928, however, catboat construction had been on the decline for years. Lathrop, however, was still offering its sturdy, two-cycle engine — such engines were referred to as "putt-putts" by island fishermen — although, like most companies, it had long since introduced a more modern four-cycle. According to Oscar, his father bought the motor from Manuel himself, who was the island's Lathrop dealer. This engine, with its make-and-

break ignition system, was used until it was replaced a decade later by a four-cycle, four-cylinder Lathrop.

"The fact that my father had a putt-putt as late as 1938," said Oscar, "indicates how successful the make-and-break engine really was." (Make-and-break referred to the ignition system. It was based on a low-tension spark coil that supplied current to contact points mounted in the cylinder. The points took the place of a spark plug and were mechanically opened and closed by a system of rods and springs. Such a system could generate a spark — when the points "broke" or opened —

even with the engine soaking wet, a big selling point for fishermen.)

Vanity herself was, in her proportion of cabin to cockpit, a traditional working-style catboat. The cockpit was built large, a roomy workspace designed so a man could make his living. The cabin was comparatively small with room for two narrow berths and a forepeak used to stow neatly coiled line and assorted gear. Small as the cabin's dimensions were, Oscar had learned to use every inch of space and spent occasional weekends aboard. Thomas Pease said that, by comparison to his previous Crosby boat, *Vanity* was more heavily built. He overcame his initial disappointment with the boat, caused by the fact that Manuel had, in a lapse, built the bow section sharper than it was supposed to be. It made *Vanity* wetter than she should have been, but faster under power. When it came time for him to paint the boat, Thomas Pease kept the hull white, but changed the original buff cabin top and decks to a paint purchased from Sears that he called dove gray. Eventually, the same color was used on the seats while dark green was applied to the cockpit sole. Those became *Vanity*'s colors for the remainder of her working life.

The fact that Pease's new boat was launched with a stub mast in place of a rig and worked purely under power for the next decade is merely one more example of the fisherman's adoption of internal combustion. In fact, had a hurricane not struck the island in 1938, *Vanity* might never have had a sailing rig. But the great storm's aftermath saw a decline in fish catches, and Thomas Pease decided to augment his income by sailing parties.

Oscar Pease, who worked with his father and eventually inherited *Vanity,* recalled every detail of the boat, its construction, and the development and building of its rig. He said that the mast was made from a spruce log washed off a coasting

schooner's deck and salvaged from an island beach by another island boatbuilder, Erford Burt. "He towed it home behind his Essex coupe," Oscar said. He also said that *Vanity*'s rig was patterned generally after that of a fast Crosby 23-footer on the island named *Four Aces*. With *Vanity*'s mast length determined as 29 feet, the traditional method of sizing the gaff and boom was also remembered by heart by Oscar.

"The boom was the same length as the mast. The gaff, when put against the mast, came aft to the boom crutch. That was the formula. Then you hoisted the peak up to where it looked good and took your measurement down for the sail leech."

Vanity's sail set perfectly, pulled like a team of draft horses, and was rigged with pennants at the clew for safe reefing. The mainsheet was rigged in a manner typical of many catboats from the 19th century. The sheet was attached to the outer end of the boom, ran to a single block on the traveler, up to a single block on the boom, and down to the cockpit. Big oak cleats were installed to which the sheet could be belayed.

Here, then, was the last of all the working catboats. For a number of years after World War Two, *Vanity* did have company. One of these boats was the Wilton Crosby-built (in 1917) *Dolphin,* owned by Joseph Mello. Oscar admired Mello both as a fisherman and boat keeper, for Mello kept *Dolphin* looking like a yacht, protecting her varnished coamings with special flannel covers and the staving and cockpit sole with tailored canvas. When *Dolphin* went ashore in the hurricane of 1954, Mr. Mello repaired her as best he could and kept her for five more years until he sold her, with tears in his eyes, to Captain Bob Douglas.

By the early '60s, one could have probably counted the working catboats left on the Vineyard on the fingers of one hand. After researching the island's

A stout breeze from the right direction was helpful when dragging for scallops under sail power. Here are the deeply reefed Crimson *and another boat scouring Nantucket harbor circa 1910.*

catboats, John Leavens concluded that one of the last remaining boats was *Doris,* which had also been built by Manuel Swartz Roberts. He reported that her owner, who had used the boat for scalloping, "chopped her up for firewood" in 1963.

But *Vanity* endured. Even after his official retirement, Oscar still kept *Vanity* rigged for fishing. As one of the most respected fishermen on the island, he was watched closely by others when he ventured forth — "just for fun" — for a morning of scalloping in Cape Pogue Pond. *Vanity,* dutifully hauling her scallop drags back and forth along the

pond's bottom, was as capable, if not far more capable, than the variety of skiffs and other work-boats engaged in the same task. It was, on a clear, cold day, hard but satisfying work, and it was easy to see how much more difficult it would have been under sail alone.

Although Oscar had not scalloped under sail himself, Nantucket's George Andrews remembered the method clearly. "What they'd do," he said, "was to tow the dredges off the stern and on the weather side of the boat. They might have two off the stern and four off the side, but sometimes towed as many as eight or ten dredges. They'd start with the sail out shaking on the port side, as they generally had the dredges to starboard. Then they'd trim the sail to get the speed and power they needed. Of course, you needed the wind from the right direction, depending on where you were dredging. The sheet and centerboard were adjusted so that as the boat gained too much headway, it would luff up, lose headway, and fall off again. This put a lot of wear on the sail."

Martha's Vineyard fisherman Leonard Vanderhoop remembered scalloping under sail with his brother Bill in their catboat *Three Friends* in Menemsha Pond before World War One.

"We had four drags on a side," he told John Leavens, "and it took a good two-reef breeze to do it. When you came along on the port tack, you'd throw the drags out to port, then when you'd come about, you'd luff her up and pull those drags. Then you would set the starboard drags when you fell off again on the starboard tack. As long as the wind was up, it was easier than pulling with power. You'd just get your drags full and then let your sail luff while you pulled your drags. The best part was that there was no cost to it."

When *Vanity* was new, it was typical to use the stub mast as the base for rigging to which the drags were attached. Later, this evolved into the efficient metal framework that Oscar assembled in the late fall in preparation for the opening of the scalloping season. When rigged to work under engine power alone, *Vanity* was fitted with a tiny pilothouse atop her hatch from which the boat could be steered in harsh weather. It was a typical arrangement. A big culling board across the cockpit, the dredges, and wire baskets for the scallops completed the scalloping rig.

Oscar Pease died at age 83 in 1995. With him passed, finally, the sight of a catboat working its native waters and skippered by a man who carried within him all those traditions and skills of a now vanished breed of fisherman — the catboat man.

Here is Vanity, *age 54, immaculate as always. It is November, 1982 and Oscar Pease has equipped the Lathrop-powered boat with her scalloping rig.*

Here is Nib, *a 21-footer built, probably at Newport, in 1896.* Nib *carries a typically large rig and won a number of first prizes before she was put up for sale in 1898.*

CHAPTER THREE

YACHT

—— •◦• ——

"The Mascot *is an old-fashioned Cape Cod catboat, 30 years old. Her dimensions are, length overall 24 ft. 6 in., waterline 23 ft., draught 3 ft. 6 in. With self-bailing cockpit, she is as safe and able a little ship as a man could want to go to sea in."*
—HENRY M. PLUMMER, *The Boy, Me, and the Cat,* 1913

I N 1852, when Bob Fish's 16-foot cat-rigged centerboarder was acquired by an English nobleman, sailing was a sport reserved almost entirely for the very wealthy. It was not until a decade after the American Civil War that "yachting" — the terminology of that epoch — began to emerge as an activity for middle-class professionals and even for some working men. Still, the idea of a cruise on one's own small boat or an afternoon's day sailing took awhile to develop. Instead, there was racing and, during the late 1860s through the 1870s and even afterwards, this meant the racing of sloop-rigged or mainsail-only sandbaggers. These boats — which ranged in size from 20 to 35 feet and carried vastly over-sized rigs — were kept right side up primarily by the shifting of 50 – 100 pound sandbags by sturdy crewmen. The boats were owned variously by both wealthy and a few professional or working class men. But the whole scene was really domi-

nated by physically punishing racing and by wagering. The sandbaggers were a rough crowd.

Although yacht clubs either accepted sandbaggers into the membership rosters — upon which they were entered as cat-rigged or jib-and-mainsail-rigged "boats" — or were formed as sandbag-racing organizations, the failure to establish any meaningful rules and the free-for-all nature of the races eventually saw the whole thing gradually sink under its own weight. Just after Christmas, 1896, *Field & Stream* noted the belated and more or less official passing of the sandbagger: "Granted that it was at one time a necessity, and that those who survived to graduate from its severe curriculum have been a credit to it as a teacher of sailormen, the harm that has been done to American yachting by the long and close adherence to sandbag models and sandbag methods, to say nothing of the direct loss of life is even yet felt in yachting. . . . It will *never* be missed." Memories of the sandbaggers

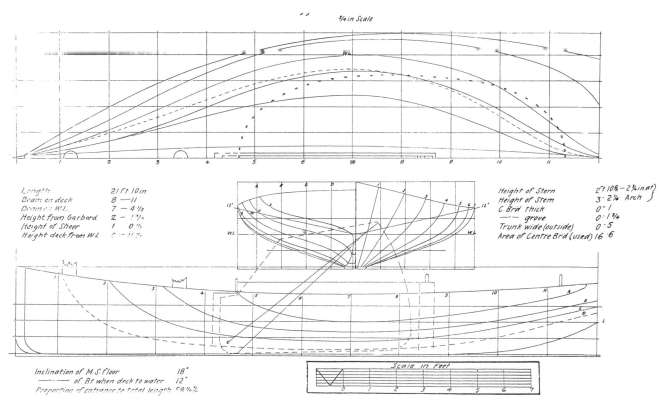

Length	21 ft 10 in
Beam on deck	8 — 11
Beam at W.L.	7 — 4 1/2
Height from Garbord	2 - 1 3/4
Height of Sheer	1 0 1/2
Height deck from W.L.	0 - 11 1/2

Height of Stern	2 ft 10 5/8 — 2 3/4 in at
Height of Stem	3 - 2 3/4 Arch
C. Brd thick	0 - 1
— grove	0 - 1 3/4
Trunk wide (outside)	0 - 5
Area of Centre Brd (used)	16 - 6

Scale in Feet

Inclination of M.S. floor	18°
— of Bt when deck to water	12°
Proportion of entrance to total length	59 1/2%

The sandbagger Oriole *could be raced as a jib-and-mainsail or mainsail-only boat. The shallow, curving lines of the hull are typical of boats built up to the early 1870s.* Oriole's *hull with its absence of a defined bilge was of a type likened to a "skimming dish" — a shallow dish in which milk was poured so that cream could be skimmed off the top. The boat's transom shape is not unlike that of* Una *or the committee boat painted by Buttersworth that appears later in this book.* Oriole *has an enormous 16 1/2-sq. ft. centerboard and sailing her must have offered demanding sport for her crew. Dimensions: 21' 10" long x 8' 11" beam on deck x 7' 4 1/2" beam at waterline.*

with their shiftable ballast and shallow, centerboard hulls, very likely prompted some negative sentiment about centerboard yachts in general.

The Catboat Comes of Age

In 1845, when he was 28 years old, the English-born painter James E. Buttersworth emigrated to the United States and settled in New Jersey opposite Manhattan. Like any painter of marine subjects, Buttersworth depicted vessels whose owners might be interested in buying the work. For years, this meant he painted square-riggers and large yachts. But later, Buttersworth began painting the occasional sandbagger, probably boats owned by wealthy men who either raced themselves or, more likely, watched and bet on the outcome from the deck of their steam yacht. In 1870,

Buttersworth painted a Great South Bay sandbagger flying the burgee of the Brooklyn Yacht Club. He painted cat-rigged sandbaggers of the Columbia Yacht Club in 1876.

At some point during this period — probably between 1868 and the early 1870s — Buttersworth also painted a picture that he called "Catboats with Committee Boat" (see Chapter 11). Although the precise year of the work is unknown, another misfortune when it comes to dating the evolution of the catboat, the sidedecks of the boats in Buttersworth's painting are too narrow for sandbags which, as "moveable ballast," were generally arranged along the edge of the weather deck. But this moveable ballast was, by the 1870s, already being discouraged in some racing venues.

40 · CAPE COD CATBOATS

Did the boats in "Catboats with Committee Boat" have moveable ballast? If so, why did Buttersworth call the painting "Catboats with Committee Boat" instead of "Sandbaggers with Committee Boat?" No sandbags are evident during examination of the painting, which is in the collection of the Cahoon Museum of American Art in Cotuit, Massachusetts. Instead, these boats appear to be open cockpit catboats of 23 to 25 feet in length, built as yachts and racing in a group. The primary boat in the painting flies a private signal or the burgee of a now unidentifiable yacht club. What can be said with certainty is that the boats in Buttersworth's painting are primitive. The curves of the committee boat's shallow transom exhibit much the same shape as Fish's *Una*. What's more, the rudders are extraordinarily long, looking to be almost 20 percent of the length of the boat, and operated by a very long tiller that might be handled by two men, if necessary. This suggests boats that, if fast, were poorly balanced. In his 1935 correspondence with Nathanael Greene Herreshoff, W. P. Stephens referred to such New York area catboats as "the very bad breed of cats prevalent 60 years ago."

Whatever their deficiencies, such boats formed a basis upon which the whole sport of small yacht racing would grow. Rather quickly, probably beginning in the late 1860s after the Civil War, boats like these — boats that came to be called catboats — grew in popularity. *The American Yacht List* of 1875 records at least 70 of from 12 to 21 feet sailing in Massachusetts Bay. And there were others, like those in Buttersworth's picture, in New York as well, not to mention New Jersey and Great South Bay. On the Gulf Coast, the racing of "Biloxi catboats" — vee-bottom, hard-chine boats descended from the area's working models — also began in the 1870s.

What did one of the early New York area catboats look like? What we have to go by are rare paintings like Buttersworth's and an occasional drawing. In 1888, C. G. Davis, a capable draftsman and illustrator, yacht designer, and regular contributor to *The Rudder*, bought such a boat. Built at Rockaway and originally named *Ada R*, the boat

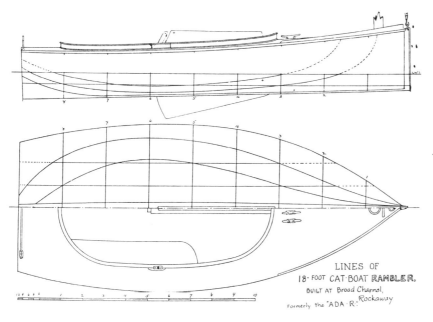

LINES OF
18-FOOT CAT-BOAT RAMBLER.
BUILT AT Broad Channel,
Rockaway
Formerly the "ADA·R."

Here are the lines of C. G. Davis's leaky but much-loved Rambler. Davis reported that the boat was "old and worn out" when he purchased her for $75. However, her lines may be the best that exist of a New York area catboat of the late 1860s or early 1870s.

had an absolutely plumb stem and stern, and the low, rounded hull form that led some to call such craft a "skimming dish." It was 18 feet long, about 8 1/2-feet wide, and had a board-up draft of about one foot. The boat was old, leaky, somewhat worm-eaten, and with rot here and there. We may suppose it had been built between the late 1860s and the early 1870s. Davis's drawing of *Rambler,* as he named her, indicates that oarlocks were mounted on the low cockpit coaming and cleats just in front of the coaming served to belay the halyards. Unfortunately, Davis did not draw the boat's rudder or details of her hardware or rigging. It was with boats of this general type that the catboat began a rapid ascent to popularity. By the mid-1880s, when the cash-strapped Davis was engaged in wet yet apparently enjoyable cruises on the Hudson in *Rambler,* the catboat entered a period that, in retrospect, can be judged a kind of Golden Age.

The Golden Age

By 1896 and the death of the sandbagger, the broad outlines of sailing as it is still enjoyed today had been in place for about 20 years. "Cabin yachts," as distinct from open cockpit boats, emerged during the 1870s both as centerboard and keel designs. Still, one of the day's most exclusive yacht clubs, perhaps recognizing that new forces were emerging that would change the nature of the sport, took steps to preserve the status quo. At Marblehead's Eastern Yacht Club, the membership approved the exclusion from its races of any yacht under 25-feet waterline length, and they later increased this to 30 feet.

One result of such attitudes was the founding in 1872 of the Beverly Yacht Club, an organization whose dues were five dollars a year and whose

youthful members were dedicated to racing. Records indicate that the club's first race in 1872 drew 11 boats, 10 of which were catboats. The club operated without a permanent clubhouse until 1895 when it leased a facility at Monument Beach. In 1898, the Club roster listed 132 boats, 70 of which were catboats.

Not only did the racing of smaller boats, catboats in particular, become increasingly popular, but so did debates about the advantages of different boat types. "Cutter cranks," for example, espoused the virtues of a type as unlike the sandbagger as possible — a narrow, deep-keel boat such as was popular in England. As the debate progressed, keel-type yachts began to become increasingly popular north of Cape Cod while centerboard boats were staunchly adhered to from the Cape south to New York. The yachting press of the day was replete with letters from enthusiasts of the various types, each pointing out the other's deficiencies. Sometimes, though, boats of different types entered the same race and, for that reason, the debate about the supremacy of keel vs. centerboard or vice-versa, was occasionally put to a direct test.

In the summer of 1889, one of these races was sponsored by the Eastern Yacht Club. Focal points were 30-foot waterline cutters from the drawing boards of two of the day's top naval architects. *Saracen* was designed by Edward Burgess. *Kathleen* was designed by William Gardner. The boats had seven-foot keels, could spread some 2,000 square feet of sail, and their racing against each other had produced a rivalry known to most who followed the sport. Also in the race was a pair of 40-foot waterline yachts. All in all, this race was widely anticipated and several reporters were on hand to chronicle the event. Then, into this arena, there appeared a catboat. In those days, there was not yet a Cape Cod Canal so *Harbinger,* which had been designed and built by Charles C. Hanley in his Monument Beach boat shop on Buzzards Bay, made the initial voyage to Boston's North Shore by rounding the Cape. The boat was owned by Joseph Hooper of the Hull Yacht Club.

July 15, 1889 was a rainy day with a strong and gusty northeast wind. Right away, the skippers of the cutters decided it was no day for topsails and they housed (lowered) their boats' topmasts. The course took the boats along the North Shore past Graves Light to the turning mark at Hardings Ledge off Hull, and it was rough going. *Kathleen* sailed the downwind leg with her main and a jib topsail after failing to set her spinnaker. *Harbinger* did set her spinnaker — a big triangular sail set on a long pole with jaws like that of the gaff — and managed to keep it up until the pole broke in four places. Still, at the turning mark, *Harbinger* was only 35 seconds behind *Saracen* and four minutes ahead of the third place yacht.

Now, it was time to begin the long beat back to Marblehead against the powerful seas that a strong northeast breeze always produces in that area. One of the boats in *Harbinger*'s class sprung her topmast and had to be towed home. Another gave up. At some point between Nahant and Swampscott, the owner of one of the 40-footers was knocked overboard and almost drowned. *Harbinger* and *Kathleen* were, meanwhile, slicing to windward in apparently fine fashion. And then *Harbinger*'s skipper took advantage of his boat's shallow draft in one of the few spots where it could make a difference. Judging the tide was high enough, he sailed *Harbinger* over the rocks between Tinker's Island and Marblehead Neck, saving just enough time to win the race on both

elapsed time and corrected time. When the latter was computed, *Harbinger,* with a waterline just over two-feet shorter than that of the 30-foot cutters, and a board-up draft of three feet, won by 20 minutes.

People were astonished. And they were people who mattered. "Under such conditions of wind and water," one observer noted, "the two keel cracks should, if modern theories are correct, have soaked out to windward three feet to her two . . . Did the *Harbinger* really show as good ability to windward as her rivals, and if so, how do the experts account for it? Was it her board or her beam or her small displacement or her rig, or all combined, or what?" The answer to this question lay in the genius of *Harbinger*'s designer but that fact was then known to a relative handful of people.

W. P. Stephens wrote that, when the famous cutters "were defeated by an unknown craft, interest shifted to the newer type." Stephens' comment is of interest if only because it is one of the few times that a catboat is referred to as a "newer type!" But the catboat, by comparison to other types including the sandbaggers, had a lot to offer. In 1897, Stephens summed it up like this: "They are handy, safe, and roomy, and men that have owned sloops, sandbaggers, and schooners, when they want a good sail often choose a Cape catboat."

Beginning in the late 1870s and escalating during the period 1885 to 1900, catboat racing attracted new enthusiasts and the finest of all catboats were designed and built during these years. Many were ordered by wealthy men whose desire to win supported advances in catboat design and construction. Ultimately, the dominance of a few of these extraordinary catboats discouraged competition but that was still in the future when

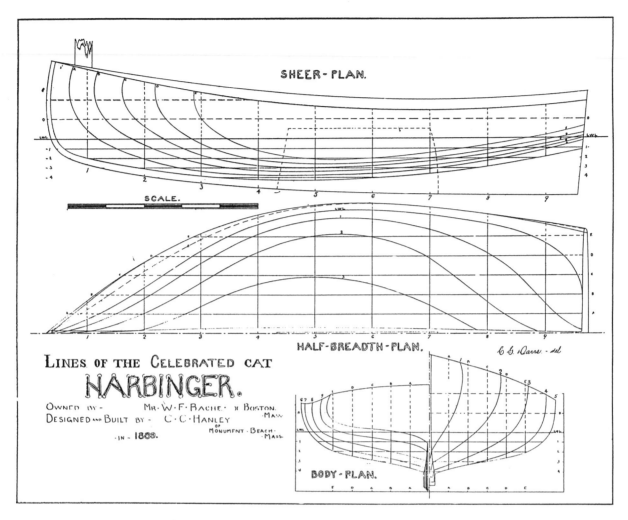

SHEER-PLAN.

SCALE.

HALF-BREADTH-PLAN.

C. G. Davis - del

LINES OF THE CELEBRATED CAT

HARBINGER.

OWNED BY - MR. W. F. BACHE. OF BOSTON. MASS.
DESIGNED AND BUILT BY - C. C. HANLEY OF MONUMENT BEACH. MASS.
- IN 1889 -

BODY-PLAN.

SAIL PLAN OF CAT BOAT
HARBINGER.

Here are the lines, profile, and sail plan of "the celebrated cat"
Harbinger as drawn by Charles G. Davis in 1889. In the proportions
of the hull, particularly in its centerboard placement and the manner
in which the beam was carried so far aft, lay some of the keys to C. C.
Hanley's success. The sailing qualities that derived from these lines
were unequaled by other catboats, before or since.

Harbinger

Designer/builder: Charles C. Hanley

Location: Monument Beach, Mass.

Date of Launching: 1889

Overall Length: 28 feet

Length water line: 27' 9"

Beam: 13' 6"

Draft board up/board down: 36" /approx. 6' 6"

Mast length: 40 feet

Boom length: 40 feet

Gaff length: 28 feet

Bow Sprit: 16 feet

Ballast: 4,600 lbs. of lead

Harbinger and her successors ushered in a period of yachting history in general, and catboat history in particular, that would never be seen again.

Marianna, a Half-decked Catboat of the Golden Age

Builder: Christoper ("Kit") Briggs

Location: Westport, Massachusetts

Date: Early 1890s

Length overall: 16 feet

Length of waterline: 15' 9"

Beam: 7' 2"

Draft (board up/board down) 2' 3"/5'

Sail area: 271.8 sq. ft. increased to 316.4 sq. ft

Ballast: 1,100 pounds of iron bars adjusted according to weather conditions for racing when only 500 lbs. might be carried. Centerboard weighted with 50 lbs. of lead.

Construction: cedar planking over (presumably) oak frames

Notes: Among the fastest catboats on Narragansett Bay including those several feet longer, *Marianna* was lost in a squall (the approach of which her skipper ignored) while racing at Newport in July, 1894. No fatalities were involved.

The Herreshoffs

Although Nathanael G. Herreshoff's father, Charles Frederick, had built the first of his four cat-rigged boats known as *Julia* in 1833, *Sprite* — launched at Bristol, Rhode Island, on June 28, 1860 — is the earliest centerboard catboat built as a yacht of which a meaningful record survives. A boat with an underhung rudder, a low-roofed cabin, and a 450-square foot sail, *Sprite* suffered from excessive weather helm but was unusually fast nonetheless. Nathanael G. Herreshoff wrote to W. P. Stephens of *Sprite:* "In her I sailed and won my first race [in 1860 or 1861] at 12 1/2 years of age. Even when 25 or 30 years old and we thought were building much faster boats, my brother James acquired her after being laid up many years, and gave us a real surprise."

Sprite's maiden voyage in late July was a 28-hour cruise to New York so that the Herreshoffs could inspect Isambard Kingdom Brunel's steamship, the *Great Eastern*. After 10 days in New York, the Herreshoffs started home. *Sprite* left a pier in the East River at 6 a.m. on a Saturday and arrived in Bristol at 8 a. m. on Sunday, a performance by a small boat that would be exceptional even today. What's more, *Sprite* was accompanied by Charles Frederick Herreshoff's *Julia III,* which may then have been five or six years old.

Nat Herreshoff recalled *Sprite* as the fastest 20-foot boat on Narragansett Bay. What the immediate impact of the boat was in terms of generating more of her type is unknown. Over in Osterville, as nearly as we can tell, the Crosby brothers were then just getting the initial orders for their boats, but these were intended as fishing craft. Yet, as the Herreshoff factory records prove, there were catboats racing in Narragansett Bay by the mid- to late-1860s. At least one, the 16' x 7' 3" *Henrietta,* had a centerboard. Three more followed a 16' x 7' 3" model and a 21 1/2' x 9' 2" boat in 1866 and 1867. Then, interest increased — whether abruptly or gradually it is now hard to judge — sometime around or shortly after 1870. Now, the Herreshoffs began building a variety of distinctive, highly engineered catboats for customers from Boston to Barnegat Bay.

In 1876, Nat Herreshoff designed the 25-foot overall catboat *Gleam* for George and Frederick Gower of Providence, Rhode Island. The contract stipulated that the Gowers would not have to pay for the boat unless she defeated what was then the fastest catboat on Narragansett Bay, *Wanderer*. This latter boat had been built in Providence by Benjamin Davis. "This she did in two races, with Nat at the tiller," recorded W. P. Stephens. According to Nat Herreshoff's letter to W. P. Stephens written in August 1935, this catboat, built by his brother John, "was the first craft to be built on the system I had worked out — of making a complete mould for each timber…thus having the form very exact to design…This method has been used by the H. M. Co. for all craft under 75 ft. x 15 ft. o.a., nearly 59 years."

Sprite

Length overall: 20' 3"

Beam: 8' 9"

Draft: 2' 9" board up

Sail Area: 450 sq. ft.

Ballast: 1,000 – 1,200 lbs. of cast iron plus 400 – 500 lbs. of sandbags

Note: The beam of this and subsequent Herreshoff catboats was narrow by comparison to that of a traditional Cape Cod model.

Gleam and the Herreshoff boats that followed were intended primarily for racing and each represented some design advance or nuance intended to make it faster than the previous model. The 18-foot *Nat,* for example, built for Quincy Yacht Club commodore John Shaw, was lightly built, had a lightweight hollow mast, and set 300-squre feet of sail. As was often the case in that period, Shaw ordered *Nat,* which was a winning boat for years, to replace a once fast boat that was past her prime. In this case, the older boat was the 18' 8"x 15' 10"x 7' 6" *Mab* built in 1891. (Those are *Mab's*

dimensions as recorded by the Quincy Yacht Club. Herreshoff records describe the boat as 16' 6" on the waterline x 7' 4" beam.) This was a rather typical example of why boats were replaced at that time. Wealthy owners, as soon as their winning vessel was eclipsed, promptly ordered another that would be faster than the latest competition.

It's worth noting that these Herreshoff catboats were designed exclusively as yachts with proportions quite different from the working catboats then in use, or even from the typical catboat created by other builders but based on working models. The Herreshoff boats were proportionally more narrow than one associates with a classic catboat, and the overall length often far exceeded the waterline length in order to gain an advantage under racing handicap rules. The *Merry Thought,* built in 1897, for example, was 32 feet long but had a waterline of just 26 feet and a beam of 10' 8". Such a yacht reportedly cost some $5,000, an enormous sum in that day's currency. Built for a wealthy Philadelphian named John Crozer, *Merry Thought* ended the dominance of the Manley Crosby-built *Scat* and also put an end to any hope of race wins on the part of Barnegat Bay's working catboat skippers. They, for more than a decade beginning in 1890, would show up — 40 or more at a time — at Beach Haven to race.

Wanda, a catboat of generally similar proportions to *Merry Thought* but built in 1897 for another Barnegat Bay yachtsman named Fred Bedford, was equally or more successful. But such success came at the price of catboat racing in general. Just as competitors or potential competitors around New York dwindled in the face of one wealthy individual's costly and overwhelmingly superior Manley Crosby-built boats, the same thing happened on Barnegat Bay. Few men were in a posi-

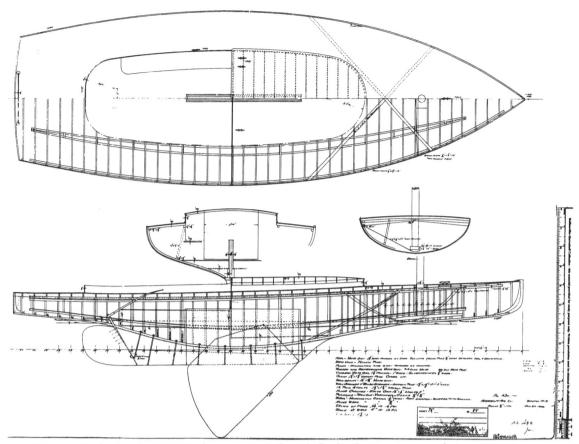

The Herreshoff Catboat Wanda: *Built in 1897, Wanda measured 21' 9" x 10' 1"x 2' 11". Although typical of other racing catboats developed by N. G. Herreshoff, Wanda had little in common with a Cape Cod catboat. With her comparatively fine ends and overhangs, a mast placed well aft, and an underhung rudder, this yacht had one principal purpose — to go very fast. Bronze strapping reinforces her hull's forward sections. A 1 3/4" white-oak keel formed the boat's backbone. The rudder and frames were also oak. The deadwood was yellow pine. The hull was double-planked with Washington cedar.*

tion to fund yachts like these, equipped with the finest sails, and interest waned.

The decline posed no threat to Herreshoffs. W. P. Stephens recorded that, in the period leading up to 1878, most of the boats built at Herreshoffs were sailboats: "many small catboats, some catboats and sloops of medium size, and a few large schooners." But then, the company began building steam launches and, as the years wore on, focused on these and the larger sailing yachts with which the Herreshoff name is principally associated. Some of the more heavily built Herreshoff catboats raced on, however. *Merry Thought* was still sailing the waters of Barnegat Bay three decades after her launching.

Little contemporary first-hand information remains about these boats. In 1900, however, *The Rudder* published an article by one Walter C. Lewis. Entitled "A Memorable Cruise," this story recounted the planned voyage of the author and a friend from Boston Harbor to Marblehead and around Cape Ann, back to Gloucester and then on to Boston. The weather did not cooperate so that the trip eventually got only as far as Marblehead, with a very near shipwreck off Boston caused by a dragging anchor. The Herreshoff 26 1/2-foot catboat involved in this story had been built in 1872 and was named *Surf*. The boat's cabin had 4' 5" of headroom and transom berths 10 feet long. Lewis recorded the following about this catboat.

Pre-1900 Catboats Designed by N. G. Herreshoff

Date	Name	Type	L.W.L	Beam	Draft
1860	*Clio*	CB	20' 11"	8' 9"	3'
1865	*Henrietta*	CB	16'	7' 3"	-
1865	*Poppasquash*	CB	16'		
1866	*Fannie (Posy)*	Cat rig	21 1/2'	9' 2"	-
1867	*Fannie (2nd)*	Cat rig	21 1/2'	9'	-
1872	*Surf*	CB	23 1/2'	9' 6"	3'
1876	*Gleam*	CB	25'	11'	-
1879	*Sabrina*	Cat rig	16'	7'	-
	Nora	Cat rig	16'	7'	-
1881	*Alice*	CB	21	9'	-
1882	*Nora II*	CB	18	8'	-
pre-1885	*Elsie*	CB	16' 2"	7' 4"	1' 7"
1889	*Calypso*	CB	16 1/2'	7'	-
1890	*Bird*	CB	16'	7' 4"	1' 4"
1891	*Mab*	CB	16'	7'4"	1' 4"
1892	*Sayonara*	CB	25'	10 1/2'	2'
1892	*Merry Thought*	CB	25'	11'	2' 3"
	Viola	CB	17'	7' 4"	1' 4"
	Mojave	CB	21'	8' 1"	2'
1894	*Acis*	Cat rig	18'	7' 5"	-
1896	*Gloria*	CB	19' 2"	7' 4"	2' 7"
1898	*Alpha*	Cat rig	14'	5' 3"	9 1/2"
	Omega	Cat rig	14'	5' 3"	9 1/2"

Notes: CB = centerboard

There is reason to believe that this list, based on information from the Herreshoff Marine Museum with some additions from magazine sources, does not include all the Herreshoff-built catboats of this period.

"So strongly was she timbered and planked that today she is in good condition, I understand, and has never needed more than ordinary repairs. She has never been replanked, nor has her frame been renewed in any part during these twenty-eight years. At the time that I bought her, I wanted a 'single-hander' and a catboat was then the only boat that could be properly so-called. I renamed her *Trojan*, and found her seaworthy, easy to handle and of a fair turn of speed. In these days she is not so far behind new boats of her general type as might be thought . . . She was the only boat that I ever sailed that would keep steadily on a course, close-hauled or free, with a lashed wheel. For a catboat, her performances in this respect were little less than miracles."

Crosbys

According to *The Rudder,* the Crosbys first began building boats intended as yachts in 1873. Typically, these boats had gracefully raked transoms, underhung rudders, and cabins that were bigger in proportion compared to the working boats. Although these catboats were raced for years under various owners and at various yacht clubs, their basic hull forms did not deviate to any great degree from the proven Crosby working model. A specific boat intended for racing might, perhaps, be a bit lighter and more fine-lined than the standard product, but it looked like one still expects a catboat to look. In 1890, *Mudjekeewis* was built by Daniel and C. H. Crosby for William P. Whitmarsh. In a letter to a subsequent owner,

Mr. Whitmarsh wrote that: "She was the first boat they had built with the small cockpit, strip deck, etc. and was rather heavily constructed for racing; in fact, she was not built for racing."

Despite her heavy construction, which made her slow in light air and downwind, the boat had spars worthy of a racer — a 40-foot mast, 39' 6" boom, and 27-foot gaff. As desired, a 13-foot bowsprit could also be fitted. Whitmarsh reported that the boat might have fared better in the hands of a professional skipper but, even so, won the championship of the Dorchester Yacht Club.

It took one of the era's wealthier catboat enthusiasts to entice a Crosby away from Osterville to focus on building boats purely as racing yachts that broke the traditional Crosby design styles. The wealthy man was Frank M. Randall, a member of

Low tide at Osterville. Wilton Crosby's shop is to the left and Worthington's is to the right. Orchid *is a typical yacht-built Crosby catboat with an underhung rudder and bright-finished coamings.*

Although built with an oversized cabin for comfortable cruising, Mudjekeewis *carried a large rig and was a frequent entrant in racing events. She was said to be slow in light air thanks to her weight, and difficult to handle off the wind, but was an excellent boat to windward.*

several yacht clubs in the New York–New Jersey area and Boston. He had been sailing catboats since the late 1870s, and had been a Crosby repeat customer since at least 1893. In 1895, Randall persuaded Horace Crosby's sons — 36-year-old Manley and 25-year-old Joseph — to move to New York where they could build catboats specifically to race in those waters. Thus was established the Crosby Catboat and Yacht Building Company of which Randall became a stockholder and the treasurer. The two Crosbys lived on a grounded-out steamboat in the Bay Ridge section of Brooklyn.

This sole off-Cape venture by members of Crosby family enjoyed some short-lived success. Young Joseph soon returned to Osterville but Manley stayed on. The first boat built at Bay Ridge

was *Step Lively,* which was launched on Memorial Day 1896. Like subsequent Crosby yachts built by Manley Crosby in New York, *Step Lively* was not a typical Cape Cod cat. Built to take advantage of racing measurement rules, the boat had long over-hangs at bow and stern so that, although the waterline length was 25 feet, the boat was actually 34' 9" overall. The result of such design was that the boat was awarded a favorable handicap. The boat's beam was also comparatively narrow. *Step Lively* finished second in her first race in light air to the Gil Smith catboat *Squaw* but then went on to a series of wins in a variety of conditions. The class for "cabin cats" in which she raced (and which Randall apparently hoped to build up) was apparently small, for reports speak of only three to seven starters.

Step Lively

Length Overall: 34'9"

Length of Waterline: 25 feet

Beam: 11'3"

Draft (board up): 1' 9"

Area of mainsail: 1,050 sq. ft.

Note: A removable bowsprit so that jibs or a spinnaker could be hoisted was part of the boat's specification, although most likely for cruising.

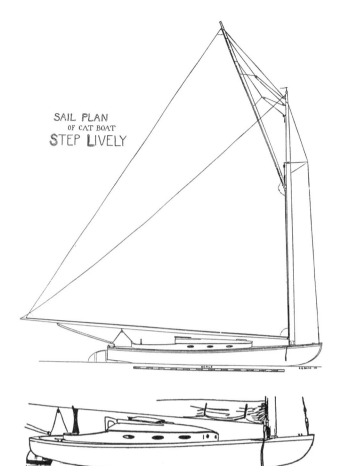

SAIL PLAN
OF CAT BOAT
STEP LIVELY

Despite her racing orientation, *Step Lively* was built with cruising accommodations that included an enclosed head or "toilet room." In fact, Frank Randall had provisioned the boat for a cruise in her first summer and was ready to depart when he accepted an unsolicited offer for her from a fellow racer named George Hill who renamed the boat *Dorothy*. Hill had rather less success with *Step Lively*, perhaps because he skippered the boat himself. For his larger catboats, at least, Randall was

Step Lively *was one of H. Manley Crosby's most successful racers.*

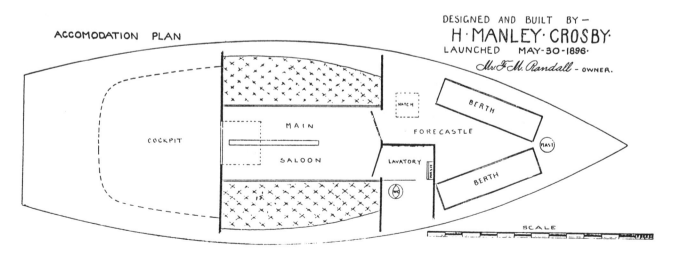

ACCOMODATION PLAN

DESIGNED AND BUILT BY —
H·MANLEY·CROSBY·
LAUNCHED   MAY·30·1896·
Mr F. M. Randall - OWNER.

COCKPIT

MAIN

SALOON

HATCH

FORECASTLE

BERTH

LAVATORY

BERTH

MAST

SCALE

Despite her racing pedigree, Step Lively *had a cabin intended to provide some cruising comforts. If a paid hand were aboard, he'd have been berthed up forward.*

more than willing to employ a professional to assist in the vessel's maintenance and operation, an attitude that did not endear him to other catboat sailors.

Frank Randall was not left without a catboat when he parted with *Step Lively*. He had another Manley Crosby catboat under construction at the same time. This boat, *Scat* — a 25-footer with 20-foot waterline — was launched in July. *Scat*'s lightweight mast was located slightly farther aft than that of previous boats, and was supported by shrouds. This detail was typical of race-oriented catboats, Crosby or otherwise, designed with overhanging bows. The boat was lightly but strongly built and had a self-bailing cockpit. *Scat* was entered in her first race in mid-August and took first place. Two days later, sailing in another event in what was described as a northwest gale, *Scat* finished a half-hour ahead of the second-place boat. In fact, *Scat* may have been the most successful of all the Crosby racing catboats built for Frank Randall. (*Scat*'s profile and sail plan appear in Chapter Five.)

How long Randall maintained ownership of the boat is unclear. Edwin Schoettle, a New Jersey sailor and author of *Sailing Craft* in 1928 reported that the boat came to Barnegat Bay in 1900. In fact, Schoettle bought the boat and owned it for years. Considering the fact that boats like *Scat* have since been labeled as "unwholesome types" that contributed to the decline in popularity of catboats, its delivery trip from Larchmont, New York to Barnegat Bay as described by Schoettle makes for an interesting counterpoint.

> . . . the boat was single-handed on the trip down the East River, through Hell Gate and New York Harbor to Sandy Hook, and then on the ocean 100 miles to Atlantic City. [The sailor] knew nothing of the lay of the land, was without charts, had the boat loaded with extra spars on deck, three extra sails stored in the cabin, and a rowboat in tow. Despite this handicap and the further fact that he was caught in a storm on the ocean and was three days going from Sandy Hook to Atlantic City, *Scat*'s delivery skipper made port with boat and cargo in good shape.

Scat immediately went on to one race win after the other.

Up in Osterville, meanwhile, some racing catboats with overhangs were built as well. Among these boats were *Agnostic* and the 28-foot *Mblem*. The latter, built circa 1905, was said to have placed first or second in 71 races by the time she was advertised for sale in 1910. But, as things worked out, Frank Randall's hopes that a big class of racing cabin catboats would develop in New York did not materialize. Randall's success, his willingness to employ a professional captain and, perhaps, crew, discouraged other catboat sailors. In the end, there were not enough men of Randall's means to support his vision of a big fleet of dramatic, racing boats. Manley Crosby returned to Osterville in 1900 and, with the rest of the family, focused on building more traditional models.

By the early 1900s, the building of catboats had become a well-established industry for the Crosbys, and the part of town that their shops dominated became known as "Crosby Town." There were five shops in operation in 1902 when F. E. Newell visited Osterville for *The Rudder*. These included Daniel Crosby & Son (Ralph), Charles H. Crosby (A partnership between Daniel and Charles Crosby had been dissolved in 1901.), Wilton Crosby, H. Manley Crosby, and H. F. Crosby, later H. F. Crosby and Sons. There is no published evidence regarding whether or not the shops cooperated with each other but it seems most likely that they operated as independent businesses owned by competitive members of a large family in which occasional feuding about real estate or other matters was not unknown. It is thought that a customer, having seen a boat with the shape that interested him, sought out the particular shop that had built it.

A Crosby Catboat of 1900

Length overall: 25 feet

Length of waterline: 22 feet

Beam: 11' 6"

Draft, board up: 27"

Length of cabin: 12 feet

Headroom: 5 feet

Cockpit size: 6 1/2' x 6 1/2'

Interior: Mohair-covered cushions, hanging lockers, dish and provision lockers. Sleeping space for up to four people.

Finish: white with bright decks, cockpit staving, and trim. Varnished interior.

The sparse available material on the subject indicates that, up until 1892, the Crosbys' boats were built almost entirely of pine and oak cut from the abundant supply of timber on Little Island, just off Osterville. White cedar for planking was obtained from anywhere possible. The keel and stem were oak, and the frames were made of rot-resistant pitch pine, sawn to shape from natural crooks. According to family records and to historian W. P. Stephens, the Crosbys did not begin using steam-bent oak frames until H. Manley Crosby bought a steam-powered saw in 1892 and simultaneously decided to steam oak to replace the pitch-pine frames. Such a saw represented a major time saver by comparison to taking logs to one of the nearby, tidal-powered sawmills. Eventually, the oak frames were overlaid with the cypress planking for which Crosby boats became so well known. Galvanized iron boat nails were the typical fastener although some boats were copper-fastened.

Ballast was generally beach stones, inexpensive by comparison to any other material and, according to the Crosbys, entirely suitable for boats that did not require weight to be concentrated at the boat's lowest points. It is clear, however, that whatever the Crosbys' feelings were about stone ballast, some Crosby yachts were ballasted with other material. The 29-foot *Kalama*, built in 1894 by Daniel and C. H. Crosby, was one such boat. This 29-footer had a centerboard ballasted with 300 pounds of lead and carried 4,500 pounds of "moulded iron" inside ballast. Doubtless, iron or lead would have concentrated weight more successfully than stones and helped *Kalama* carry a sail that measured 40 feet on the boom, 23 feet on the gaff, and had a 21 foot hoist.

By the late 1890s, the various Crosby-family members had the building of a catboat down to a science. Time and again one finds references to a boat being ordered in January or February and being completed and ready for launching in the spring. In part, this was because the builders had so much experience with boats of various sizes that there were "stock models." In 1910, for example, Daniel's offerings included: 22-foot catboat for $700, 23-foot catboat for $725, 24-foot catboat for $750, and the 25-footer for $800. A higher-grade than standard finish added $50 to the price. These were for boats with the deadwood

This trio of Crosby catboats is sailing through a mooring area not far from the shops.

drilled for a propeller shaft but without a motor.

Boston journalist and lifelong catboat sailor Winfield M. Thompson bought one of these stock 25-footers, which became famous to readers of *The Rudder* everywhere as *Twister,* and wrote entertainingly about his experiences. His boat was sailed around the Cape to Boston by a delivery crew of a man and a boy. Upon arrival in Boston, the skipper said of the boat that "He had tried her under all canvas, from whole sail to three reefs, and had found her 'a fine, able boat, and dry in a seaway,' and he added that she 'steered easy.'"

In terms of maintenance, Thompson reported that three coats of paint sufficed to keep the topsides looking good for a season, although he noted that his boat's hard pine planking did not hold paint as well as soft pine, cedar, or cypress.

The latter eventually became the preferred planking material at the Crosby shops. Thompson painted *Twister*'s canvas-covered deck and cabin top with two coats of "warm buff" that lasted all summer. But his varnished sliding hatch, he said, required an additional coat every couple of weeks. He was glad that the cabin sides, cockpit sole and seats were painted a light brown color.

Boats like *Twister* were popular as stock models because they were just about the perfect size in terms of accommodations, performance, and the ability of a working man to maintain. A 24- to 26-foot catboat represented the heart of the market, a century ago, for a sailing cruiser, or sailing auxiliary. That's not to say that bigger models weren't also turned out by the Crosbys and others. Those seeking extra accommodations might opt for a 28-

foot catboat or, as the accompanying graphic illustrates, one much larger.

Twister, a Stock 25-foot Crosby Catboat of 1906

Model: Overhang stern

Length overall: 25' 3"

Length of waterline: 22 feet

Beam: 10'6"

Draft: Approx. 2' 6" board up

Freeboard at stem: 4 feet

Cabin length inside: 9' 7"

Cabin width inside: 8' 5"

Headroom: 4' 5 1/2"

Mast length: 34 feet

Sail area: Approx. 600 sq. ft. (18 feet hoist x 20 feet gaff x 29 feet boom)

Keel and frames: Oak

Planking: Hard pine

Cabin sides: There is some indication that "standard grade" models had oak cabin sides while the "finer grade" boats had mahogany.

Fasteners: Galvanized iron nails

Finish: White hull, varnished coamings and cockpit staving, buff decks and cabin top, varnished spars, varnished cabin (cypress and pine with oak trim)

Ballast: Approx. 2,500 lbs. of beach stones

Equipment: 25 lb. anchor, 25 fathoms anchor rode, boathook, 12-foot oar and oarlock (convenient, especially on boats without motors).

Engine: As delivered, no engine although shaft log and bearers were installed. Subsequently, a 5 hp, single-cylinder, two-cycle Lathrop was mounted that turned a 17" x 18" propeller.

Price: $650 – $675

A Big Auxiliary Catboat

Builder: Crosby

Model: Overhang stern w/underhung rudder

Length overall: 42 feet

Length of waterline: 32' 6"

Beam: Not specified

Draft (board up): 3' 6"

Length of cabin trunk: 20 feet

Engine: 15 hp Murray & Tregurtha

Rig: Mainsail and jib set on bowsprit

Notes: Copper fastened and coppered bottom. This boat was similar in dimension to the *Nickerson* and, by 1910, had twice cruised from New England to Florida. The cabin had two toilets. The boat was sold with an 18-foot "dinghy."

Just as the question of power arose for the owner of a working catboat, it also became most topical for recreational sailors. The inevitable questions were — what brand engine and how much horsepower? Information on how knowledgeable men of the first decade of the 1900s viewed these issues has been almost entirely lost. Reviews of engine specifications and literature from the period suggest that, while each brand possessed some interesting or even unique features, they all appear to have offered the same potential for reliability and performance. The correspondence between Daniel Crosby and John Killam Murphy attendant to the latter's purchase of a Crosby catboat in 1910 does, however, include Daniel's general thoughts on motors. Whether because of experience or pricing arrangements with the maker, Daniel Crosby recommended Bridgeport motors. He even noted to John Killam Murphy that "The Palmer engine is not so good an engine as the Bridgeport, but is very satisfactory and we believe will give you good service for your money." Daniel quoted a Bridgeport 5 1/2 hp [$250 installed] and 3 1/2 hp [$190 installed] to Murphy, noting "we believe them to be the best value for your money when everything has been considered." But he added that the 3 1/2-hp Bridgeport would be useful only in light weather.

It is clear from reading Daniel's thoughts on the subject, that his customers had varying ideas about motors and that usually these were bad ideas. Daniel warned regularly, it seems, against underpowering a boat. At the time he wrote to Murphy, he had in his boatshop an almost new, two-cylinder, seven-horsepower Bridgeport. The reason? Although he had recommended a 12-horsepower model to a customer, the latter had insisted on the seven. When it proved unsatisfactory, it had to be removed and a 12-horsepower installed.

Lucidly, Daniel Crosby advised John Killam Murphy to buy the nearly new, seven-horsepower, two-cylinder Bridgeport at a good price.

> We would advise that this boat, with the 7 H.P. engine mentioned above, will make an ideal boat for you. For if you should ever be caught out when it comes up to blow and you are without help, you have only to lower your sail and start your engine and you have ample power to take you home in any weather, or you can tie the wheel and let her run, taking your time about reefing, when you can then change back to sail power, or use both if you like.

In the end, Murphy ordered a five-horsepower Lathrop — a heavily built, proven favorite with fishermen — for his new *Sea Mew*.

In addition to its "big boats," Crosby also offered what sounds like a very nice tender. Daniel Crosby described this skiff as

> about 10' 6" long, 3' 6" wide and 15" deep amidships, which makes as good all around tender as you could have. They weigh on the average about 80 lbs. and are built of the same stock we use in our best boats and will practically last a lifetime, are very comfortable to use with either one, two or three persons, and are very able and dry in towing as well as rowing. They are painted white outside and varnished inside, price with two sets of rowlocks and one pair of oars is $30.

Maturity

The course of the catboat's emergence and development as a yacht spanned approximately five decades beginning, for our purposes, with the Herreshoff-built *Sprite* in 1859 and entering a decline around 1910. The cat-rigged sandbaggers evolved into more wholesome, open-cockpit boats used predominantly for racing throughout the 1870s. Such boats were joined in the 1880s by improved designs with cabins intended for racing and cruising and by a variety of half-decked models like *Marianna* and others.

In his loving chronicle, *Sailing Days at Mattapoisett* 1870 – 1960, Edward F. R. Wood, Jr., captured the spirit of that era's catboat racing.

> Racing in the eighties was an important feature of village life. The men of towns like Mattapoisett . . . spent winters altering their boats, trying to extract every particle of speed by changes in hull form and rig . . . Racing proved a spectacle for watchers on the shore, and the new summer residents quickly caught the spirit, chartering catboats for entire seasons. The owners then hired

out as skippers on their own boats, continuing to take the helm and to advise on racing strategy despite their new professional status.

The period of the late 1880s through the late 1890s saw racing-oriented designs emerge, some with overhangs fore and aft that departed from the traditional type. But it should be remembered that the racing, although not conducted at the level of the sandbaggers, was still intense. In his description of the racing scene in Buzzards Bay, Wood noted that it was "loud and sometimes bitter, accompanied by fouls and breaches of common sense and the rules of the road which a later and more sophisticated era would not tolerate [so he thought!]. Wagering was prevalent among the large crews that manned the catboats."

Although many of these catboats were occasionally used for cruising as well as racing, the period of about 1895 – 1910 saw the cruising catboat reach its highest state of development. Such boats included the addition of an engine to what was still primarily a sailing yacht. The Crosby yacht *Sea Wolf* built about 1909 is a good example of the cruising catboat in its most-evolved form. At last, the low-freeboard demanded by fishermen but not conducive to spaciousness in a yacht gave way to higher topsides. Here was a boat suited not merely to cope with the tides, currents and winds of her natural habitat, but a boat equipped to meet the needs of an owner who had the time constraints and responsibilities of a working man. Writing in *The Rudder* in 1911, Winfield M. Thompson set forth the timeless virtues of a perfect catboat.

In order to avail himself of every minute of a weekly respite from labor of thirty-six hours, the owner of *Sea Wolf* wanted a boat that would present these features: (a) ease in getting underway; (b) ease in handling (c) power to proceed in any kind of weather; (d) light draught, admitting her to small harbors; (e) habitability with a considerable degree of comfort; (f) moderate initial cost and operating expense...

To insure perfect dependability in all kinds of weather, and particularly to overcome the impediment of calms and head tides, insuring prompt return to business at a required hour, the boat was fitted with auxiliary power from a gasoline engine but primarily she was designed for a sailboat, with good spread of canvas, and lines to give her a fine turn of speed in a breeze, in spite of the drag of her propeller.

Was it difficult to raise *Sea Wolf*'s 800 square-foot sail? The boat was equipped with ball-bearing blocks, and Thompson reported that "a man of ordinary strength can run up the sail with both halyards at once." How did *Sea Wolf* perform? Thompson reported a 49-mile trip from Block Island's west harbor to Hadley Harbor triple-reefed in winds that sometimes exceeded 33 mph and with the final 19 miles bucking a head tide. The boat averaged seven knots for a trip that took seven hours. Thompson reported that he and the boat's owner could reef *Sea Wolf* in five minutes and shake out the reef in three minutes. And he noted that "In heavy weather, when off the wind, we topped up the boom in good shape. If it came on to blow hard, we settled throat and peak. There is magic in the effect on steering of settling the peak. Many catboat owners do not attach half enough importance to the part played in maneuvering this type of boat by the halyards and topping lift."

Here was an extraordinary boat by any meas-ure. The fact is, when it comes to cruising cat-boats, things never got any better than boats like *Sea Wolf.*

Crosby Catboat *Sea Wolf* (circa 1909)

Model: Square-stern w/barn-door rudder

Length overall: 28 feet

Length of waterline: 26' 9"

Beam: 11' 6"

Draft (board up) 2' 8"

Freeboard at bow: 5 feet

Length of cabin trunk: 10' 6"

Headroom: 6 feet

Length of cockpit: 10 feet

Sail area: 800 sq. ft. (20' 6" hoist, 21' 3" gaff, 45' 5" leech). Sail made of 8-ounce "special yacht duck" at cost of $80.

Keel: Oak, 8" thick, 10" deep

Deadwood and sternpost: Oak

Frames: Oak, 2" square, steambent

Planking: Cypress, 1" thick

Fasteners: Galvanized nails

Deck: Clear white pine strips 1" x 1 1/8" caulked with "light-colored composition"

Interior trim: White pine, cypress, mahogany

Cockpit seats: Cypress

Wheelbox: Oak with mahogany trim

Rudder dimensions: 4 feet high by 4 1/2 feet long

Ballast: 3,000 lbs. of field stone

Engine: 7 1/2-hp, single-cylinder, two-cycle

Price: $1,000 plus $400 for engine, cushions, dishes, compass, horn, anchors and an 11-foot $85 dollar round-bottom tender

---

Whatever their virtues, boats like *Sea Wolf* did not continue to draw new buyers as the years marched on. Demand tapered off quite steadily

Daniel Crosby inspects the stem of Sea Wolf.

and so did the steady stream of customers who rode the trains to Cape Cod, booked a room at the East Bay Lodge or at the Crosby House, which had been opened by Horace Crosby and his wife Lucy in 1880 when Horace retired from boat-building. Once settled in, customers then visited the shops to examine boats and, perhaps, order one. What appears to be the next-to-last Crosby catboat built was commissioned by a 64-year-old retired busi-nessman named George I. Rockwood in 1931. Mr. Rockwood owned a summer home in Harwichport, and he approached the then 78-year-old Herbert F. Crosby about building a yacht. Herbert had been building boats since 1880 and was then doing business as Herbert F. Crosby and Sons, the sons being Herbert B. and Andrew W., who died of a heart-attack at age 48 during the Rockwood boat's construction. Because this boat came into the possession of Catboat Association founder John Leavens, its history was saved and all its particulars recorded. Today, rebuilt by her current owner, Bill Sayle of Nantucket, *Pinkletink* — the name Leavens gave her — is still sailing.

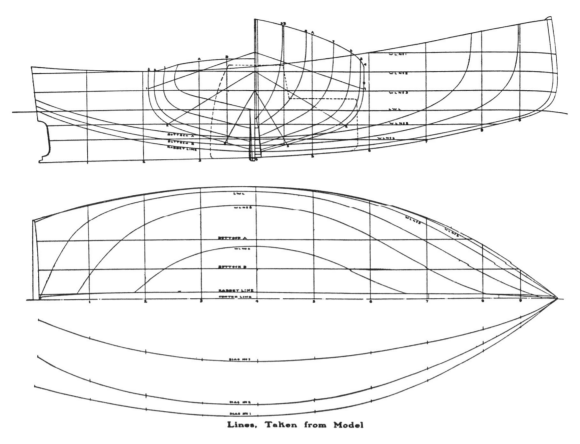

Lines, Taken from Model

A big, able vessel, Sea Wolf *was built from a half model, not lines. These lines were taken from the model — a practice the Crosbys generally discouraged — and published in* The Rudder.

That Crosby catboats were well-regarded in the marketplace of their day is indicated in the correspondence between Daniel Crosby and prospective purchaser John Killam Murphy in 1910. Daniel wrote: "We had some correspondence last winter with a man who had one of our boats 10 years old stating that if he could sell the old boat he would order a larger boat. We asked his price for the old boat, which was $600, and upon looking the price up, we found that he had paid us $575 for her. This goes to show, in a manner, the appreciation in value and also the reluctance to part with one of our boats."

From first catboat to last, built in the mid-'30s, the Crosbys worked from half-models. Eventually, some blueprints were made but they were not detailed and did not include the boats' lines. In 1910, Winfield Thompson reported that Daniel Crosby's son Ralph had "introduced drafting into the Osterville shops" but noted that "the approved Osterville model" had been developed long before. In 1931, when George Rockwood ordered *Charlotte,* he also asked if he could borrow enough drawings so that a model of his new boat could be made. The answer was "no." Mr. Rockwood's son recalled that his father was told that "neither he nor anyone else would ever be able to copy the hull form exactly; it was a Crosby family secret." This was not, in fact, accurate, for the lines of a Crosby working catboat accompanied the article written by William Lambert Barnard and published in *Boating* in 1907. Even had he been aware

Crosby Catboat of 1931

Builder: Herbert F. Crosby

Owner: George Rockwood

Style: Square stern

Length overall: 21' 10 1/2"

Length of waterline: 21' 7 1/2"

Beam: 10 feet

Draft: 2 feet board up/7 1/2' board down

Freeboard at stem: 3' 7 1/2"

Keel: "Pasture oak"

Frames: White oak

Planking: Cypress

Fasteners: Galvanized iron boat nails

Cockpit staving and seats: Mahogany

Cabin house: Steam-bent oak

Cabin dimensions: 8' 3" long x 7' 4" wide x 4' 1" headroom

Centerboard: Oak

Deck: Mahogany strips, edge-nailed

Mast: Sitka spruce 27' 1" overall length (7 1/2" diameter at deck)

Boom: Sitka spruce 24' 9" long

Gaff: Sitka spruce: 16' 10 1/2" long

Sail: 350 sq. ft.

Headstay: 5/16" stainless steel wire rope

Throat/peak halyard: 1/2" dacron

Main sheet: 1/2" dacron (3-part purchase plus removable snatch block)

Blocks: two-inch diameter sheaves

Engine: 20 hp Redwing (replaced with 22 hp Palmer with reduction gear and Paragon reverse gear in 1955)

Propeller (for Palmer): Two-blade 16" x 9" bronze on bronze shaft

Water capacity: 18 gallons, stainless sink

Head: Winner

Stove: Two-burner alcohol

Anchors: "Large" and "small" yachtsman type

Special equipment: Four sealed copper flotation tanks under cockpit and two more inside the cockpit staving.

Note: Boat originally named *Charlotte,* now *Pinkletink*

---

of those lines, they would not have been what Mr. Rockwood sought. Mr. Rockwood had his boat hauled and took off her lines himself. He then spent nine years building a model that was acknowledged by Manley Crosby as being perfect. The "secret" was out but, by then, nobody paid much attention.

Local Builders and a Famous Boat

The market for catboats during the type's golden age was large enough to help support numerous boatbuilders along the East Coast from New Jersey to New England. If the Herreshoffs and C. C. Hanley served the top end of enthusiasts and the Crosbys catered to the market's broadest segment, other builders also found ready buyers among a very local clientele. These builders all offered a variety of boat types, but some became particularly well known for their catboats. William Wallace Phinney was one of them.

Born on Cape Cod at South Monument in 1865, Phinney built his first boat at age 13, was sailing parties aboard a 24-foot catboat by age 16, and was fishing from his own catboat a year later. Rather than graduate from Wareham High School,

Here is Frederick Dunn's elegant Daisy, *built in 1888 for racing in Buzzard's Bay. The International Yacht Restoration School in Newport, Rhode Island, has restored this boat, and* Daisy *is the only known Dunn-built boat to survive. Appendix A contains more details.*

Phinney instead became an apprentice to Frederick Dunn in Monument Beach, a skilled catboat builder. A few years later, when he was 21, Phinney built his own shop at Monument Beach and, with the help of Dunn and a partner named William Buzzell, built *Superior,* a boat that he raced successfully. It was the beginning of a long racing career. In 1911, Phinney won the Atlantic Coast Catboat Championship. "He would rather race than eat," remembered Merton Long who was one of the many neighborhood boys who hung around Phinney's shop and learned to build boats them-selves. Phinney always enjoyed socializing with his young admirers who, when he became elderly, called him "Gramps." He helped with their model sailboats, scallop boxes, and quahog rakes, but he also worked very hard, 12-hour days being the norm. Occasionally, Phinney went over to Osterville to visit with his friend, Wilton Crosby.

In 1913, Phinney sold his yard in Monument Beach. He spent a year working for another builder, Benjamin F. Berry, before establishing a new yard at Falmouth Heights (now MacDougall's) where he continued working and

Launch day 1940, Falmouth, Massachusetts: W.W. Phinney stands beside his last catboat, Oriole. In the winter of 2002, the 29-footer, now named Ghost and ashore on Nantucket, was reported to be in need of a total rebuild.

built his last catboat in 1940. By then, Phinney guessed that he'd built about 100 boats, from pulling boats used by life savers at the Charles River Basin to catboats of all sizes to a 53-foot schooner. He had been around long enough, in fact, to witness a change in the skills and attitudes of many boatbuilders. Phinney thought rather little of the workmanship that boatyards were turning out on the eve of World War Two. "It's disgusting," he told a reporter in 1940, "the way boats are slapped together today." William Phinney died on December 7, 1946.

Across Buzzards Bay from Phinney's, in Wareham, stood the shop established by another all-around builder well known for his catboats. This was the yard of Charles A. Anderson. Like Phinney, Anderson — who was brought to the U.S. by his parents when he was nine years old in 1879 — quit school. At age 14, he went to work in an iron foundry and, at age 18, got a job in a shipyard in East Boston. In 1890, Anderson returned home and began building skiffs and, soon, larger boats. Thus began a career that saw

the design and building of boats as diverse as a 57-foot motorsailer for Henry DuPont, the ferry *Alert* that for decades ran from New Bedford to Cuttyhunk, and catboats ranging from half-decked daysailors to 30-footers. On the side, he made violins and banjos.

Phinney, Long, and Anderson were merely a few of the Massachusetts boatbuilders who designed and built catboats in the period beginning in the early to mid-1880s and continuing for as long as commissions could be had. There were also, to name just a few: Phinney's colleague in Monument Beach, Frederick J. Dunn, "Kit" Briggs in Westport, Smalley in Hyannis, George Shiverick (who learned his craft from C. C. Hanley) in Kingston, Manuel Swartz Roberts at Edgartown, Nelson Huckins, Jr., at Onset, J. C. Small in Chatham, George Wells in Chelsea, Wood Brothers in East Boston and, in Boston, the Pierce Brothers. What's more, there were dozens of other capable builders located from New Jersey to Maine. In fact, the Hull Yacht Club's 1885 roster of catboats lists a total of 77 builders including the Crosbys. The output of these men, when added to that of the Crosbys and, doubtless, many others, ensured that catboats would continue to attract sailors for many years after the last boat had left her builder's yard.

As time passed on, it was a vessel built by a man little known beyond the village in which he lived, worked, and died, that was destined to become among the most famous catboats ever made. The builder's name was Alonzo Melville Jenney. Mr. Jenney was born on April 16, 1830 in Rochester, Massachusetts, which then included Marion and Mattapoisett. It is likely that Jenney learned his trade building whaleships in Mattapoisett, but he also became aware of the growing market for pleasure boats. Jenney was said to have been the first shipbuilder in the town who built a yacht, a 26-foot sloop launched in 1879. At least 15 more catboats followed. Catboat racing was then emerging as an important sport in Buzzards Bay. At Mattapoisett, where a catboat regatta was held in August 1878, there were four classes. These were: 1st class for boats over 24 feet, 2nd class for those 20 to 24 feet, 3rd class for boats of 16 - 20 feet, and 4th class for boats under 16 feet, and the races attracted sizeable fleets. Among the racers was J. Malcolm Forbes who would sail over from Naushon Island to compete.

Zingara, an A. M. Jenney Catboat

Year built: 1884

Owner: Edward V. Bird of Boston and
   Mattapoisett

Length overall: 26 1/2 feet

Beam: Approx. 12 feet

Draft: 3 feet

Mast length: 39 feet

Boom length: 34 feet

Gaff length: 22 feet

Frames: White oak

Planking: Cypress

Cabin trunk: Mahogany

Cockpit trim: Cherry

Sail maker: Job Almy, New Bedford

Notes: This boat was built at a time when Jenney
   was in partnership with shipwright George W.
   Lewis and did business as Jenney & Lewis.
   She was handled by a professional captain,
   James R. Blankinship. In 1888, the boat was
   remodeled to become a sloop.

Alonzo Jenney became an important figure in Mattapoisett. His yard on Prospect Road was a busy place and it was the training ground for John and Edgar Dexter, two cousins in the town. In 1894, when Jenney scaled back his activity a year before his death, John Dexter took over the business and went on to earn a good reputation of his own. Although most of the detailed information about Jenney-built catboats has been lost, the boats were staunchly built of top-quality materials. We know this because, in 1883, Jenney built a catboat for a well-to-do Bostonian named Francis E. Bacon, Jr.

Unfortunately, Mr. Bacon died just two years later, and his catboat was sold. Twenty-seven years later, however, and 17 years after Alonzo Jenney's death, this catboat made a voyage from her home waters, which had remained Buzzards Bay, to Florida and back. The trip was recorded in a still-fascinating book written by the boat's owner, Henry M. Plummer. The book was entitled *The Boy, Me, and the Cat.* The catboat, built by Alonzo Jenney in Mattapoisett, still carried her original name — *Mascot.*

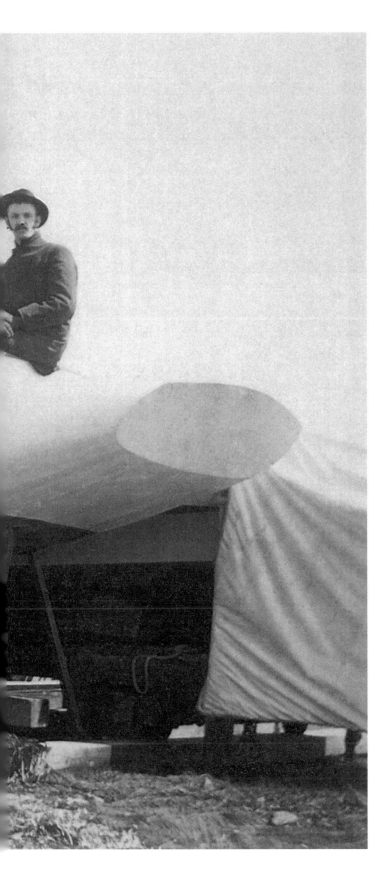

CHAPTER FOUR
THE ARTISTS

—◆—

"Hanley boats and Hanley designs are becoming things to be sought after and treasured by the small-boat connoisseur. Being in a class by themselves, their like will not be seen again when they have had their day."
—THE RUDDER, March 1919

WIDESPREAD ACTIVITY in any endeavor, whether it be painting, athletics, or boat designing, always sees the emergence of seemingly natural talents. From out of nowhere, apparently, come those who somehow manage to transcend the best efforts of everyone else, without any apparent effort. Many catboats were designed and built by highly capable rule-of-thumb designers, and some university-trained designers from New Jersey to New England, men who made good names for themselves and good boats. But, in general, the greatest boats came from the hands of a relatively few men who had "the touch" and who produced what were essentially floating works of art. These were all, essentially, "rule-of-thumb" men who could have been subject to criticism from those who held that they were wed to ignorant and outmoded

Boatyard of Charles C. Hanley on the Back River at Monument Neck in Bourne, Massachusetts, circa 1895. Neither the boat nor the men in the photo can yet be identified with certainty. (Hanley and his crew appear on page 70.) This yard was destroyed by fire in 1897 after which Hanley reestablished himself in Quincy. Upon his death in 1934, Hanley was buried at Gray Gables cemetery in Bourne, not far from where this photograph was taken.

beliefs without scientific foundations. In fact, however, they were simply geniuses, and this was recognized by their colleagues, competitors, and the sailors of that time. They were Charles C. Hanley on Cape Cod, Gilbert Smith of Patchogue on Long Island, and Archibald Cary Smith of New York and New Jersey.

C. C. Hanley

Charles C. Hanley's emergence onto the scene as a designer and builder had no logical basis in education or training. Yet, MIT professor and naval architect George Owen called him "a master craftsman and an epoch maker in American yachting." Hanley was born in Warren, Maine, in 1851. His father was inspector of prisons at the time but later became superintendent of lighthouses on the New England coast. Although he received some education, Hanley was apprenticed to a piano-case builder, a craft he mastered without dedicating his life to it. Instead, in 1875, Hanley moved to Monument Beach on Cape Cod and set himself up in business as a blacksmith. It was a moment in time when the racing of small craft, and catboats in particular, had become a popular activity, and Hanley became involved.

"My catboats are all made from one model," Hanley told *The Rudder* in 1919. "I made the model when I was new to the business, forty years ago, and built the *Surprise* from it. It was the fourth boat I ever built, and I never built better."

Surprise (24' 3" x 24' x 11' 3" x 22") was built in 1884 and made an impressive showing wherever Hanley raced her. The boat was sold to James M. Codman of the Beverly Yacht Club in 1885, won the club's championship for four years straight and, according to the club yearbook, "many other races in all kinds of weather." This was the design that established Hanley's "rules of thumb" relating to the shape and proportions of a catboat. Chief among these were that the proportion of beam to overall length would be 47 percent, that the boat would carry its maximum beam very far aft, possess moderate freeboard forward, and have a relatively low-roofed cabin. The freeboard and low-roofed cabins were driven in large part by Hanley's desire to reduce weight.

It was fashionable, in Hanley's own time, for some formally educated naval architects to look down on the "rule-of-thumb men" and even Thomas Fleming Day made occasional fun of some of such designers. Yet, a trained naval architect, even given Hanley's rules to work with, would have had little chance of duplicating Hanley's own results. Hanley, at least, was perceived as a genius in his chosen specialty, and each Hanley catboat was recognized for what it was, a work of art.

The Rudder's 1919 article on Hanley included drawings of a catboat designed for a client in South Africa. This 28-footer had a 890-square foot sail, raising the obvious question of how such a boat could be handled. The answer, according to the article was that "experience has shown that the Hanley cats carry their sail extremely well in a blow; in fact, a Hanley cat of 27 feet over-all has been known to carry 900 square feet through a breeze that has smothered smaller craft, and some that were larger. It is a characteristic of Hanley cats that the harder it blows, the better they settle down to business. . . . No analysis of a Hanley cat on paper can give an idea of the boat's best points under sail." Perhaps the most telling thing about the balance of this boat, however, is that Hanley drew it with tiller steering, rather than a wheel.

In what now seems like rapid succession, Hanley built the three post-*Surprise* catboats,

The 24-foot Surprise, *built in 1884, set forth the overall proportions and shape that reflected C. C. Hanley's genius.* Surprise *was an immediate race winner and, like all Hanley boats, was renowned for her ability to comfortably carry sail in all weather.*

Probably still a superb sailer despite a rather baggy looking sail, Harbinger *initially brought wide attention to her creator, C. C. Hanley, after she defeated larger keel boats in heavy wind and seas in a Marblehead race sailed in 1889.*

ing up a paper as he passes a newsstand." In the summer of 1888, Morgan picked up *Mucilage*. He renamed her *Iris,* and immediately defeated his nearest competitor (quite possibly a Herreshoff boat) by 30 minutes in a race at Newport, winning what Winfield Thompson only called a "liberal purse." Morgan's patronage of Hanley put the builder on the yacht-racing map.

Mucilage (1888)

Model: Square stern w/barn-door rudder

Length overall: 26' 6"

Beam: 12 feet

Draft: 2' 6" board up

Freeboard at stem: 3' 9"

Outside length of cabin: 8 feet

Headroom: 4' 3"

Cockpit dimensions: 10 1/2' long x 9' 7" wide

Sail area: 998 sq. ft.

Boom: 39' 6"

Gaff: 25' 6"

Construction: Pine over oak, strip pine decks

Ballast: 4,000 lbs. of copper dross

Notes: Successfully campaigned by Hanley in 1888. E. D. Morgan, Jr. bought the boat (renamed her *Iris*) to sail in one race, which he won. Then he soon sold it to Elbridge T. Gerry, commodore of the New York Yacht Club, who kept the boat at his Newport home for 16 years, although she saw little use.

---

which thoroughly established him as a force in yacht design and construction. These boats were 26 1/2-foot *Mucilage* (1888), 28 1/2-foot *Harbinger* (1889) and 26 1/2-foot *Almira* (1890). It was *Mucilage,* perhaps, that really launched Hanley. Despite the boat's name, suggesting perhaps, the stickiness of glue and slow speed, Hanley demonstrated that his creation was faster than any competition. This attracted the interest of the then rear commodore of the New York Yacht Club, Edwin D. Morgan, Jr. A distant relative of J. P. Morgan, and grandson of a namesake who had been New York governor during the Civil War, Edwin Morgan owned the magnificent Newport estate, Beacon Rock, overlooking the harbor. He was an important patron of the Herreshoff Manufacturing Company who commissioned at least a dozen yachts from Nathanael. W. P. Stephens wrote that Morgan "thought no more of buying a yacht than the average man does of pick-

Hanley's boats were built of the finest materials with Hanley himself doing much of the work. Materials were white oak frame and clear white pine planking, with brass screw fasteners. Men capable of making an educated assessment of these boats said they were finished as finely as one of

Renowned for her speed and balance, Almira *remained a force in catboat racing for a quarter of a century.*

Hanley's piano cases. *Surprise,* the recipient of good care, was still sound 40 years after her launching.

In short, Hanley's boats were considered to be as finely built as any yacht in the country, but reputedly cost about a third more than a comparable Crosby model. They became the dominant boats in Narragansett Bay, Buzzards Bay, and Massachusetts Bay.

It might be noted that although the atmosphere around the races was quite different from that of the sandbaggers, bets were placed, and prize money was offered. It was racing conducted, more and more, in the new spirit of "Corinthianism," which espoused high ideals of amateur sportsmanship rather than the paying of professionals. Still, some successful amateurs occasionally reported that they paid their entire season's sailing expenses out of winnings. It was not unusual for the designers to race their own boats to demonstrate their mastery. Hanley followed *Mucilage* with another winner, *Harbinger.* Then, not content to rest on *Harbinger'*s laurels,

Hanley set about to build an even faster catboat, which he launched in 1890. He won $250 when he sailed his new *Almira* to a win over the longer *Harbinger.*

Almira

Model: Overhang stern with underhung rudder

Length overall: 26' 2"

Length of waterline: 25' 4"

Beam: 12' 2"

Draft: 2' 1/2' board up/7 1/2' board down

Original sail area: Main and jib: 1,125 sq. ft.

Sail area for D Class, circa 1915: 950 sq. ft.

Construction: 5/8" North Carolina pine over oak

Length of cabin: 16 feet

Rudder: Originally under transom to comply with 25-foot waterline rule. Later changed to barndoor, improving balance. (As a Class D champion, *Almira* was reportedly able to sail to windward in light air without a finger on the wheel.)

It was reported that Hanley sailed home from this race with a bottle of rum in one hand (an unfortunately telling observation), the boat's wheel in the other, and with a loaf of bread nearby on which to snack. He was now on a rising curve of success that would be sustained by the patronage of wealthy men from New York to Newport and Boston. He soon was living in a new and sprawling Victorian-style home (built by Hanley himself) near the Cape Cod summer residence of President Grover Cleveland. In the summer of 1898, Cleveland's three daughters were photographed on the porch of Hanley's house, where they had gone to visit his wife, Deborah, and daughter, Saidee. By the mid-1890s, Hanley was employing a small work force of nine men whom he drove hard to produce work of only the finest caliber. He had come a long way from his birthplace in Warren, Maine, and his original training as a builder of piano cases.

In 1897, two important events occurred in C. C. Hanley's life. One was the launching of the 33' 4" x 23' 11" x 11' 3" *Thordis* (rigged initially as a catboat but later as a sloop), which won every one of the 17 races in which she was entered. At the time, some Buzzards Bay-area sailors believed *Thordis* to be the finest boat ever launched in the area. She had sleeping accommodations for four, a head, and a mahogany-trimmed interior. This big yacht carried 3,000 pounds of internal ballast and her sizable centerboard reportedly "works to a charm, without even a double block."

The other event of 1897 was that Hanley's boat shop was destroyed by fire. All that Hanley salvaged was his precious box of tools. The fire was important news in the little Cape Cod village of Monument Beach, for Hanley — as the "genius of Monument Beach" — was something of a celebrity. The local paper reported Hanley would rebuild the shop, and they were right. He did rebuild, but up the coast on Boston's South Shore in Quincy. It is presumed that Hanley made this move to place himself in closer proximity to the wealthy Boston

Charles C. Hanley (left) and his boatbuilding crew including, in the front row (l.- r.): Mr. Godet (with axe), Harry Storms, and Reuben Bigelow. The other names were unfortunately not recorded; however, as Hanley was known as a demanding and hardworking boss, one presumes the men in this photograph were a select bunch. The pneumatic tire, safety bicycle was state-of-the-art, two-wheel technology when this photograph was taken in 1895–1896.

men who patronized the day's finest yacht builders such as Lawley's. Hanley must have set his sights on extending his work far beyond catboats, for he immediately received two orders for enlarged versions of *Thordis.* It was a great start, for both boats were highly successful. Then things went bad.

In 1898, Hanley designed and built four boats for a new 25-foot class adopted by the Massachusetts Yacht Racing Association. Two others were built to the same class rules by B. B. Crowninshield. When the boats were officially measured, however, Hanley's boats were declared illegal because their draft fell an inch short of a rule. The boats had to race among themselves and became known as "Hanley's Orphans." Hanley lost out to Crowninshield in another way, too. It was the latter whose design was chosen for an America's Cup contender by a syndicate that was also considering Hanley's bold proposal for a 90-foot centerboarder with a 36-foot beam. The Crowninshield yacht, *Independence,* had a 20-foot deep keep that, it was discovered, had been placed too far back for proper balance. Nat Herreshoff's *Columbia* successfully defended the Cup and Hanley stated that he had lost "the chance of my life."

C. C. Hanley's personal life also took a significant turn when he moved to Quincy. His wife Deborah didn't move with him. With his marriage broken, Hanley lived with his housekeeper, Susan Smyth, whom he later made his heir. He now took on a monied partner, Lorenzo Baker, president of the Standard Fruit Company, and the Hanley Construction Company was formed, probably in 1900. This firm became a major industry in Quincy, a sprawling layout of electrically serviced shops, sheds, lofts, and marine railways. From here, a successful 49-foot yacht, *Cadillac,* soon emerged to defeat a Crowninshield design and

defend the Canada's Cup in 1901. None of this, somehow, was enough to make the Construction Company a success. Hanley quit the partnership in 1903 when it entered receivership. Now 53 years old, Hanley was, once again, left with nothing but his toolbox.

According to C. Willis Garey, who, as a boat-loving Quincy teenager knew and rather idolized Hanley, the partnership "just didn't work out." Was it because of a personality clash between Hanley and Baker? Or was it because Hanley had a drinking problem that was recognized by everyone from his estranged wife to the catboat builder on Martha's Vineyard, Manuel Swartz Roberts, and from the Cape to Quincy? Whatever the case, Hanley, who should have been at the top of his game and enjoying the fruits of well-recognized genius, was instead, according to a *Boston Sunday Herald* article of January 1904, needing "to begin life again at the bottom of the ladder." Still, when he received a commission to design and build a new 25-foot sloop, that is just what Hanley did. He bought two acres across the Town River from his previous yard, dug a well, set up a tent and, as business grew, built himself a small house. He received additional commissions and grew his new boatyard over a period of time thanks to his incredible energy and physical stamina. It was reported that, in the fall of 1918, the 71-year-old Hanley hauled and stored 76 boats with little or no help. Then, in 1920, boatyard, house, and all were again lost to a fire.

This latest disaster prompted Hanley to rebuild yet again. Five years later, he sold out to his neighbor, Fred Lawley, and retired. He focused on gardening and on a basement distillery known for turning out a very fine rum, Prohibition notwithstanding. Visiting newspapermen referred to the old boatbuilder as "a merry old boy," and when he died on July 4, 1934, Nathanael Herreshoff said, "Captain Hanley was the hardest nut I had to crack." Might C. C. Hanley's vision for a giant centerboard America's Cup yacht have proven successful? Or might it have fallen short of the sophisticated engineering needed to translate one of his smaller boats to that size? These are questions that will never be answered.

Duster

Designer: Charles C. Hanley

Year built: 1891 – 1892

Model: Square stern with barndoor rudder

Length overall: 22 1/2 feet

Length of waterline: 22 feet

Beam: 10 1/2 feet

Draft: 2'

Freeboard at stem: 37 inches

Least freeboard: 15 inches

Mast height: 35 feet (32 feet from deck to masthead)

Boom length: 32 feet (reduced to 30 feet in 1911)

Gaff length: 18 1/2 feet

Sail area when fitted with bowsprit and jib: Approx. 900 sq. ft.

History to 1911: Built for William K. Nickerson of Provincetown; sold in 1894 to Harry E. Mapes of Cohasset; sold by Mapes to James T. Ball of Boston who added a larger cabin that was 10 feet long and 16 inches high at the aft bulkhead, giving 4' 5" headroom. Also added a water tight cockpit 6' 8" long x 8' 3" wide and a 21" x 27" lazarette in the cockpit floor. Sold to John Burroughs and Frank I. Smith of Boston; purchased by journalist Winfield Thompson in 1910.

Gilbert Smith

Slender and lightweight, graceful and artfully constructed of dozens of species of timber, Gil Smith catboats dominated racing on Great South Bay. These boats became treasures that were recognized as such in their own time. Eventually they would be recognized as the impressive legacy of a slender, sturdy, blue-eyed man who had begun his working life as a seaman and commercial waterman before he ever became a boatbuilder. Gilbert Smith was born in Manorville, New York, in 1843, and grew up on Long Island's south shore, where he worked the waters of

Portrait of the artist: Here is Gil Smith, a skilled sailor as well as boatbuilder, at the wheel of one of his yachts.

Shinnecock and Peconic bays as a commercial gunner, clammer, crabber, and fisherman. He went to sea as a young man on trading schooners and spent the Civil War on supply ships for the Union Army. After the war, Smith worked as a hunting guide, and carved decoys, which are now highly regarded treasures, having survived the years rather more successfully than his boats.

Gil Smith's first boats were probably those he built for himself for duck hunting, but he also built a number of boats for local baymen. When wealthy families began summering in Westhampton — New York's governor John Dix was among the first to build a summer home there — sailing became popular and Smith took notice. He decided to move his family from what is now

Hampton Bays to Patchogue, which was where he would have easier access to the new summer crowd at the Hamptons, suddenly made accessible by the Long Island Railroad. In 1876, Gil Smith loaded his wife, Miriam, who was a teacher, their four children, luggage, and the kitchen table aboard the 24- or 25-foot catboat he had built. Then the Smith family cast off for Patchogue.

Al Terry, a lifelong student of Smith's career, believes that despite an article that claimed Smith worked for several yards in Patchogue before establishing himself, there is no record of Gil Smith working for another boatbuilder. In an article on Smith in *Yachting* in 1966, Ham deFontaine wrote that Smith "was self-taught, a natural designer and builder and never worked as an

Gilbert Smith boatyard: At this yard in Patchogue, Smith built work boats and then yachts that were recognized as vessels of exceptional artistic merit by Smith's Great South Bay clientele.

apprentice." What all agreed upon was that Smith worked from beautifully carved half models from which lines were taken and laid down on the floor.

Whichever view is accurate, Smith's skills were highly enough developed for him to be confident of supporting his family in Patchogue. According to his wife, the whole plan almost failed not because of any lack of ability on her husband's part but because he was unsuccessful in his effort to find a client. While he searched, the family ran out of money and was about to sail back home in their catboat. Miriam Smith said that her husband's disappointment was so great that she persuaded their landlord to extend them credit. Then, at last, there came a commission for a boat and Smith began building it from a half-model at a shop on the west side of the Patchogue River. Al Terry believes the landowner may have been an initial partner of Smith's. In 1881, Smith moved to a new location on the river's east side and established Smith's Boat Yard.

Initially many of Smith's boats were workboats, but he moved into the building of pleasure craft as increasing numbers of summer people began to come to the area. These Smith-built boats went through an evolution that saw their shapes change from rather blunt, plumb-stem, heavily built boats to slimmer models with an emphasis on lightweight and speed. It's worth noting that although they were catboats, the Gil Smith designs did not have the beamy proportions typical of what we now think of as those of the classic Cape Cod catboat. Rather like the Herreshoff boats, Smith's were generally a foot or more slimmer in beam than what one might expect, with modest freeboard. There was about them a certain artful delicacy.

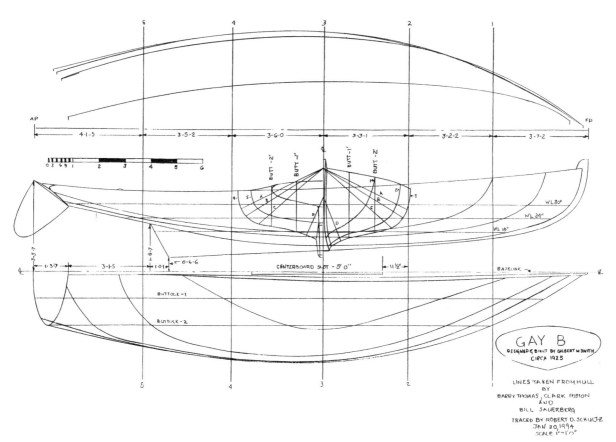

The entrancing and beautiful lines of a Gil Smith catboat are evident here in Gay B, *built in 1925.*

"He always went for lightness and would sacrifice strength," said Terry. "That's what the people wanted. As his designs progressed, he did away with every other sawn frame and put in a light, steam-bent frame in its place."

Among the highlights of Gil Smith's boats was the wide variety of woods that the builder employed in their construction. The 28-foot catboat *Kittery,* built in 1928, was but one example. The son of her owner told *Yachting* editor Ham deFontaine that the $800 boat had "about 30 varieties of wood . . . each selected to best serve its purpose." The steam-bent planking was fastened not with iron boat nails with with longer-lasting copper rivets. One can imagine the impression such a boat must have made as she first emerged from the shop with decks of varnished white cedar with seams neatly caulked with white compound, a wonderfully graceful cockpit and cabin coaming

Moonbeam was a BB Class racing catboat built by Gil Smith in 1909 but still race-worthy three decades later when this picture was taken.

of gleaming mahogany or cherry, the smooth, white-painted planks of the hull and the slender, brightly varnished spars.

Smith catboats included those designed for class racing on Great South Bay and Shinnecock Bay, the 22-foot Class B, the 25-foot Class BB, and the 28-foot Class A. These and Smith's other boats were built in a shop that never had electricity. Depending on the workload, Smith could call on a group of some six builders, all capable of extremely fine work done quickly. "The old timers," said Al Terry, "were both good and *fast.*" Smith's wife, who sewed many of the sails for the boats, accompanied him on local deliveries. Gilbert Smith built his last boat at age 92 and died in 1940 at age 97.

Lucile

Designer/builder: Gilbert Smith

Planking: Cedar

Location: Patchoque, New York

Frames: Sawn oak

Date of Launching: 1891

Fastenings: Iron

Overall Length: 21 1/2'

Cockpit: Two benches removable for racing

Length water line: 17' 9"

Beam: 7 feet

Storage: Ceiling under fore and aft deck for stowage area

Draft board up: 1' 9"

Mast length: 22 feet

Finish: Black hull w/gold cove stripe, bright decks

Boom length: 21 feet

Gaff length: 12 1/2'

Fittings: Brass blocks

Sail area: 343 sq. ft.

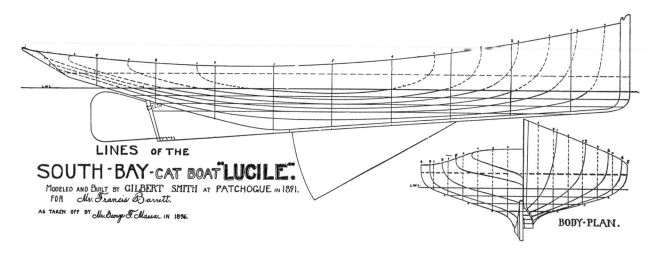

LINES OF THE
SOUTH·BAY·CAT BOAT "LUCILE".
MODELED AND BUILT BY GILBERT SMITH AT PATCHOGUE IN 1891.
FOR *Mr. Francis Barrett.*
AS TAKEN OFF BY *Mr. George F. Massa* IN 1896.

BODY·PLAN.

Designed in 1891. Lucile was more curvaceous in her stern sections than forward. Smith's designs evolved to embody different bow forms that bore no resemblance to Lucile's plumb stem.

Squaw

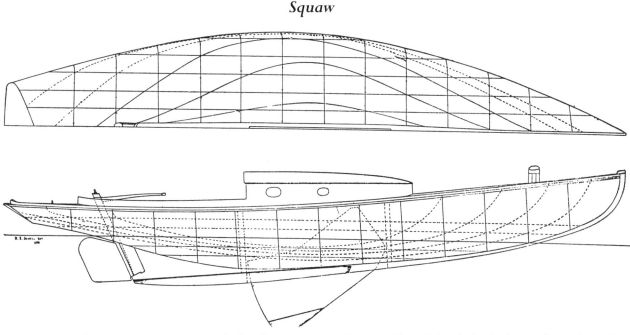

Built in the spring of 1893, Squaw was designed specifically to be a race winner. In her original form, the boat had a plumb stem. After much initial success, Squaw was "modernized." The bow was remodeled in 1896 to the form seen in these lines. Squaw was lightly sparred but her mast was well-supported by forestays and shrouds made of steel rigging wire. She carried 2,000 pounds of outside lead ballast and her lead-weighted centerboard was smoothly operated by a 19:1 winch. Like Smith's other boats, Squaw employed a variety of wood in her construction. Her keel was oak, timbers were oak or hackmatack; planking was white cedar, deck was cypress, and the sheer plank and coaming were mahogany.

Archibald Cary Smith

If Gilbert Smith and C. C. Hanley were artists in their chosen craft — the design and construction of yachts, including catboats — Archibald Cary Smith possessed rather similar talent, but he was an artist with paint and easel as well. In fact, at some point around 1870, Smith devoted himself entirely to marine painting in a studio on West Tenth Street in New York, the city of his birth in 1837. W. P. Stephens, who considered Smith as a dear friend, said that he was an "artist and philosopher . . . in no way fitted for [the]rough-and-tumble of successful business naval architecture. His natural disposition was such that he would much rather have clients seek him out to place an order for a picture than for him to seek them for an order for a design."

But Smith was a gifted and well-trained designer. He became fascinated by boats as a boy, exploring the New York docks, and he was taken by his father, a minister, to see the yacht *America* as she was being built. He told Stephens that he and his childhood friends would plug up the gutter near his house, and create a pool in the street in which to test their model boats. When he grew older, he joined a model yacht club in Hoboken. This put him in rather close proximity to Captain Bob Fish in Bayonne, and when Smith was 18 years old in 1855, he was apprenticed to Fish. There, he learned to sail, to design according to Fish's rules of thumb, and to build. What's more, he moved beyond the traditional method of design by carving a half-model. He paid a shipbuilder to teach him to draw lines plans. Subsequently, according to Stephens, Smith accompanied the lines for his boats with detailed construction drawings and these "paper plans" did much to establish his reputation. He became best known for his schooners.

Stephens recorded that Smith's first boat was a 16 footer soon followed by an 18-foot cat-rigged boat named *Comet*. This is, however, at odds with the *Comet* described by Smith himself. Writing in *The Rudder*

many years after the event, Smith said he built *Comet* in 1860 and that she was 26' 9" overall with a 26' 7" waterline, 10' 7" beam and board-up draft of 1 1/2 feet. Smith said the cat-rigged boat "came about like a rabbit." It raced successfully under both cat and sloop rigs. How many catboats Smith designed is unknown. His hope of establishing himself as an artist eventually foundered on his own design abilities, for wealthy patrons began seeking him out in his studio and interrupting his marine painting with commissions for all manner of sloops and schooners. Many of these were later sketched by artist Frederic S. Cozzens for publication in *The Rudder*. Throughout his life, however, Smith apparently stood ready to design catboats. One of these boats, *Bouquet*, was among the fastest catboats on Barnegat Bay in 1900 when she won one of the chief races in the area, a cup named for Senator William J. Sewell.

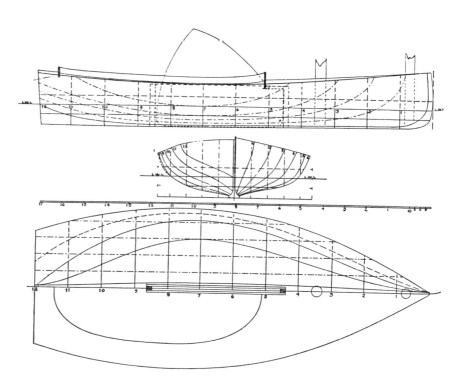

Here is Cary Smith's Comet *of 1862 as presented in the work of W. P. Stephens. Although a close friend of the designer, Stephens had a different memory of* Comet's *dimensions than did Cary Smith himself. The boat raced successfully under both cat and sloop rigs.*

By then Smith enjoyed a position of enormous respect and admiration throughout the yachting world. Although not really a "yacht club type," he belonged to the New York Yacht Club, where he served as measurer for eight years. He lived simply with his wife and daughter in Pamrapo, in a house not far from that of his old mentor, Bob Fish. W. P. Stephens said that the house's "plain and unpretentious exterior gives little hint of the comfortable interior, whose books and pictures suggest the artist or the poet rather than the prosaic planner of lead keels."

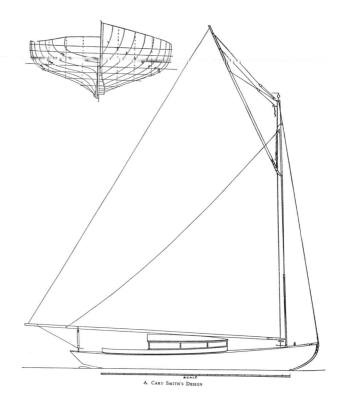

A. CARY SMITH'S DESIGN

"Just put your duffel in the summer cabin and go" is how Thomas Fleming Day introduced this A. Cary Smith 33-foot catboat in The Rudder *in 1897. Smith designed the boat with a "modest" 722 square-foot sail for a client in Port Tampa, Florida. The boat's hull was long and shallow, with no centerboard, and drew 2 1/2'.*

Archibald Cary Smith Cruising Catboat (circa 1896)

Length overall: 33 feet

Length of waterline: 25 feet

Draft (board up): 2' 6"

Mast length: 31 feet

Boom: 31 feet

Gaff: 19' 9"

Sail area: 722 sq. ft.

Note: Boat designed for Florida (Port Tampa) waters with a "summer cabin"

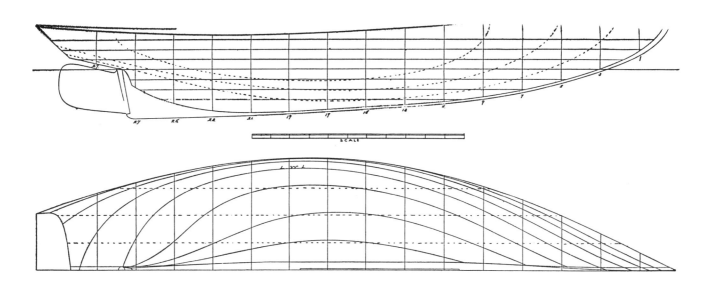

Squaw: *Here are the sail plan and hull sections of Gilbert Smith's speedy boat. The comparatively light mast was supported by steel wire shrouds and forestays. The drawing shows the boat as she appeared in 1896 with the upswept, overhanging bow that replaced the original plumb stem. The hull sections show modest deadrise amidships, and Squaw must have been a powerful boat. She was said to possess exceptional windward ability.*

981-Alma- July 19 1894

CHAPTER FIVE

RIG

— •◆• —

*"The bowsprit is always an excrescence, a false note
appended to what had been a harmonious whole."*
—WINFIELD THOMPSON, *The Rudder*, 1908

"The Piscator *carried her reef clew outhauls all rove
which is quite customary in catboats; and as she had
reef points instead of reef lace lines, the reef was put
in within a few minutes which is only possible
as the result of practice."*
—*THE COMPLEAT CRUISER*, L. Francis Herreshoff

A LTHOUGH THE DEFINITION of a catboat
has always included the statement that it's
a boat with only one sail, this matter of
rig is not as straightforward as it seems. The fact is
that jibs were rigged on ungainly bowsprits in the
old days somewhat more often than one might
suspect. Locale had much to do with whether or
not headsails were carried. In 1896, when designer, artist, and yachting journalist C. G. Davis
sketched a variety of catboats for *The Rudder*'s
series on the type, he labeled a drawing of C. C.
Hanley's *Almira* without a jib as "Almira New
York." However, his sketch "Almira Boston" shows

*Alma, photographed in the summer of 1894, has what it takes when it
comes to a practical rig. Her peak halyard runs through two blocks on the
gaff to equalize loads on the spar and to minimize the effort of raising
sail. Permanent reefing pennants are rigged for the first two reef points
that would otherwise not be reachable from the cockpit. Her mainsheet
runs through two large single blocks and is unlikely to become fouled on
itself. Her halyards and topping lift run through turning blocks on deck.
It is a model catboat rig!*

the boat with a long bowsprit and jib. Typically, catboats that raced north of Cape Cod carried a headsail, and so did some working and cruising boats irrespective of location. There was always, however, controversy about the real value of jibs, and whether such changes really meant the catboat was now a sloop. When a reader posed just this question to *The Rudder* in 1896, editor Day's answer was unequivocal: "No; the boat is no longer cat-rigged if she is fitted, as you say, with a bowsprit for carrying a jib, and does carry such a sail. She is a jib and mainsail boat."

Bowsprits and Jibs

Among the most controversial and confusing of all issues relating to catboats of the golden age and the immediately subsequent years, roughly 1888 – 1908, is the matter of headsails. It is a subject that caught up and frustrated both sailors of the period and yachting writers of that and subsequent eras. What is one to make of a boat whose most distinctive feature, its rig, was suddenly changed in such a dramatic and, to most eyes, such an ungainly manner? When did this aberration occur, and why?

Before the late 1880s, any bowsprit on a catboat appears to have been a short one intended to improve the angle of the headstay and serve as a handy place to stow the anchor. Most catboats built for pleasure had no bowsprit at all, and neither did the vast majority of fishing boats. The sudden arrival on the racing of scene of C. C. Hanley's boats, however, changed matters. The wealthy men who initially bought yachts like *Mucilage, Harbinger,* and *Almira* usually did so to prove they owned the fastest boat, win a bet, and move on to the next challenge. Nothing forbade them hiring a professional crew and crowding on as much extra sail area as possible. That accounted for the sudden sprouting of bowsprits of 10 – 13

feet in length so that a jib, balloon jib, and triangular spinnaker could be set. Once the initial race or series had been won, the boats were usually sold, most going to new owners in and around Boston. They retained the bowsprit.

Later, when the Cape Catboat Association was formed in 1904, its regulations — written in part in the hope of encouraging new construction — specifically forbade overhangs and reverse curves associated with the most "modern" racing catboats. They mandated how much freeboard was required and even how many crew could be carried — "not more than one person to every four feet of waterline length." But the rules did specifically permit "working sails," which meant the mainsail and the jib, but not the balloon jibs and spinnakers of the previous years.

Generally, the jibs were about 15 percent of the mainsail's area. They were set with a small sprit running diagonally from about a third of the way up the sail's luff to the clew. Perhaps because of a combination of the lack of backstays to keep the mast tensioned, and because only narrow sheeting angles were possible, the sprits were necessary to add tension to the luff of the sail and prevent it from sagging. Most of the sails look like half of an upside down kite. When beating, the jib was sheeted rather flat and apparently served its purpose of balancing a boat whose boom might extend six feet or more beyond the transom. Off the wind, the effect would have been more pronounced, and the jib also added some modest drive. There is conflicting commentary on the benefits of these jibs. William Lambert Barnard said they had "some advantages as a steering sail with the wind abeam or free" but were of "little value when close hauled." Winfield Thompson reported that "those jib men went by me, while steering with one hand."

SAIL-PLAN OF CAPE COD CAT, DESIGNED BY V. D. BACON.

According to the commentary that accompanied this catboat designed by V. D. Bacon of Barnstable, Massachusetts: ". . . the jib is merely an auxiliary sail, and can be used or not, as the owner may see fit. This rig is used on nearly all boats north of Chatham, and at that point, while on the south shore they use the 'Straight Cat.'" This 31-foot boat had a 905 sq.-ft. mainsail and 161 sq.-ft. jib on a 12-foot bowsprit.

Often photographed and also widely seen by Boston area sailors, these jib-equipped racing machines influenced some men to add bowsprits to their "regular" catboats. One who did was Winfield Thompson. After his acquisition of a fine Crosby catboat that he named *Twister* in 1906, Thompson admitted that, toward the end of his first season with the boat, "Another thing that began to trouble me was the jib question. When I first got the boat I was opposed to the jib on principle. 'Ah,' said I, 'these fellows who put jibs on Cape cats are degrading the type.'"

But, surrounded by the bowsprit-equipped racing craft of the Cape Catboat Association, Thompson convinced himself that, because *Twister* wasn't intended to be a fishing craft where additional sheets and hardware would only be in the way, a bowsprit and jib would be a good modification. For various reasons, Thompson sold *Twister,* apparently in 1907 or 1908 but wound up buying

her back in 1914, and she still had the bowsprit. By then, however, Thompson had owned and sold a bowsprit-equipped Hanley boat named *Duster* and his attitude toward bowsprits and jibs had changed dramatically.

"I may remark in passing," Winfield Thompson wrote in 1914, "that the Cape Cod builders have no use for a bowsprit on a cat. They never design a boat with one. If an owner insists, they put one on; but they usually state that beyond its convenience in getting the anchor, a bowsprit is a useless appendage on one of their boats. Experience has led me to agree with that view, and to bring myself to the point of offering the advice to a man who would have a boat with a bowsprit, that he would do better to buy a sloop than to spoil a good catboat with a bowsprit." The first thing he did when he repurchased *Twister* was to remove her bowsprit. He concluded that "artificial appendages, not intended in a boat's original design, are rarely good for the hull, and never seem to belong to it. It is well to keep a boat as the makers made her. . . ."

But how did the "makers make her?" The simple answer is that catboats as they left the builder's yard generally but not always did so under a pure cat rig. This was certainly true of working boats in all the popular sizes, although it is possible, even likely, that boats of 30 feet or greater length may have originally been rigged to carry a small jib for improved balance. There were, however, exceptions. As fishermen in a relatively few specific towns — Hyannis, Massachusetts, being a key example — sought maximum speed from their boats, jibs began to be used. Manley Crosby said that "In regard to the jib on these boats, this was to offset the long booms which were used to drive the boats for fishing." A few such boats left the Crosby yards with a bowsprit. But mostly, if a fishing boat carried a bowsprit, it was likely to have been added by the fisherman himself. "Around 1905 to 1910," said Joe Nickerson, whose family had fished out of Chatham for generations, "some put on bowsprits. They just took a 2" x 8" plank, rounded it off and spiked it to the deck. The jib helped a bit with steering."

Winfield Thompson once interviewed C. C. Hanley about bowsprits on catboats and came away believing that Hanley had little more use for a jib on a catboat than did the Crosbys. Thompson specifically questioned Hanley about *Duster*, which was fitted with a bowsprit and jib. He reported: "Hanley had never intended the boat for a bowsprit rig. He has a proper dislike of bowsprits on cats. But the style of rig was different on the north side of Cape Cod than on the south. . . ." Hanley's great *Thordis* is a perfect example. Built in the winter of 1897 for Thomas Wales of Wellesley Hills, Massachusetts, who also owned a summer home in Cataumet, *Thordis* was photographed during the following season. A picture in *The Rudder* shows the boat slicing easily through

the water under a cat rig. A stumpy bowsprit was fitted to aid in supporting the mast, which looks lighter than Hanley's typical spar, perhaps because *Thordis* had longer overhangs than the previous catboats, and has spreaders and shrouds. Later, under a different owner, a long bowsprit was added and a jib was rigged.

As he eventually did with *Twister's* bowsprit, Winfield Thompson removed the one on *Duster*. He reported that the moment the bowsprit was off, *Duster* emerged "from a long undeserved period of disgrace. She looked like another boat the moment it dropped to the ground. The graceful lines of her bow and the contour of her stem had been completely obscured by the contraption of that bowsprit and its gear."

As if to prove that for most racing, a well-designed catboat had no need for additional sails, Boston sailor Walter Burgess sailed his catboat just as Hanley had designed it. This 28 1/2-foot boat was *Clara,* built by Hanley in 1895 primarily as a cruising yacht. At the height of the catboat-racing era around Boston, Burgess sailed *Clara* under

Here is the bowsprit — "excresence" as Winfield Thompson came to believe — on his Hanley-built Duster. *Thompson removed the bowsprit to return the boat to her original form.*

mainsail alone against boats with jibs, balloon jibs, and spinnakers. According to a brief report in *The Rudder, Clara* "never had a racing crew on board, being sailed by her owner, sometimes *alone,* and sometimes with a lady or other friend. To windward in a strong breeze, she proved to have no equal of her size, and almost always caught the next larger class, which started five minutes ahead of her." In 13 races in 1895, Burgess — brother of the naval architect Edward and a founder of the Beverly Yacht Club —won eight prizes, including five first-place finishes.

Clara

Designer / Builder: C. C. Hanley
Model: Fantail stern with underhung rudder
Date built: 1895
Length overall: 28' 6"
Length of waterline: 23' 11"
Beam: 11' 6"
Draft, board up: 24"
Mast length: 36' 1"
Boom: 33'

Winfield Thompson, in an effort to summarize the whole issue of jibs on catboats, wrote the following:

Bowsprit and jib do not belong to the catboat. In the native waters of the cat, Cape Cod, they are never carried. Boston [probably, he was referring to the Cape Catboat Association] has long employed them, thus debasing the cat, the simplest of all rigs, into a mongrel sloop. The bowsprit allows larger rigs to be carried than the type is built to carry. . . . The matter of bowsprits on the Massachusetts Bay cats is mentioned here as the only fault of an otherwise admirable class,

in the hope that the boat owners in the class may see the esthetic and logical considerations urging their abandonment, and a reversion to the pure type that, in spite of this corruption at their hands, has given them so much sport.

Much of Thompson's effort was directed at the rulemakers of the Cape Catboat Association. In 1908, Thompson wrote that the association was going to consider abolishing bowsprits. This they did, and later photographs of the old D Class competitors like *Almira* and *Iris* show no bowsprit.

Perhaps the best single piece of evidence we have regarding the whole matter of when and by whom the great Hanley catboats were fitted with bowsprits is a handwritten letter on the stationery of the Quincy Yacht Club regarding *Mucilage.* The letter, which bears no signature but is clearly of the era, puts everything into perspective.

The *Mucilage* was sold by Capt. C. C. Hanley of Monument Beach to E. D. Morgan of New York for a special purpose just before the 4th of July race of 1888. It was said to Mr. Morgan that a cat-boat could not be produced that would beat the Newport cat-boats. Mr. Morgan did not believe that they were invincible and purchased the *Mucilage* of C. C. Hanley especially for that race. The *Mucilage* defeated this class by about 30 minutes. Mr. Morgan sailed the *Mucilage* in a very few unimportant races and sold her to Com. Elbridge T. Gerry of the New York Yacht Club who purchased her for one of his sons. The young man did not care for yachting and the *Mucilage* now named the *Iris* was used very little until the spring of 1906 when she was purchased by Com. Frank Fessenden Crane of the Quincy Yacht Club who had a small jib added to her rig and was sailed by her owner in all the races of 1906.

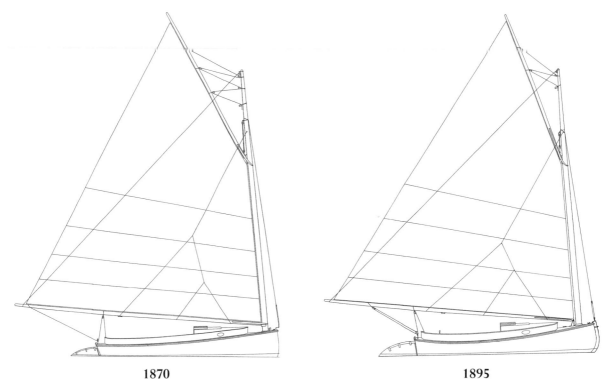

| 1870 | 1895 |

Although the classic single-sail cat rig changed but little over the years, it did evolve along with the boats. Perhaps the most basic changes were the intro-
duction of higher peaks as the centerboard was enlarged and moved more forward in the boat, and the increased use of hardware throughout the rig. These
two sailplans drawn by Howard Chapelle show three basic differences between the boat of 1870 (l.) and that of 1895 (r.). The 1895 model has a higher
peak, a boom mounted on a pedestal rather than with jaws, and a mainsheet with an extra part to improve handling. On both boats, blocks on the forestay
and stem permitted the stay's tension to be adjusted.

South of the Cape, at Newport, the boat raced without a jib in the form Hanley had built her. North of the Cape, at Boston, a bowsprit was added and a jib flown.

The Mast

In the late 1800s and early 1900s, as a new generation of formally trained designers began designing occasional catboats, tried and true aspects of the rig were changed, usually to the detriment of the boat. Consider, for example, the addition of standing rigging to support the mast. Shrouds became rather common around the turn of the last century. Here is what Winfield Thompson had to say about a Mower catboat designed to race in the 1910 season: "She had a hollow mast, and shrouds to hold it up, things in themselves that

would cause a Cape Cod catboat skipper to laugh himself into a fit. A stiff mast, stayed hard and fast, is contrary to the theory of the down-east [he meant Massachusetts] builders as to what makes a Cape cat go to windward." One could say that this was simply a reaction against something new made by an overly traditional sailor who was not even a yacht designer. But Thompson went on to provide the basis for his beliefs. These grew out of his understanding of the rigs of the boats he ceaselessly examined, boats built by the Crosbys and by Hanley, examples of which he himself owned.

They believe the mast should have play at the top, and do not encourage struts or shrouds. A good stick, which will bend more or less, is believed to lift a boat into the wind. The value of one of this sort was well illustrated . . . when *Iris* carried away her forestay, and kept on, in a hard breeze, going to windward as if nothing had happened. The masthead bent, but her speed did not fall off, except when a man went forward to put a whip on the broken stay, and she won. The action of the mast and the boat under this situation was in exact accord with the belief of her designer and builder, C. C. Hanley, who told me only last Winter, 'You really don't need a forestay on a catboat's mast. They're only convenient to hang on by when you go forward. Don't put on a strut anyway. They put your mast in danger.' I had thought this a pretty strong view, until the accident to *Iris*. Then I saw it was the stick itself that took the strain.

The fact is, too, that in every recorded instance in which the mast in one of Hanley's boats was replaced or modified, the boat's performance was never again what it had been.

The whole subject of mast bend on catboats, and the effect of this bending on the set of the sail, presented a challenge to sailmakers. What little information survives about this problem suggests that matching sail to spar involved more art than science. C. G. Davis noted that it was a sailmaker's experience "knowing about how much the local builders allow their boat's spars to bend" that permitted the sail to be cut so they would "come out nice and flat when the spars are bent, and in consequence, in a light air of wind, the sails have excessive bagginess, or draft. They cut the sweep or 'roaches' on the edges of the sails so the sails will not pull tight in one spot but flatten all over as it breezes up."

Although typical Crosby, Hanley, or other Cape Cod model catboats had a stout mast usually supported only by a headstay, such a system was certainly not universal. Gil Smith boats, so different in model from the Cape Cod cat, were comparatively lightly sparred and the masts were supported

by shrouds. Forestay and shrouds were also found on the various racing and cruising boats designed for owners around New York and Barnegat Bay. Some Cape Cod catboats, intended primarily for racing, also had a hollow mast.

Gracie

Builder: Herbert F. Crosby
Model: Counter stern with underhung rudder
Date built: 1886 – 1887
Length overall: 24' 4"
Length of waterline: 21' 5"
Beam: 10' 11"
Draft, board up: 30"
Length of cabin: 6 feet
Length of cockpit: 9 feet
Mast length deck to truck: 30' 10"
Boom: 22' 4"
Gaff: 19''
Spinnaker boom: 23' 6"
Bowsprit: 9' 9"
Mainsail area: 657 sq. ft.
Jib area: 104 sq. ft.
Total sail area: 751 sq. ft.

The mast of a well-built catboat was, and is, an impressive spar. C. C. Hanley's colleague, Erland Debes, called *Almira*'s mast "the stiffest and toughest piece of black spruce ever seen." *Gracie*'s mast formed an eight-inch octagon at the partners. This was slightly greater than the general rule stated by Fenwick Williams in his catboat design treatise suggesting that mast diameter at the deck should roughly be eight tenths of an inch for every foot of beam.

When he described the building of his *Ring Dove* design in *The Rudder* in 1904, Charles Mower wrote that the mast should be made "from spruce timber which is straight-grained and free from bad knots, shakes, or sappy places." Two decades later, describing how to build another catboat, he advised "Mast, boom, and gaff to be solid spruce spars. Mast to be a natural growth stick, sound and free from large knots."

Mast length was dependent on sail area. *Gracie's* mast rose above the deck to a height that was almost seven feet longer than the boat. According to well-accepted practice, the mast had to be high enough for the upper peak halyard block to be located somewhat above a point opposite the gaff's midway point. Additional length was then needed for locating the topping lift block which, with the lift itself, was recognized as a vital part of the catboat's rig. Williams wrote that mast diameter at the topmost halyard block would be a "little less than half the diameter at the deck." The blocks themselves were shackled to substantial eyebolts in the mast, each bolt backed with a pad that distributed loads and kept the bolt from pulling out under great strain.

The masts of working boats were usually treated with a mixture of tar and turpentine, while boats for yachting purposes often had a varnished mast. Mast hoops — 20 to 25 percent larger than the mast's diameter — were the most common method of affixing the sail to the spar. Sail track and slides were also used on some boats. According to the writer William Lambert Barnard, the introduction of seine fishing resulted in some fishermen replacing their mast hoops with track and slides, and that the gaff itself was mounted in the track. "This permitted the adoption of a feature common on all Cape cats as late as 1888, namely, cleats nailed athwartship to the foreside of the mast and leading, like the rungs of a ladder, to a crow's nest, about twelve inches

square, and placed about three fourths the length of the mast above the deck, on which stood a lookout for the schools of fish sought by the seiners."

Track was also sometimes installed on catboats used as yachts. The Daniel and C. H. Crosby *Kalama* built in 1894 had a "slide rig" on a track long enough to accommodate the sail's 21-foot hoist. Winfield Thompson commented on a Maine-built catboat that had sailed with "sliding hoisting gear" since 1884. Thompson noted that this boat's sail was easily hoisted and lowered while his own boat's lower hoops tended to stick on occasion. He wrote that he was considering fitting *Twister* with a similar arrangement but acknowledged that his Crosby catboat had a much longer and heavier gaff, which might have presented a problem.

Fenwick Williams wrote that "the track restricts free movement of the gaff . . . and puts undue strains on the spar. It also cramps the gaff jaws and, in addition, destroys the airfoil near the mast in the most important part of the sail. . . . Hoops allow the gaff and the whole luff of the sail to fall free so that the luff and driving part of the sail can settle itself." When he described the building of his *Ring Dove* design, Charles Mower wrote that "A patent slide may be used on the mast if desired, but for all-around hard service, the good old-fashioned mast hoops cannot be much improved upon."

Boom

The boom of a typical catboat was made from a solid length of spruce. On occasion, a racing boat might have the boom made hollow. For example, the Crosby-built *Mblem,* which was regularly raced, was eventually fitted with a hollow boom (and gaff) built by spar maker Fraser. Although unusual, a hollow boom like *Mblem's* was not unique. Other fine, racing-oriented catboats like the George Shiverick-built *Arawak* and Crosby-built *Kalama* also had hollow booms (and gaffs).

Traditionally, the boom was not attached to the mast but mounted instead on a pedestal, tripod, or "crab." Made of several flat pieces of galvanized iron (or, sometimes on yachts, bronze), the crab was securely fastened to the deck and the boom could swivel atop it. Barnard described this type of gooseneck as consisting of "four or five flat, galvanized iron rods, with lower ends screwed to the deck just aft of the mast, and the upper ends united around a socket that held a pin hinged to a spike which was driven into the end of the boom."

Such pedestals offered several advantages. A crab was readily fabricated locally and therefore not as expensive as a gooseneck based on bronze castings purchased from a foundry or supplier. Perhaps the arrangement's chief virtue was that it saved the mast itself from strains imposed by the long boom. Fenwick Williams also suggested that a crab avoided the "danger of crushing the vital outer fibers of the mast." Eventually, splendidly cast gooseneck fittings were used as well, and stock castings such as those from the C. D. Durkee company, which had been founded in New York in 1894, could be purchased according to different mast diameters. Even so, the boom crab was always a common catboat feature. Although boom crabs and, later, gooseneck fittings were most typical, some booms were attached with jaws.

In addition to whatever oak cleats and eye straps were necessary to secure blocks, lazy jacks, and topping lift, booms also carried a line of bronze eye screws. These matched thimbles seized to the bolt rope on the foot of the sail, which was then attached to the boom by threading a "jack line" through both sets of eyes from tack to clew. These bronze eyes seem to be the one piece of manufactured hardware found even on fishing catboats that may otherwise have carried an absolute minimum of purchased, cast fittings. The jack line was often made of wire rope to resist stretch and maintain tension along the sail's foot.

Gaff

A catboat's gaff had to be made so that it combined minimum weight without sacrificing durability, and these should remain principal objectives on boats built today. They are achieved with greater success in some instances more than others. It is clear that 19th-century builders had a reasonably good sense about what would work and what wouldn't. The great majority of gaffs were solid spars, but sometimes, to reduce weight aloft, a hollow gaff was constructed. In either instance, it was typical to stiffen the gaff with a slotted jackstay fitted to the underside. Failure to build a stiff enough gaff would, particularly on boats used for racing, result in a gaff that would not remain straight under great tension and in a good breeze. If the gaff could "buckle" (bend) or otherwise get out of line, the sail's peak and leach could be affected. On Hanley's *Almira*, a special fitting was eventually engineered to keep the hollow gaff straight even when peaked up to a near-vertical position. There is no indication such a device was ever needed aboard *Almira* as Hanley originally rigged her.

The sail was attached to the gaff with line that passed through eyelets in the sail and the slots in the jackstay. Many gaffs, however, had no jackstay. On these, the sail was attached with a continuous laceline. The accompanying drawing by C. G. Davis suggests that, particularly in the days of cotton sails, there was a right and wrong way to bend the sail to the gaff. He noted that harm could be done to the sail by permitting uneven strain as it was laced to the gaff. "Not lacing it on with a rolling hitch or running hitch, which holds the sail firmly at each grommet as it should, but lacing it around and around, so the greatest strain and sag comes in the middle of the sail, and all the strain is put upon the upper outer clew lashing. This generally develops a fan-like set of wrinkles from the peak down through the upper part of the sail, the

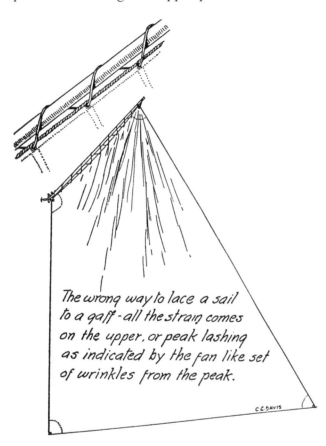

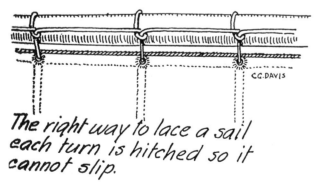

Right and wrong ways to lace a cotton sail to the gaff, as presented by Charles G. Davis.

lacing not supporting the sail uniformly along the gaff as it should." One suspects that a jackstay, with narrow slots, would have performed much the same function as the sort of lacing that Davis advised for spars without a jackstay.

Photographs of some boats suggest that cast, circular fittings were also used, one for each grommet, and sized according to the diameter of the gaff. Tension could then be adjusted with the outhaul. At the front of the gaff, oak jaws lined with rawhide were the most common method of locating the spar on the mast. Sometimes, locust or hackmatack was used for the jaws which, in their best form, always had a pronounced upward curvature. In general, the gaff was fitted with one or two bridles or "slings" positioned so as to support the gaff in areas of stress and help it resist bending. Larger boats with heavier sails would employ two bridles so that the mechanical advantage of a second set of peak halyard blocks eased hoisting the sail while evenly distributing loads along the gaff. Occasionally, particularly on earlier working boats, the bridle was eliminated when, by the experience of the builder, the attachment points for the peak halyard block and end fitting could be set in a fixed location where eye screws were placed.

Reefing Rigging

The long overhang of a catboat's boom posed an obvious problem when it came time to reef the big sail and to furl it. Although one encounters occasional references to reefing the clew while standing on a dock or in the boat's tender, it was typical to rig any clew that one couldn't safely reach from the cockpit with a pennant. This usually meant that at least the first two clews were so rigged. Basically, the pennant was secured on one side of the boom beneath the clew, ran up through the clew's grommet, and then back down on the other side and then forward to an easily reached cleat. Not to have so rigged the boat, particularly in the days before motors became popular, would have been foolhardy indeed. The adoption of motors did not end the need for permanently rigged clew reefing lines, and they remain useful today although they do hang awkwardly during the period when one is raising and lowering the sail. Although there is little indication that boats in the old days were rigged with reefing pennants for the tack fittings, these are also good to have to avoid having to go forward in poor conditions.

Running Rigging

Even at the turn of the last century, references were sometimes made to the simplicity of the catboat's rig, a popular but sometimes misleading sentiment echoed today. Usually, these remarks have to do merely with the fact that there was only a mainsheet to tend when tacking — no jib sheet, staysail sheet, mizzen sheet, foresail sheet, or running backstays. In hindsight, however, such remarks about simplicity need to be put into context. The catboat was once so prevalent that details of its rigging were taken for granted. To several generations of sailors, the rig may have appeared to require no explanation at all. But this ceased to be the case by the early 1900s when newer rigs became popular and new sailors were attracted to the sport. Hearsay, experimentation, and inexperience resulted in the gradual loss of collective knowledge and wisdom regarding details of the rig that has continued down to the present day.

In 1907, William Lambert Barnard succinctly listed the catboat's running rigging as follows:

"Two halliards, two lazy jacks, a single topping lift (usually rigged with a gun tackle to double the purchase) and a sheet, constitute the entire running rigging."

Barnard did not supply details of how each of these pieces of rigging was arranged. He didn't mention, for example, that the turning blocks for the halyards and topping lift were shackled to pad eyes mounted on the deck, not the mast itself, as is typical of today's production catboats. This traditional method resulted in much less opportunity for the lift, in particular, to bind the mast hoops as the sail was raised and lowered. Nor were specific details given of where the bridles were placed on the gaff and how the various peak halyard blocks were arranged. Mainsheet arrangements were likewise taken for granted. Today, these setups are worthy of study, for there are few production catboats that would not benefit from their adoption.

The accompanying drawings show a variety of mainsheet arrangements. In almost every case, the sheet is attached to the boom at a minimum of two points. Very often, single blocks are used, greatly reducing any chance of the sheet fouling itself. These blocks were also generally larger in diameter than those fitted today, with 3 1/2" and four-inch blocks being typical on boats of 19 feet or more.

Finally, the topping lift was recognized for the vital role it played. This was especially so in days before boats carried motors and reefing under sail in rough conditions was a fact of life. In order to produce the mechanical advantage needed to lift up the often immense boom of a 19th-century catboat, the topping lift was, as Barnard noted, rigged with tackle. This also permitted the long boom to be more easily raised to clear seas that might otherwise "trip" the boat when running in heavy conditions. Mower stressed the topping

The system of three single blocks as shown on Scat was among the most popular ways of rigging the main sheet, and remains an excellent method.

lift's importance even when presenting his 20-foot *Ring Dove*. "It is very important that the topping lift should be very strong as there are many trying times, such as reefing in rough water, when light gear would surely be carried away, perhaps with disastrous results."

In conclusion, it can be seen that the cat rig, while simple by comparison to others, involves its own complexity and need for understanding. A boat rigged according to traditional methods, with deck-mounted blocks at the mast, a proper mainsheet with blocks sized to give good advantage, and a stout topping lift, perhaps with intermediate blocks to increase leverage, can all add to the pleasure, performance, and safety of sailing a catboat.

Although this Edson Schock catboat has a double block on the traveler, the sheet dead ends at the aft end of the boom to minimize the chance of a slack sheet fouling itself.

The rig of C. C. Hanley's Mouser *looked more or less like this rendering by Wilton B. Crosby, Jr. who developed the drawing based on the recollections of yacht broker E.V. Rosemond. Assuming the drawing to be generally accurate, the boat possessed a 33 1/2-foot boom, 21-foot gaff, and the sail had a 19-foot hoist. That means that the 24-footer carried a sail of some 750 sq. ft. As was typical, the mainsheet ran through three single blocks. The peak halyard was belayed to a becket on the masthead block and then ran through a block on each of the two bridles. The boat was equipped with a balanced rudder. As was typical of Hanley catboats, the forestay attached to a fitting on the mast rather than to a spreader.*

The mainsheet of this Fenwick Williams catboat is sensibly rigged with a trio of single blocks.

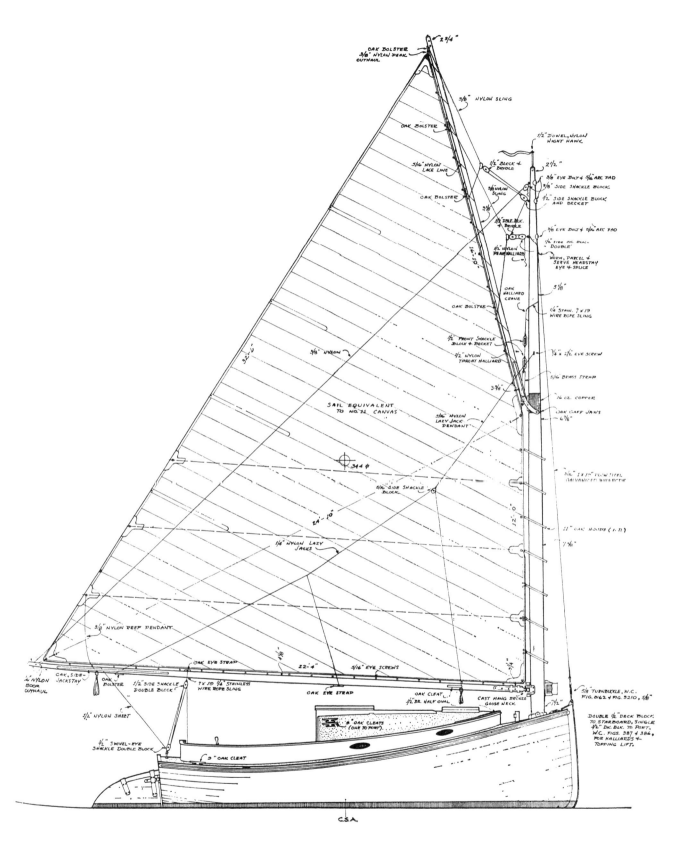

This design by W. J. Skinner was published in 1961 but its rig is extremely well presented and worthy of close study. The only off-key note is the suggestion for "nylon" line. Any modern low-stretch material would suffice.

The clean appearance and graceful proportions of this catboat are typical of Charles C. Hanley's work. In fact, Iris, *ex-*Mucilage, *was among the great builder's most famous boats. Built in 1888 and an immediate race winner for Hanley,* Mucilage *was sold the following year to the wealthy E. D. Morgan, Jr., for the express purpose of winning a race and a bet. Here,* Mucilage *is seen circa 1905 racing as D-Class catboat number 34 and still dominant. While still a beauty, the boat had been modified from her original appearance. Originally, the cabin was longer and had three portlights.* Iris's *sail sets wonderfully. A block attached to her topping lift increases mechanical advantage for the crew member assigned the task of raising and lowering the boom.*

CHAPTER SIX

DECLINE AND RENEWAL

— ◦◆◦ —

"What has become of all the big old Crosby cats? I have not seen any in years, must be some stowed away in barns, and boat houses up Buzzards Bay that should be shaken out of their nests, or they will dry up and blow away."
—E. V. ROSEMOND LETTER TO H. MANLEY CROSBY, Aug. 2, 1921

"Most of the older cats eventually expire of trunk sickness, having fallen into the hands of people who are too busy to do anything right, too ignorant to find out how, or who just don't care . . . The worms really make themselves at home, and the first evidence the owner has of this is a miserable leak that he can't seem to locate."
— WILLIAM B. OERHLE, *Yachting,* April 1944

HOW WAS IT that a boat type as pervasive as the catboat lost popularity? When one examines the decline of general interest in the catboat, there appears to be no single event that triggered it. Rather, there are at least *three separate* time periods on which to focus. First, there was the reduction in enthusiasm for the open cockpit catboats so popular from the early 1870s through the mid-1880s.

Second, there was a decline in the building of expensive, racing-oriented, cabin catboats, some designed with long overhangs to gain favorable ratings under racing regulations. In later years, these designs were often called "extreme," but they were not regularly referred to in that manner in their own time. In fact, quite the opposite is true. However, the heyday of these boats and of the great Hanley, Herreshoff, and Crosby racing catboats ended rather abruptly shortly before 1900, before ceasing to exist altogether around the early 1920s.

Finally, there was the dwindling of interest in the catboat as a cruising yacht, a lingering trend that was sparked to a great degree by the development of marine engines and the growing popularity of motorboats. As America emerged into the early 1900s, motorboats began to attract an increasing portion of the market. "I must confess," naval architect Charles D. Mower told *Motor Boating* in 1910, "that most of the sailing craft now built are for racing purposes, and the sailing cruiser has to a large extent given way to the modern power cruiser and the craft known as the auxiliary cruiser."

Catboats by the dozen now had their centerboard trunks removed, the slot filled in or planked over, and an engine installed, usually with the flywheel positioned at about the cabin steps. The shape of the hull actually made for a comparatively respectable, if not ideal, motorboat. There was too much deadrise aft to be truly efficient under power but many recreational and even commercial fishermen, and engine-oriented cruising enthusiasts bought a relatively inexpensive older catboat with no thought of ever sailing it.

When Gregory Mason visited Osterville in 1928 to do his story for *Motor Boating,* he observed "graceful knockabouts and trim, fast motor boats . . . for the Crosbys no longer confine themselves to the construction of the cats which made them famous first from Provincetown to Boston, and later wherever there was appreciation for a sailboat . . ."

That same year, *The Rudder* carried a brief feature on the Crosby Yacht Building and Storage Company. It noted that while 15 workmen were then employed year-round, "There is little demand now for the famous cat but the plant is kept busy building one-design sailboats, power boats and outboards." The last catboat built before World War Two at Crosbys left the shop in 1935 or '36 but by then, the building of catboats had long since ceased to be a viable commercial enterprise.

In short, the catboat gradually lost favor as times and tastes changed, but even in decline, because so many catboats had been built and because new catboat designs kept appearing, the type was never really without adherents. This view of the catboat's decline is quite different from what has long been the usual answer to the question about why the type lost popularity. The generally accepted reason seems to have grown out of Howard Chapelle's statement, and others like it, regarding "loss of life at summer resorts." In *American Sailing Craft,* published in 1936, Chapelle wrote that "inexperienced handling, combined with too much sail, was undoubtedly the cause of the loss of life at summer resorts, which has been one of the reasons for the prejudice against catboats among modern yachtsmen."

Yet, there is little evidence to support such conclusions. In 1911, the journalist Winfield Thompson bought a 22-foot Hanley-built catboat and, in writing of the vessel, noted the warnings and prejudice against the general type that he encountered. Among the warnings was one involving the number of people drowned in catboats. Thompson noted, however, that "as for the people drowned, or the date of the fatality, he could say nothing."

If numerous drownings were behind a loss of interest, the catboat would have lost favor abruptly rather than gradually and in stages over a period of some three decades. Certainly, racing catboats were occasionally capsized, as were other boats then and now. But there was no drumbeat of headlines — "Another Catboat Party Is Drowned" — chronicled in the press of the day. This is quite unlike the press notice given to accidents that befell several big centerboard schooners. The most infamous of these was the 150-foot *Mohawk.*

On July 20, 1876, *Mohawk's* professional crew — then anchored at Staten Island — hoisted the vessel's mainsail, foresail and two topsails in preparation for raising the anchor. Instead, the yacht — which drew only six feet with her board up — was struck by two big puffs of wind. When *Mohawk* capsized, unsecured ballast and lavish furnishings trapped people below. Five were drowned. The cutter cranks who advocated abandoning centerboard yachts in favor of keel models quickly blasted *Mohawk's* design. But it was later discovered that *Mohawk's* captain had permitted the sails to be raised without uncleating the main sheet. (At his trial, Captain Oliver P. Rowland claimed he had cast off the sheet but that it had jammed.) Earlier that month, another centerboard schooner had suffered a similar fate, although with no fatalities. Later, in the 1880s, at least two more centerboard schooners were unexpectedly capsized.

W. P. Stephens described these terrible mishaps in some detail, and also noted that "these major disasters were multiplied almost innumerably in the capsizes not only of half-decked racing craft, but of cabin cruisers of all sizes; matters of almost weekly occurrence throughout the yachting season." Ultimately, the centerboard schooner and big centerboard sloops did lose favor to keel models. But whatever "disasters" Stephens was referring to regarding half-decked boats, he never suggested that they had anything to do with any decline of the catboat. Instead, Stephens looked at the obvious to suggest why the racing of open cockpit catboats, at least, which had been widespread for some 15 years, began to lose favor by the mid-1880s. His conclusion: ". . . there came into existence new types, the 21-foot restricted sloops, the knockabout classes, various sizes of fin-keels, dories, and a number of one-design classes, the small open catboat gradually losing favor." He also went on to add: "A powerful factor in the eclipse of the type was the advent in yachting of the 'Cape cat'. . . ."

So, initially, one sort of catboat lost favor as another, the "Cape cat," gained support. But interests and styles of all sorts often run in cycles and what Stephens called the Cape cat was not immune to dwindling enthusiasm either. These splendid boats, which had basically been perfected by the late 1890s, were often the property, initially, of very wealthy men whose primary aim was to defeat a specific other boat, after which interest usually switched to the next yacht.

Doubtless, too, the catboats began to seem old-fashioned even before the turn of the last century. Here were yachts that looked pretty much the same as they had for years. By contrast, the emerging one-design classes were all distinct and also seemed to offer some special brand of performance imbued by the hand of designers who worked not with carved half-models but with mathematical calculations and paper plans. Class rules eliminated any need to handicap different boats within the same race. By the eve of World War One, there was literally an alphabet soup of racing classes from A to X that drew attention away from the variety of catboat classes that had existed for years. Even the Crosbys became involved. They developed the Wianno, Sr. for Osterville's Wianno Yacht Club in 1913. However, although the one-design movement attracted many sailors, it also generated a reaction among the most independent-minded, who always yearned for a distinctive boat unlike the next man's. As the years wore on, the once commonly seen catboat certainly became ever more distinctive!

Boston journalist Winfield Thompson lived through much of this period and was a thoughtful witness and inspired chronicler of both his own experiences and those of others. Although Thompson never overcame his fascination with catboats, he was not immune to the allure of new yachting types. Once, he even bought a Lawley-built knockabout but he never was satisfied with the boat or its small cockpit and admitted to himself and his readers "that I was not a knockabout man." Later, he suffered a "misadventure" with a powerboat that he never forgot. His conclusion was that a good catboat was such a perfect answer to the question of a small cruising boat for New England waters that, for him at least, there really was no alternative.

"Every little while a catboat sailor encounters a yawl-sailor or a cutter-sailor, or a glass-house [powerboat] sailor, who assumes a suspicious air, and says: 'Why a catboat?' The catboat sailor, being a philosopher, replies: 'Why a yawl, why a sharpie, why an oyster sloop, why a marine street car called a power boat, why a schooner, why a steamer? Why anything distinctive? Why not have all boats one type?'"

Extreme Types and the Response

One reason regularly put forth for the decline in popularity of catboats was the development of "extreme types." This seemed to have been applied not merely to boats with very large rigs but to boats that combined large sail plans with hulls that had reverse curves and/or long overhangs to gain favorable ratings. *Step Lively* was but one example of the type and these boats may, in fact, have done more to discourage catboat racing than to promote it. But this was because of their specialized nature, not because they were dangerous or unseaworthy.

That said, these were expensive boats, often designed with the knowledge that they would be crewed by professionals. They would have done little to foster their own ongoing popularity.

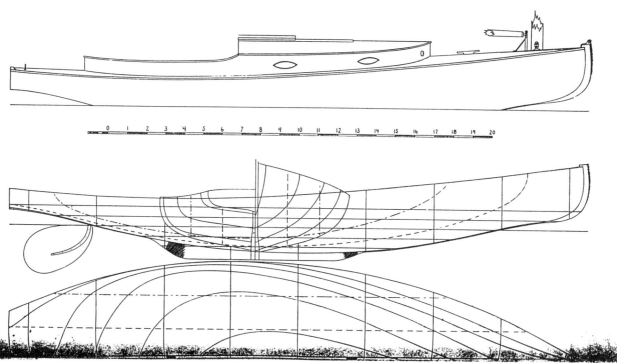

Designed for The Rudder *in 1897 by Vaughan D. Bacon, this racing catboat has the overhangs that characterized the genre. Thirty feet overall, the boat had a waterline of just 21' 3". A 1,200 pound lead molding was inset into the keel and the boat had a 467-pound bronze centerboard. Her sail area was 808.5 sq. ft. The boat's cockpit was eight feet long and the cabin offered four feet of headroom.*

It was fortunate for the better class of racing catboats that the Cape Catboat Association of Massachusetts Bay was formed in 1904 under the impetus of Frank Fessenden Crane. Crane was commodore of the Quincy Yacht Club, a man in his 50s who admired antique furniture and fast catboats and who indulged his interest in both when he wasn't selling real estate.

The Association's inclusion of the name "Cape Catboat" gives a good clue to the sort of boats it wanted and did not want, and makes clear the extremes to which catboat racing had gone in the previous decade. Explicitly forbidden were overhangs of more than 20 percent of the load water line. Neither were reverse curves permitted or "any unusual features. . . . The forward side of the mast shall not be more than one foot aft of the forward end of the waterline [this to mitigate against the boats with shrouds or even backstays]. . . . Working sails only shall be used (Jib and Mainsail)." This latter rule did away with big triangular spinnakers that had once been a part of catboat racing. The Association defined a boat legal for inclusion if it was 22 to 27 feet long overall and was "a seaworthy cruising and racing yacht, of the centerboard type, strongly constructed, properly ballasted with fixed ballast, having good freeboard, and substantial cabin trunk with suitable cabin accommodations for cruising." The rules required the boats to be usable cruisers with transom berths, a blanket for each crew member, lockers, a bucket, and other assorted equipment.

The Association attracted a good number of men who shared Crane's enthusiasm for catboats and it soon became the new home for over two dozen of the sport's fastest boats. When racing, they flew the Cape Catboat Association burgee, a black cat with arched back on a yellow field. While a variety of awards could be won in Association races, the most highly coveted, in 1907, was a silver serving tray on which a portrait of the top boat would be engraved. As it happened, the award was won by Crane himself sailing his Hanley-built *Iris* (ex-*Mucilage*).

By now, the Association was the center of catboat racing in Massachusetts. Here were gathered many of the fastest racing catboats ever built. Besides *Iris,* there were Hanley's *Almira, Busy Bee,* and *Dartwell.* Crosby-built boats included the 24-foot *Ariel,* 25-foot *Dolly II, Grayling, Mudjekeewis,* and *Hustler,* a former fishing catboat from Chatham. Others included *Stranger,* which had been built in Providence, Rhode Island, by Davis Brothers, and *Moondyne,* built by Smalley in Hyannis.

The owners were workingmen, dentists, manufacturers, and salesmen. Winfield Thompson described them as eager and dedicated sailors who handled their boats entirely on their own with no thought of paid crews. "Corinthians" was the word coined to distinguish the amateur sportsman from those who sailed with professionals aboard. These amateur sailors, heirs to history's best catboats, were often highly skilled, having studied the craft of yacht racing in general, and the demanding nuances of catboat handling in particular. Each boat was typically raced with a crew of four to six men, and physical size and strength were much in demand. The Daniel Crosby-built *Dolly III,* for example, had a core crew consisting of a 210-pound helmsman, 240-pound mainsheet man, a 205-pound generalist, and the others weighing at least 160 pounds.

Winfield Thompson described in colorful detail the sailing of an Association race at Quincy in July 1907, an event characterized by a rather unusual, fall-like northwesterly breeze of such weight that Frank Crane put four reefs into *Iris*'s sail before he left his mooring. Thompson described the efforts of the 250-pound mainsheet man, sitting on the cockpit floor and controlling the sheet by feeding it around a floor-mounted cleat while others tailed and green water flooded the cockpit as the boat, despite its 12-foot beam, heeled when tacking. He also described how a crew member aboard *Almira* helped take out a reef when the skipper mistakenly assumed a brief drop in wind velocity was permanent.

The boom was well off, rising and dipping regularly over the steep, hard chop. The man walked out nimbly, balancing himself with his left hand against the hard, contoured surface of the sail. At the leech he let go the pennant and then, still supported by the sail, he backed carefully inboard, casting off the stops as he came. It was a graceful act of first-class seamanship in small boat sailing, the sort of thing that can be accomplished only by use of brains as well as manual dexterity.

The result, however, was that *Almira,* with three reefs now in instead of four, was overpowered, could no longer point up high enough, and lost several minutes and the race.

All the Association's boats, built primarily by Hanley and the Crosbys but also including one built by Hanley's understudy, George Shiverick, (*Arawak*) and a scattering of other builders, were by then in the hands of their second, third, or more owners. Most existed, however, in rather highly modi-fied versions of their originally splendid selves. Some suffered more than others, most of the damage having been done before an Association member acquired a boat. Even *Almira* ran into trouble and had so deteriorated by 1914 that she was "sold out of the Association." But she came back the following year.

It took at least two seasons to restore *Almira* to some semblance of her former glory, and this was accomplished only with the help of naval architect Erland Debes who was then closely associated with Hanley in Quincy. Purchased by Dr. H. A. Jones in 1914 when she was 26 years old, *Almira* was given a new set of sails in 1915. Her under-hung rudder was replaced with a barndoor rudder and all her ballast was removed when it was decided to fit a lead keel shoe that ran along the bottom from the front of the centerboard trunk to the stern. Some 300 pounds of inside ballast was retained for trimming. Mast hoops were replaced

Arawak was the D Class champ in 1906. An impressive catboat built by George Shiverick in his Kingston, Massachusetts, shop, Arawak *measured 27' x 23' x 11' x 3' 1". She was ballasted with 2,600 pounds of lead. This boat's boom was 34 feet long, her gaff 25 feet.* Arawak *had a 923 sq. ft. sail and could set a 125 sq. ft. jib on her 13 1/2-foot bowsprit.*

with sail track and the peak halyard was re-rigged with a new system of blocks intended to reduce the spar's tendency to buckle and destroy the sail's shape. By 1916, *Almira* — using "only" her new 998 sq. ft. mainsail — was not only defeating the other catboats, but new R-boats and Sonder boats as well.

The rules of the Cape Catboat Association sought not only to preserve the catboats the members owned but even to encourage new construction by adopting sensible rules aimed at ensuring a practical boat. Two boats were, in fact, built. The Small brothers designed one of these new catboats, *Atalanta,* probably in 1906. The boat turned out to be too long in some measurement and had to race in a class other than the one she'd been designed for, but did so successfully. A second boat, *Mellwood,* met the class rules but was not competitive with the older catboats and was eventually converted and re-rigged.

Atalanta

Designer / Builder: Small Brothers, Quincy

Model: Overhang stern

Length overall: 27 feet

Length of waterline: 25 feet

Beam: 10' 8"

Draft: Approx. 3' 2" board up

Headroom: 5' 8"

Planking: Pine and cedar

Notes: This boat was probably launched with its long bowsprit as original equipment. When advertised for sale in 1910, it was stated that owner had lived aboard the boat for the previous two summers and cruised from Boston to Block Island.

Before America's entry into World War One, the Association's "D Class" catboats were enthusiastically campaigned on a circuit from Annisquam to Gloucester to Marblehead to Boston to Provincetown. What's more, even before the opening of the Cape Cod Canal in 1914, an effort was made, beginning in 1909 or 1910 to promote more diverse competition. The Interbay Catboat Association was developed to have catboats from Massachusets Bay, Narragansett Bay, and Barnegat Bay compete with one another. It was a grand, if unwieldly, idea.

Surviving photographs show the D Class catboats being handled with a surprisingly casual air, and they were clearly used for cruising as well as racing. C. Willis Garey reported that, as a 98-pound teenager, he had single-handed *Almira* many times. *Almira* and her cohorts were still being raced in the early '20s but by then, they were racing against time as much as against one another.

A Growing Scarcity

One day in 1969, H. Manley Crosby's grandson, Wilton B. Crosby, Jr., discovered a file of letters written to Manley by E. V. Rosemond, a retired hatter and catboat enthusiast who had lived in Greenport on Long Island. In retirement, Rosemond busied himself with buying and selling catboats. Although the letters, which were later published by John Leavens in the *Catboat Association Bulletin,* are limited to a seven-month period in 1921, they provide a unique glimpse into the state of catboats at that time. In general, it was not a pretty picture. Rosemond found boats with centerboard trunks totally removed, with worm-eaten keels, rudderposts, and centerboard trunks, broken exhaust pipes, and leaky bottoms. Once he described the colors someone had painted a catboat: "Sea green interior, barn red slide [hatch], rail, s—- color carlins [cabin beams], doors, etc. . . . "

Rosemond believed he would have had a good market for any Crosby 25-footer with a good cabin, or for the bigger boats. He wrote Manley that I "could sell many of those old big cats, but dare say they have all been converted into beam trawlers." He was right. Still, Rosemond turned up the occasional serviceable old Crosby boat, seeking them out from Boston to the Cape to Cuttyhunk or anywhere else that he got a likely tip. Sometimes, he even acquired an old Hanley cat like this one described by her owner:

Built 1892. Hull is sound and smooth; no rot in timbers or plank; and no leaks, no worms; board worn, but will last a year; sail old, can get a new one for $60. Staving a little punky in one place. Decks scraped down pretty fine in places, cabin house not canvassed but ought to be (leaks), cushions need new covers; she is a good old fast cat, 24 feet with 21-foot waterline, 11-foot beam that can sail. She is waiting an appreciative owner. I cuss the luck that won't permit me to sail her; has a ton of lead ballast — Price $450.

One of the things that may have saved this boat, believed to have been Hanley's *Mouser,* was that the deadwood was only three inches wide, too slim to bore it for a propeller shaft. Rosemond took the boat out in what he called a gale of wind and reported "she is the smoothest, fastest thing I ever sailed . . . smooth and slick as the day she was launched, not a check, mar, rot, or crack to her, she had been kept in a private boat house."

With Rosemond urging him on, H. Manley Crosby began working on a new 23 1/2- x 10 1/2-foot catboat intended to be a stock design with the features demanded by that generation of sailor. Chief among these were a large cabin with

five feet of headroom and a reliable 10 - 14 horse-power Red Wing, four-cycle motor. Apparently, *Fair One* was not available to show at the New York Motor Boat Show in 1922 where, Rosemond believed, it would have been a big hit. Nor did it lead to the hoped-for series of orders. Up in Osterville, Daniel Crosby & Son stopped building new boats about 1926. Daniel had died in 1920 during the construction of a big keel catboat named *Sea Fox.* Charles H. Crosby also closed in the mid-to-late '20s. H. Manley continued for a while longer and Crosby Yacht Building and Storage Company remained in the family until 1972, although catboat building was no longer part of the business.

Sea Fox

Style: Keel with overhang stern

Year built: 1919 – 1920

Length overall: 40 feet

Beam: 14 feet

Draft: 3' 8"

Engine: Lathrop jump-spark 40 hp

Fuel capacity: 240 gallons

Price: $9,600

Notes: Re-rigged as a sloop in 1936 with 980 sq. ft. mainsail and 250 sq. ft. jib

---

Into the Modern Era

It is perfectly clear that, as America entered the 1920s, gaff-rigged catboats were no longer going to be a big part of yachting. There was simply too much competition from one-designs of all sorts, easy-to-handle knockabouts with their comparatively modest sloop rigs, motorboats, and larger sailing yachts. *The Rudder,* which had earlier published catboat material on a regular basis, now carried almost nothing. The boat plans published included those for big yachts, and there were frequent articles about Gold Cup motorboat racing, and engine technology.

All this did not mean the catboat didn't continue its long evolution. It simply fell into step with prevailing trends as, at the drawings boards of a new generation of designers, a new generation of catboats began to emerge. They weren't traditional Cape Cod catboats. Rather, many were usually one-designs aimed at breathing new life into the type by standardizing specifications and often switching from gaff to what was called either a Bermudan, marconi, or a "jib-headed" rig. In some cases, such as the 15-foot class of catboats raced at the Quincy Yacht Club, the boats were converted from gaff to marconi rigs.

Among the newer generation of designers who always maintained a lively interest in catboats was Charles Mower, who had been born in Lynn, Massachusetts, in 1880. Catboats were still a common sight on Boston's North Shore during the years Mower was growing up. He took note of many of them even as he built his own first boat in his backyard. His son remembered that, for Charles Mower, boats were "a pastime, vocation,

everything." When he was 15 in 1895, Mower began a three-year apprenticeship in Boston with naval architect Arthur Binney and followed this with a year's work with Bowdoin Crowninshield. Then, when he was 19, Mower went to work for Thomas Fleming Day at *The Rudder* where he was called the "designing editor" and began to publish his work.

Among Mower's catboats was a 20-footer published in *The Rudder* as a how-to-build series in 1903. Mower introduced the boat as follows:

> For many waters, the catboat has much to recommend it over any other type, and while the ever-growing craze for the knockabout has had the effect of placing the cat among the ranks of the old-fashioned craft, far behind the modern idea of what a yacht should be, the type still exists and its usefulness is proven by the fact that down around Cape Cod, on Barnegat Bay and similar waters, the cat is still used by the fishermen and yachtsmen in preference to the various types of knockabout.

Mower was forthright in telling readers that his new design was based on his study of earlier boats. He specifically mentioned A. B. Babbitt's *Varuna*

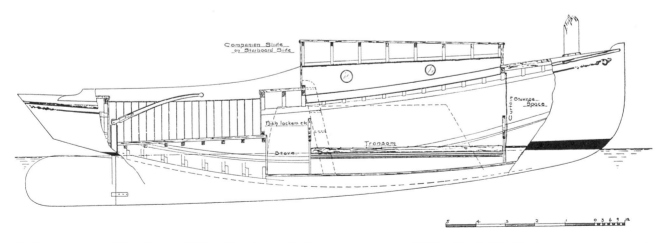

Charles Mower designed Ring Dove *in 1903 and her plans and building instructions were published in* The Rudder. *The design was meant to provide amateur builders with a wholesome, practical catboat designed for a new generation of sailors.*

and C. C. Hanley's *Harbinger* and stressed that his design "has plenty of freeboard, especially forward, good beam, a bilge that will make her able and a bottom that will give her a good turn of speed." In fact, Mower's design, which he named *Ring Dove,* was rather modern by comparison to the classic catboat. Although 20 feet long, *Ring Dove*'s water line was just 16' 4", and her rig was admittedly short although Mower noted that she would "not need reefing very often." The need to reef a catboat's big sail was something that 20th-century sailors apparently found much less appetizing than had their predecessors and shows up on occasion as another reason for the catboat's decline in general favor. *Ring Dove* was an early example of quite a number of catboat designs or plans that would appear in *The Rudder,* and other magazines, pretty much without interruption for many years.

The Rudder's New York offices placed Mower in handy proximity to sailors with the means to support his design ambitions. In 1904, he designed a modern racing catboat for the mayor of Philadelphia, who planned to race her in Barnegat Bay. *Empress* was 30 feet overall but had a waterline of just 18' 9". Spars were hollow and the mast had shrouds and a spreader for the forestay. The boat was lightly built and there was no ballast other than a weighted centerboard. This was the sort of "modern racing machine," as *The Rudder* called it, which finally displaced the older Barnegat Bay champions like A. Cary Smith's *Bouquet.* But such boats seem to have dominated the older models without inspiring real enthusiasm or long-term support for themselves.

In January 1906, Mower left *The Rudder* and opened a design office at 29 Broadway. There he specialized in designing a variety of racing yachts and auxiliaries although, by 1910, Mower found he was receiving an increasing number of commissions to design powerboats. In 1922, Mower designed the first of the Barnegat Bay A Cats, a boat commissioned by Edwin Schoettle. By then, Schoettle had owned several fine racing catboats,

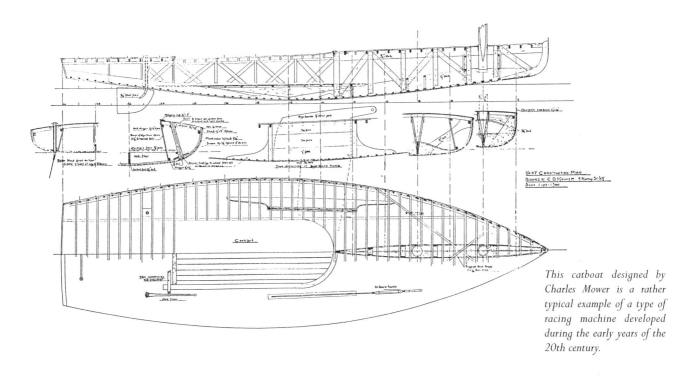

This catboat designed by Charles Mower is a rather typical example of a type of racing machine developed during the early years of the 20th century.

including Frank Randall's Wilton Crosby-built *Scat*, which he acquired when he was 24 years old in 1900. Schoettle's new boat, *Mary Ann*, embodied what Mower and his client believed to be the necessary elements of a "modern" catboat. The 28-footer had a shallow, centerboard hull, and an underhung rudder operated by a tiller. The 48' 6" mast was supported by triple forestays, shrouds, and running backstays. The sail, slightly over 600 square feet in area, had a short gaff, a style then referred to as a "Swedish rig" (replaced by a triangular sail in the late '20s). The cabin was fitted with a berth on each side, a stove, and toilet.

Mary Ann impressed all who saw her and soon was followed by other generally similar boats that would make up the A-Cat class and race for one of the oldest trophies in American sport, the Toms River Challenge Cup, which had been crafted at

Barnegat Bay circa 1920s: (l. - r.) Tamwock, Mary Ann, Bat, *and* Spy *are seen here, their original "Swedish rigs" (with a very short gaff) having been replaced by a jib-headed sail. A tall spar, spreaders, and running backstays typified this "modern" generation of racing catboat first designed by Charles Mower in 1922.* Mary Ann *and* Spy *were known as good heavy-air boats and* Spy *was noted for better windward than downwind speed. Lovingly rebuilt and raced by devoted crews, the original A cats are being joined by an increasing number of new boats. By 2002, the fleet reportedly numbered 13, a testament to the enduring appeal and challenge of the class.*

Tiffany's in 1871. Mower's subsequent A Cats —
Bat, Spy, Lotus, and *Helen* — differed in detail from
Mary Ann and each was known for particular performance traits. *Mary Ann* and *Spy* had the reputation as good heavy-air models but *Spy* was said to
be slow downwind. *Bat* was always reputed to be
a fine all-around sailor. *Helen,* built in 1923 with a
somewhat narrower beam than the others, was
not successful.

These A Cats attracted enough attention that
two area sailors arranged for boats to be developed by another New York-based designer, Francis
Sweisguth, who would go on to design the famous
Star. The first of these boats, *Foresome,* was said to
have been improperly built and improperly rigged
and was unsuccessful. The second boat, *Tamwock*
("seagull" in the language of the native Americans
who once lived in what became New Jersey),
raced successfully for many years until destroyed
in an Island Heights boatyard fire in the 1940s.

Francis Sweisguth was born in Union City, New
Jersey, in 1882 and was graduated from Cooper
Union and the Pratt Institute. He worked for
some 20 years for designer William Gardner in
New York before moving to City Island, where he
became part of the firm Ford, Payne and
Sweisguth. His partner, Gerald Ford, remembered Sweisguth as "very reserved and quiet . . . so
close-mouthed as to be gloomy." But Sweisguth
was also very capable. Edwin Schoettle wrote of
him that he was "so thorough and painstaking in
his work that it would be almost impossible for
him to design a poor boat."

Sweisguth had been exposed to catboats during
the time he lived in Point Pleasant, New Jersey. In
1920, he designed for Schoettle the 30' x 12' *Scat
II,* an immediate racing success. She was eventually replaced in Schoettle's affections by *Silent Maid,*
a boat he owned until his death in 1947.

Here is the Sweisguth-designed Silent Maid *sailing in Barnegat Bay
nearly 60 years after her launching.*

Silent Maid, a cruising catboat of 1925

Designer: Francis Sweisguth

Builder: Morton Johnson, Bay Head, New Jersey

Length overall: 33 feet

Length of waterline: 28' 6"

Beam: 12' 6"

Draft (board up): 2' 6"

Sail area: 950 sq. ft. (Originally intended as a
marconi rig, this was changed to gaff.)

Headroom: Six feet

Cockpit: Self-bailing

Finish: Bright hull, cabin sides and coamings

Engine: None (hence the boat's name!)

Boats like the Barnegat Bay A Class, *Scat II,* and
Silent Maid serve to demonstrate that, although

the classic 19th-century catboat had given way to a variety of new designs and types, the catboat could still evolve and attract sailors in the new century. While Schoettle and his colleagues were wealthy men who had no thought of switching their interest in catboats to other types, less affluent but independent-minded sailors with an interest in practicality and proven sailing qualities either purchased old catboats, built catboats at home, or had one built to plans published in one of the yachting magazines of the day.

Charles Mower's *Ring Dove* was merely one early example of this trend to publish plans and even include detailed instructions, making it possible for those of modest means to have a professionally designed boat without having to pay the architect's fee. How many Mower catboat plans were published in magazines is not known, but he contributed at least three more to *Motor Boating* in the '20s. These included, in 1921, an 18-foot, half-decked, marconi-rigged model that he called *Frances* and intended for club racing; a C. C. Hanley-inspired 20' 9" x 9' 3" cabin model named *Grace* that was intended to have a pair of outboard motors for auxiliary power; and *Caper,* a 22' x 10' x 2' cabin catboat whose plans were published in 1926.

Whether to drum up excitement or because he recognized an upsurge of interest in catboats, Mower introduced *Caper* by noting that "Cat boats are returning to favor in many localities where a shallow draft boat is required. . . . The cat rig makes a boat that is easy to handle and the large cockpit makes a very comfortable boat for day sailing while the small cabin gives shelter in bad weather or a sudden rain squall and provides accommodations for short cruises." Mower included color schemes in his plans, and they seemed to be consistent. Hulls were to be white,

the bottom green, the decks and cabin top either a salmon or gray color that he called "lead." For *Caper,* he suggested the decks and cabin sides be varnished and the cabin top be buff. Interiors were to be white with varnished trim.

Mower was not alone in publishing designs, of course, and some rather peculiar boats also emerged. *Little Pal* was a marconi-rigged 28-foot catboat designed by one J. B. Barrington and published in *Motor Boating* in January, 1920. Mr. Barrington's catboat had a 785 sq. ft. sail, which he justified by saying that eliminating the gaff would make it relatively simply to handle. The boat had an iron tiller and what appeared to be a barndoor rudder but which, on close examination, was actually a kind of balanced rudder that was cut to fit under the hull and into the propeller aperture. It's unlikely that *Little Pal* spawned much in the way of interest or much enthusiasm for modern catboats.

Outboard profile of Little Pal. Scale, ⅛-inch equals 1 foot

Little Pal — *how many friends she earned is unknown.*

More intriguing was a vee-bottom 20-footer designed for amateur construction and published in *Motor Boating* in March 1921, by William J. Deed, creator of many a beguiling little motor cruiser. This was a practical and friendly-looking little catboat that Deed named *Porpoise*. Cost of materials was said to be about a thousand dollars. This boat, with its 265 sq. ft. sail, five- or six-horsepower two-cycle engine, and a cozy cabin with five feet of headroom would have been a most satisfactory little craft for many a Roaring Twenties sailor. *Porpoise*'s comparatively narrow beam of 8' 1", which was judged to be "liberal", would have contributed to good performance under power. The centerboard, however, looks a bit small, although the boat's hard chines and ample skeg may have contributed to windward ability.

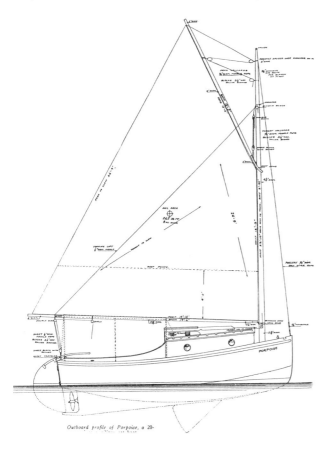

Outboard profile of Porpoise, a 20-

Best known for his appealing motor boats, William Deed designed Porpoise *as a practical catboat that could be built by the amateur enthusiast.*

As the '20s progressed, the catboat retained a small but enduring niche in the recreational boating scene. It was a niche peopled by wealthy men at one extreme, who accounted for a comparatively small number of commissioned designs, and the amateur builder for whom budgets were a primary concern. In between were those who sailed a variety of half-decked one-design, cat-rigged boats often specific to a given locale or yacht club, and the scattering of sailors who sought out an older and usually leaky catboat because they simply liked the type. This, in fact, was the general catboat scene right up to and through World War Two. The Depression did little to boost any sort of boating, although its true impact on the sport is somewhat difficult to assess. Dire predictions for emptied harbors and lack of racing contestants did not prove true. In the fall of 1931, *Yachting* reported that "the season afloat on Massachusetts Bay was singularly successful," and the magazine's story on Marblehead's "Race Week" included a photograph showing the waters off Marblehead Neck crowded with boats.

It was just at this apparently most unlikely economic time that a modest and uniquely gifted 30-year-old designer in Marblehead introduced the first of a series of catboat designs that not only garnered attention then, but continue to do so today. The designer was Fenwick Williams. Exactly how Williams developed his extraordinary abilities remains something of a mystery even to those who knew him for many years. "Well, it's a complete mystery to *me*," he once told Concordia founder Waldo Howland. Of course, his genius was exceeded only by his modesty.

According to yacht broker John Killam Murphy, who met Williams at the John G. Alden office in Boston where they both worked, Fenwick left high school to devote himself to eye exercises that would improve his extreme nearsightedness. Among other things, Williams began drawing flowers, birds, and catboats, and then progressed to boat plans. By the time he was 22 years old in 1923, Williams had so developed his abilities that he was hired by John Alden, who would later remark to his staff that Williams "draws lines just the way I want them!" The staff then included Samuel Crocker, Murray Peterson, Charles MacGregor, and Carl Alberg!

By the time Williams joined Alden, in the early '20s, the catboat was clearly viewed by most as being old-fashioned. Years later, Williams would add that "it was a disaster to be known as a professional catboat designer." Within the marine trade, Williams was famous not for catboats but for his versatility. During his career, Williams worked on the design, engineering, and plans of boats as diverse as America's Cup yachts, schooners, the Concordia yawl, Boston Whaler, and even the first deep-vee powerboats of C. Raymond Hunt. Catboat design was strictly an after-hours activity, but Williams gave the whole subject great thought, and closely examined every catboat he could that visited Marblehead harbor.

In November of 1931, *Yachting* published the first of Williams's catboat plans. It was for an 18-foot model that, with its high bow and barndoor rudder, represented a new interpretation of the classic, 19th-century catboat. As was by then customary with most published plans, the boat was engineered for amateur construction "with sawn frames, which form the molds over which the boat is built, and lighter steam-bent frames between each pair of sawn timbers..." The copy accompanying Williams's design noted that: "Only those who have had catboat experience can realize how much fun can be had in these craft, with but a single sail to handle, and draft enabling one to

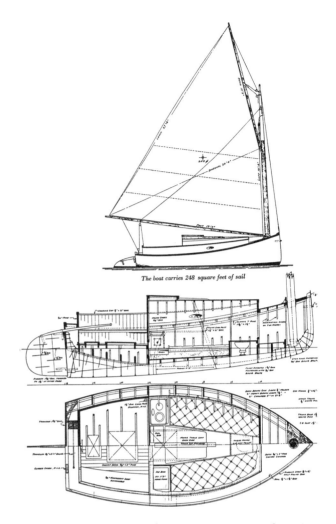

The boat carries 248 square feet of sail

Fenwick Williams published his first catboat design, the 18-footer shown here, in 1931. Wonderful in form and function, the boat remains as appealing today as it was then.

poke around in all sorts of little nooks, which are quite inaccessible to the ordinary cruiser."

Fenwick Williams Catboat of 1931

Length overall: 18 feet

Length of waterline: 17' 7"

Beam: 8' 6"

Draft: 2' 4"

Sail area: 248 sq. ft.

Engine: NA

Steering: Tiller

Williams's catboats are still known for their full bow sections, which he believed imparted good sea-keeping ability, balance, and dryness. The first of the 18-footers was built in Chicago by an owner who reported himself well-pleased with the result. But, when Williams looked at the snapshots the builder had sent, he told John Killam Murphy that "I became considerably shook, lost my nerve and redrew the lines with a somewhat finer forebody."

A year after publication of the 18-footer, a 21-footer by Williams was published in *The Rudder* in September 1932. This boat was designed for a couple who "wanted the conveniences of boats usually over 30 feet." Unlike the 18-foot model,

Fenwick C. Williams (1901 – 1992). Here, Fenwick stands at the drafting board in his Marblehead home in 1983.

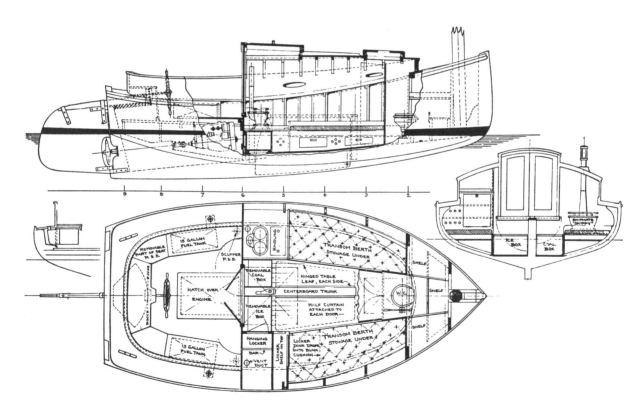

The Fenwick Williams 21-foot catboat: 21' x 20' 4" x 10' x 2' 4". The boat had a displacement of 6,500 pounds of which 1,000 was ballast. Sail area was 372 sq. ft. Among the most practical and desirable of catboats, this 21 footer — built and rigged according to the designer's specifications — will provide years of satisfying daysailing and cruising.

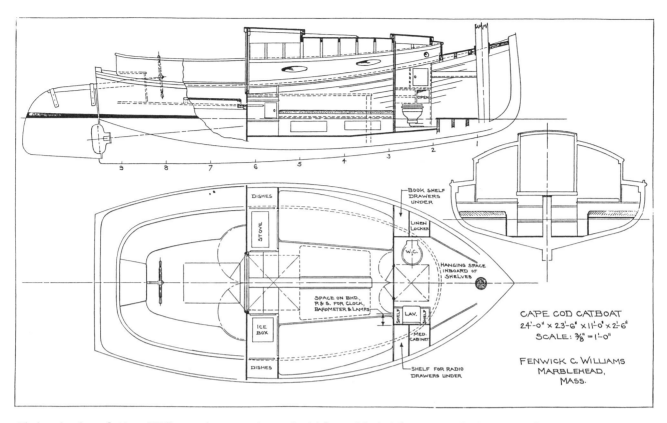

DISHES

STOVE

ICE
BOX

DISHES

BOOK SHELF
DRAWERS
UNDER

LINEN
LOCKER

W.C.

HANGING SPACE
INBOARD OF
SHELVES

SPACE ON BHD,
P. & S. FOR CLOCK,
BAROMETER & LAMPS

SHELF LAV.

MED.
CABINET

SHELF FOR RADIO
DRAWERS UNDER

CAPE COD CATBOAT
24'-0" X 23'-6" X 11'-0" X 2'-6"
SCALE: 3⁄8" = 1'-0"

FENWICK C. WILLIAMS
MARBLEHEAD,
MASS.

The beguiling lines of a Fenwick Williams catboat are evident in this 24-foot model, which features an enclosed head at the forward end of the cabin.

the larger boat's plans made provision for an engine, either a 25-horsepower Falcon with reduction gear or a Gray 4-30 (four cylinders, 30 horsepower) without. Twenty years later, Williams modified the boat by engineering a version with an off-center centerboard that would in no way compromise the strength of the keel. Eventually, Williams would adapt his catboat lines to a variety of sizes including a 15-, 16-, 24-, 25-, and 28-footer. But it was the 18 and 21 that would be the most popular. When the catboat began to be rediscovered in the years following World War Two, the appeal inherent in these boats caused their plans to be ordered by enthusiasts both in the U.S. and abroad. Even today, these remain the boats of choice for those who want to build a traditional Cape Cod catboat.

Fenwick Williams Catboat of 1932

Length overall: 21 feet

Length of waterline: 20' 4"

Beam: 10 feet

Headroom: 5' 6" under hatch, 4' 10" forward

Sail area: 372 sq. ft.

Ballast: 1,000 lbs.

Displacement: 6,500 lbs.

Steering: Wheel

Engine: Four-cylinder gasoline

Photographed in August 1963 at the Catboat Association Rendezvous at Osterville are those who did so much to restore interest in catboats. First row (l.-r.): John Leavens, Albert Rockwood, Dr. Robert Schwab, Milton Craig, Paul Birdsall, Breck Marshall. Second row (l. - r.) Herbert Stenberg, Alfred Lincoln, Arthur Northrop, Paul Drumm, Dr. Robert Ascher, S. Alex Mitchell, Graeme Elliott, Robert Winsor. The Association they founded would grow to be one of the world's largest devoted to traditional boats.

PART TWO

REBIRTH

Carl Beetle introduced his 12-foot BB Swan catboat in 1946, one of the earliest production fiberglass boats. This one is being sailed by Fred Towle, an important figure in Beetle's pioneering but unsuccessful company. The BB Swan was entirely distinct from the famous Beetle Cat.

CHAPTER SEVEN

CARL BEETLE AND THE FIBERGLASS PIONEERS

———— •◆• ————

"All Marscot hulls are glass fibre reinforced, one piece polyester resin castings, guaranteeing uniformity of strength, unequaled by other methods; producing light, efficient, resilient hulls that withstand wind, water, climate — no drying out, no rot, no caulking or injury from marine growth — smooth inside and out."

— MARSCOT PLASTIC INC, 1956

B Y THE SPRING OF 1944, articles in the boating press were looking ahead with increasing frequency to the coming of peace. The same magazines that carried big display ads showing Herreshoff-built rescue boats, Packard V-12 marine engines, and Haskelite plywood used in landing craft, also had stories about the sorts of boats that people would want in post-war America. In April 1944, *Yachting* published an article called "In Defense of the Cat — *Haidee,* a Post-War Yacht Suggesting the Revival of the Catboat." Stories about rediscovery of the catboat by then had a long tradition, for similar articles had been penned with some frequency ever since the pre-World War One days of Winfield Thompson's "I Buy an Old Cat." In 1953, *Yachting* would publish another important piece, not in "defense" of the cat but in praise of it. In fact, the theme of both articles — the timeless virtues of catboats — was the same. Although these stories often presented the attractions of the surviving

Crosby catboats, they now also offered new designs aimed at a new generation of sailors.

"Of late years hereabouts there has been a revival of interest in the catboat," wrote Rhode Islander William Oehrle in his 1944 *Yachting* piece. "I regard it as a healthy revival of a type of boat that fits the requirements of our pleasure boatmen almost perfectly, and one which has always seemed to me to be worth serious consideration by yachtsmen whose home ports are located between Cape Cod and Florida." At the time, Oehrle could never have guessed just how important one of the designs presented in his article would be. But the fact was that a good case was being made for people to buy catboats.

A new generation of designers was also emerging, many of whom added catboats to their portfolios and sought to address one or another of the problems that the type was perceived to have. In Middletown, Connecticut, in 1951, Winthrop Warner presented plans for a 24' x 11 1/2' keel-type catboat that drew 3' 10" but offered six feet of headroom and an enclosed head. In 1953, Ralph E. Winslow, working in Quincy not far from C. C. Hanley's old yard, showed a 21 1/2' x 10' 7"catboat with a board-up draft of 2' 11" — a bit more than any Crosby would have been comfortable with in a boat of similar size. A year later, Charles Wittholz published plans for a boat designed expressly to take advantage of plywood for the amateur builder. Wittholz would design several more such boats of varying size for plywood or plank-on-frame construction. In Marblehead, in 1949, Fenwick Williams released drawings of the latest version of his latest 18-footer. The boat was typically traditional but this one showed a two-cylinder Blue Jacket engine and wheel-steering rather than his engineless prewar model with its tiller.

Charles Wittholz at his Silver Spring, Maryland, drawing board in 1980. A friendly, multi-talented naval architect, Wittholz had a long interest in catboats and designed everything from an 11-foot "catboat dinghy" to the 25-foot Prudence.

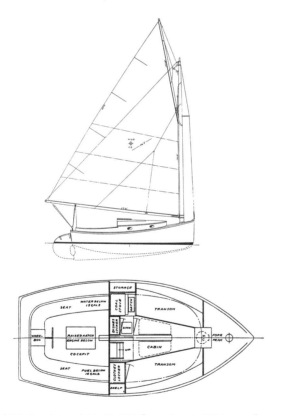

Ralph Winslow designed this 21 1/2-foot catboat in 1951, one of several post-World War Two interpretations of the type.

Even while all these new catboat designs and others began appearing, something quite dramatic was being methodically developed in states as diverse as Ohio, New Jersey, California, Massachusetts, and Rhode Island. In each of these places, a handful of visionaries was working to develop an idea whose time, they believed, had come, even if the boat-buying public in general didn't know it.

The prewar introduction of plywood as a boat-building material was a first step toward simplifying the construction of a wooden boat, to reducing its cost, and to reducing maintenance. But, whatever its virtues, plywood was still *wood.* Even before the war ended, the search was on for a new material that would speed boat construction, offer both durability and a long service life, and essentially eliminate the need for the maintenance that a wooden boat demanded. It became apparent to those involved in this effort that some sort of plastic was going to be the answer. The plastic that offered the most promise seemed to be mats made

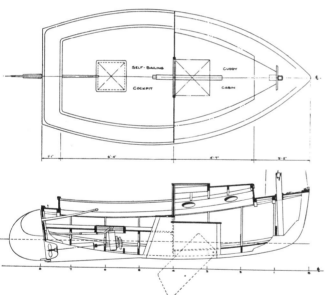

Charles Wittholz first published plans for this 15' 2" hard-chine, plywood catboat that he called Sapphire *in* The Rudder. *"The object," he wrote, "was to get the biggest possible boat utilizing 16-foot panels." The boat was only slightly larger than the 14' 11" Corvus but, according to Wittholz, "has her centerboard further forward. Because of this she handles nicely with the marconi rig whose center of effort is also further forward than on the gaff rig." These plywood Wittholz boats remain justly popular. Builders are well-advised to construct the hulls exactly as the designer intended while modifying cockpit / cabin arrangements, if desired, according to personal preference.*

of woven glass fibers that had first been developed in 1941 by Owens-Corning Fiberglas.

One of those who believed that fiberglass represented the future of boating was a New Bedford boat builder named Carl Beetle. Born in 1896 into a family famous for the design and manufacture of whale boats, Carl Beetle was a forward-looking, ambitious man who left New Bedford to gain experience in a variety of boat and shipyards. Beetle was so convinced that fiberglass represented the future of boat building that, after he returned to New Bedford, he sold the family's wooden patterns for the Beetle Cat to Waldo Howland, proprietor of Concordia, in the mid-1940s. Then he focused all his energy on building and marketing small fiberglass boats.

At his shop in New Bedford, Carl Beetle designed one of first sailboats ever engineered for production in fiberglass. It was a 12 1/2-foot, marconi-rigged catboat called the BB (Beetle Boat) Swan. The year was 1946. Once the initial difficulties were overcome, production began in 1947, the hull and deck molded at the General Electric plant in Pittsfield, Massachusetts, which had the technology needed to make the boats in expensive, matched metal dies using heat to cure the resin.

Beetle's was very much a pioneering effort, but it was not the first attempt to build and sell fiberglass boats to the public. In Trenton, New Jersey, Taylor Winner had built and advertised his PlastiCraft fiberglass boats since 1945. In California, Wizard Boats introduced a line of outboard-powered models in 1945. In Toledo, Ohio, Ray Greene had molded (but not put into series production) an eight-foot dinghy in 1942 and then introduced his famous and long-lived 16-foot Rebel sailboat in 1947. These pioneers were soon, joined by others. Not far from Beetle, in New Bedford, boatbuilder Palmer Scott molded a little pram in 1947 and then set up a plastic boat division named Marscot — a combination of the name of fiberglass pioneer, Dr. Herbert Muscat and Scott. Marscot built 18-, 22-, and 26-foot Angler powerboats, which remain available today as the Tripp Angler. In 1949, Bill Dyer, at the Anchorage in Bristol, Rhode Island, began building his Wittholz-designed Dhow dinghies in fiberglass. In 1950, in Wareham, Massachusetts, where Charles Anderson had built his catboats, the Cape Cod Shipbuilding Company began building a fiberglass version of the Herreshoff Bullseye and followed this in 1951 with a very nice, round-bottom, nine-foot dinghy.

Fiberglass, resins, and various types of molds all represented new technology at the time that Carl Beetle started his company. The use of expensive matched metal dies and heat to cure the resin gave way to female-type molds built from wooden plugs. In such molds, the fiberglass could be laid up with resin that would cure at room temperature. Those who had begun with the original method developed by Dr. Muscat, including Beetle and Palmer Scott, soon switched. Beetle, with the financial backing of Fred Towle who was the company president, now began to expand his line of models and to build them in New Bedford. The catboat was joined by the BB-24 Cabin Cruiser in 1950 and then by several dinghies.

Today, more than half a century after these first fiberglass boats were built and marketed, it is interesting to reflect upon the objections that people then raised to fiberglass. The concern that a fiberglass boat would be weak was initially widely prevalent, and countered in a variety of ways. Carl Beetle had an advertisement that showed him firing a revolver at the hull of one of his little cat-

boats, to no damaging effect. This was similar to a photograph probably done at Winner in New Jersey. It showed a state trooper examining a fiberglass panel at which he had fired a .45 caliber submachine gun from 10 feet away. The half-inch-thick panel resisted penetration. When showgoers at the Boston Boat Show routinely dirtied the hull that Palmer Scott had on display by kicking it to test its strength, Scott himself went out and bought a rubber mallet. He hung the mallet on the boat together with a sign that said "Hit Me!" More than once, magazines reported that a 12-inch cube of fiberglass "could support a Navy destroyer without being crushed."

There were other, perhaps odder, concerns as well. Dave Biddle, who worked in the industry during its formative years, remembers that, at the New York Boat Show in 1951, a man in a three-piece suit asked Scott if his 26-foot fiberglass boat would work in fresh water as well as salt water. "Palmer said that he didn't know but would be happy to analyze a sample of the water in the lake where the man intended to use the boat. Sure enough, the man sent a jar of the water, which Palmer left on his daughter Thalia's desk for several days. Then he wrote the man and said he had carefully analyzed the water and that the boat would 'float most handsomely in it.' They thought little more about this until a check showed up for *two* boats."

Carl Beetle, meanwhile, was doing his best to publicize his BB Swan which, inevitably perhaps, was also referred to in the press as a "Beetle catboat," creating persistent confusion between it and the wooden Beetle Cat, an entirely different boat. At the time, Concordia was legally required to refer to its boat as "the original Beetle cat," to ensure there would be no confusion. Today, some confusion continues to exist about the two boats and in regard to the original specifications of the BB Swan itself. It appears that the early versions molded by GE had wooden components that included the coaming, a foredeck applique, floorboards, and seats. These probably did much to dress up a boat that had a deck with exaggerated tumblehome designed to ease the molding process. Later versions did not have so many wooden parts and presented a less attractive appearance.

There appear to have been two different fiberglass foredeck configurations, one that was entirely smooth and another that had a molded-in raised area where the wooden applique had been. The BB Swan had hollow aluminum spars produced by Zephyr, a part of Cape Cod Shipbuilding in Wareham. The mast was unstayed. The spars were grooved to accept the 90 sq. ft. sail, which had

This ad for the BB Swan appeared in Yachting *in May 1949.*

three battens and a "BB" insignia. An aluminum tiller was used that could be slid backward or forward atop the rudder depending on how much leverage was required. The boat weighed 300 pounds and originally cost just under $600, although this was closer to $700 by the time production ended, probably sometime around 1954 even though the boat continued to appear in magazine ads for several years thereafter.

By then Carl Beetle was no longer involved in boatbuilding. He had sold the company in 1951 to his partner Fred Towle, and had founded Beetle Plastics around 1950. "He had a sour taste in his mouth for boats," remembers Russell Pierce, Carl Beetle's son-in-law who was involved with Beetle Plastics, which built fiberglass components for the Navy and for various industrial applications. "He didn't even want to talk about boats." Pierce disputes the suggestion, put forth on occasion, that Beetle sold his molds to Palmer Scott. "He had no connection with Scott," Pierce says simply.

Carl Beetle died in 1952 when he was 56, a man whose dreams of successfully pioneering a new postwar boating industry had unhappily eluded him. The BB Swan, however, proved to be just as durable as Beetle knew it would be. Today, the

This BB Swan was restored by the Museum of Yachting *in Newport, Rhode Island.*

boats still turn up on occasion, their odd looks often mystifying those who discover them. In fact, they are very stable and forgiving boats. In their day, they were sometimes even taken on camp-cruising expeditions; *Yachting* published a picture story about one such cruise. The two men involved slept on air mattresses placed on either side of the centerboard trunk, and had rollers they could use to haul the boat ashore.

While Carl Beetle's fiberglass boatbuilding venture was reaching its bitter conclusion, others in the immediate vicinity continued the struggle to build a commercially viable fiberglass boat. Palmer Scott expanded his line of Marscot boats and developed a dealer network to sell them. One of his dealers was from Long Island. Ted Hermann had served in the Pacific during the war and, when he returned home, decided to pursue a career in boats that would eventually include building a 17-foot Wittholz-designed catboat. "What I learned about fiberglass," said Hermann "was during the time I was a Marscot dealer. I'd drive up to New Bedford to Palmer Scott to pick up a boat in kit form and then spend time in the shop there and ask questions. Leo Telesmanick was building wooden Beetle cats there for Concordia, and his brother Angelo was there, too. He taught me how a fiberglass hull was molded. They started with gel coat, put in a layer of mat and, after it set, rolled it for maximum adhesion. Then they would lay up a layer of roving and another layer of mat and finish it off to a smooth surface."

But in 1954, a hurricane wiped out Palmer Scott's yard. "An LCVP went right through the office," remembers Scott's daughter, Tolly. "That was the end of Palmer Scott. My brother went to work with George O'Day [to keep Marscot going] and my dad finished what little he could."

By then, it seemed pretty clear to the men who had returned from the war and were working in boatbuilding that fiberglass was the technology and material of the future. What's more, by the mid-1950s, designers and builders were seriously looking at using fiberglass for much bigger sailboats than those currently in production. In 1956, one of the men considering this possibility was a 35-year-old Coast Guard veteran of the Pacific campaign named Breckenridge Marshall. Marshall had recently gone to work at Beetle Boatbuilding, but before any more of the company's BB Swans or other models were built, Marshall became involved with designer Bill Tripp in a venture to build five big fiberglass yawls, boats that eventually became known as the Block Island 40. The Beetle premises in New Bedford were too small for such a project, and a larger yard was acquired in East Greenwich, Rhode Island.

In his presentation to the Catboat Association in 1970, Marshall said that after they completed the molds for the yawl and built 10 boats, "We looked around for a smaller boat to build. This brought up the idea of a catboat . . . and now I suggested the idea to Bill Tripp. He and I had quite a hassle about the idea. He didn't want a boat that was too wide and wouldn't sail right and he thought it was a lot of money to invest."

Marshall didn't give up. As a matter of fact, he learned that, years earlier, the East Greenwich yard had built a catboat designed by a local sailor of great repute named Ernest "Pop" Arnold. In fact, this boat was the same one presented in William Oerhle's 1944 *Yachting* article. Of Arnold, Oerhle wrote that he "has forgotten more about rigging and sailing boats than I'll ever even suspect." He went on to say that Arnold had designed a marconi-rigged catboat for a friend that was

Breck Marshall, whose 18-foot Sanderling was responsible for the resurgence of interest in catboats, is seen here at his yard in 1975.

building fiberglass runabouts, canoes, and kayaks. Marshall persuaded the owner, Gil Verney, to invest in the catboat. Eighteen years later, he described how Pop Arnold's boat became the Marshall Sanderling.

We set up the boat just the way Arnold designed it . . . and we set it up upside down for convenience in working on it. The original boat was not a pretty boat. She was a flat sheer boat with a kind of tumblehome ram bow in her. She had a square house and a marconi rig. My foreman and I spent about three weeks in the visual process of modeling by eye.

First we took the Number 1 station and hollowed it out quite a bit. We pulled the stem out a bit and gave it a little overhang. We couldn't give her that tumblehome bow or we wouldn't be able to get her out of the molds very well. Then we set each succeeding station. We gave her more sheer than the original boat had. We spent a long time modeling the boat. Both when we started and when we were through, we had no lines anywhere that pictured the boat we were going to build, and that became the 18-foot Sanderling.

eighteen feet long, eight feet six inches beam, with a displacement of about twenty-five hundred pounds and a sail area of two hundred fifty-five square feet. This boat, the *Mary L,* was built by Alder, at Warren, and was very successful. The following winter, a similar boat was built by Leonard Gaucher, and these two boats were raced against each other, and all the other cats that cared to appear, at several of the N.B.Y.A. regattas. . . . Ernest Arnold, at the tender age of seventy-three, was able to win with either one.

Now, years later, Breck Marshall got the plans for Arnold's design. "Pop Arnold had designed the boat," he said, "and we had the plans and three or four of the station molds." In 1962, with the yard at East Greenwich having suffered financial reverses, it was sold. Marshall resigned his job and took the catboat plans (that only he was interested in) with him. He had an idea but not quite the means to make it reality. That means came when he accepted a job in New Hampshire as vice president of Custom Fibre Glass Products, a company

The first "Custom Catboat 18" attracted favorable comment at the 1963 Boston Boat Show, but there were few buyers. Marshall remembered that people were skeptical about a catboat built in the woods of New Hampshire. The rest of Verney's fiberglass business was not doing well, either, and he was planning to cut his losses. Marshall now bought from Verney the molds and rights to the catboat. With the investment support of two friends, Charles Chapin and Robert Truesdale,

Marshall and his wife Sarah moved the operation to the newly purchased Cuttyhunk Boat Yard in South Dartmouth. There, in its new location on Buzzards Bay, Marshall Marine began to attract attention and customers felt more comfortable about its product. Marshall's shop foreman, Howard Craig, remembered that Breck Marshall was "100 percent sure of the market and after he got out of New Hampshire, I could see, even though I didn't care much for sailing myself, that this catboat could be popular."

It's been said by those who were close to Breck Marshall that one reason for his success was that he not only knew what he was doing but that he "caught the market just right." By the mid-'60s, various boating writers had been talking about a catboat comeback for almost half a century without it ever having occurred. Certainly, there were new designs and enough new wooden construction to keep the catboat from dying off, but it took the application of a new technology to a well-designed boat to develop a newly revitalized catboat market, albeit still comparatively small. What's more, the method that Marshall relied on to build the boats proved to be highly effective. The hulls were molded in Freetown, Massachusetts by a former colleague of his, and were then finished by boat builder Alan Vaitses in nearby Mattapoisett.

"For a new company with little capital," Marshall's wife would write years later in a Catboat Bulletin article, "the method of molding and finishing off the cats worked well, with no money tied up in construction facilities." She recalled that by the end of 1964, some 18 boats — now known Marshall Sanderlings — had been built, and the numbers steady increased.

Two years after the launch of the Sanderling, Marshall took the boat's lines and had a set of blueprints made. These he brought to Vaitses in Mattapoisett with the idea of creating an enlarged version. "We lofted right from the blueprints," Vaitses remembers, "and built the tooling, the plug, for the Marshall 22. That was sent to New Bedford to have the molds made. There were problems with the materials used and the mold had to be redone, but the materials supplier picked up the tab."

There was no specific buyer for a new 22-foot catboat and Marshall hoped to find an interested customer before he actually built a boat. As things developed, Robert Jones heard about the project and, according to a reminiscence that he shared in the Catboat Bulletin in 1987, Jones called Marshall from the bar at the Royal Bermuda Yacht Club (having finished that year's Bermuda race) to discuss the 22. Jones wrote that "after returning, I called Breck and went up to see him at Alan Vaitses's yard in the piney woods of Mattapoisett . . . We arrived at a price of, I believe, $11,500, which included a great deal of additional teak trim by Vaitses, sails, and an Atomic 4."

After a brief shakedown cruise in the summer of 1965, Jones entered his new boat in a race from Newport to Block Island. Sailing with him were Breck Marshall and two crew members. Although they began the race with two reefs in because of a 30-knot breeze, it was decided to remove them both when the breeze dropped to 25. Jones reported that "Breck's eyes were about six inches out of his head waiting for the boat to self-destruct along with his reputation, but she went at it like a champ. We moved about eight cases of beer to windward, which helped."

The result was that Grimalkin placed second on elapsed time and won on corrected time. This was not well received by the race committee, which ruled that Grimalkin would not be permitted to enter subsequent races because a catboat was not self-righting. Still, the point had been made and the 22 added an important new product to Marshall's lineup. Later, in 1972, a smaller version of the 18-footer, the 15-foot Sandpiper, was also introduced.

Alan Vaitses, who possesses a lifetime of experience in the difficult world of commercial yacht building, remembers Breck Marshall as a man who had what it took to succeed in the business. "He was a smart guy, a great salesman, and he was very clever at finding sources for inexpensive materials. He was also funny."

He was also focused. Marshall had first sailed a catboat as a boy in Rhode Island where the local yacht club had a Crosby catboat. After the war, when he bought a boat, it was a catboat. It was a big 28 1/2-foot Charles Anderson-built boat with a 33-foot boom, and he modified this vessel until it had much in common with a 19th-century racing catboat with a long bowsprit and a big jib (and spinnaker). Later, when he seriously went into the boatbuilding business, Marshall remained focused solely on catboats. At least once, it was suggested to him that he broaden his product line.

Before Maitland Edey decided to start his own boatbuilding company with Peter Duff, he suggested to Breck Marshall "that he build Stone Horses, or something similar." In a brief article in *Messing About in Boats*, Edey said he told Breck that "it seemed to me he couldn't lose with a small cruising sloop so outrageously superior to the competition. He agreed that the Stone Horse was an excellent design, but thought me naïve for supposing people would buy something merely because it was better. . . . He attributed his own survival to the uniqueness of catboats."

That focus on the special appeal of catboats to a specific market ultimately resulted in Marshall's

long-term success. Even after Breck Marshall's death in 1976, the company retained his vision of offering a line of good-performing boats with a timeless appeal. It was a formula that sustained the business through years when much bigger companies came and went. What's more, it demonstrated the catboat's marketability to other would-be builders. Former Marscot dealer Ted Hermann began building the fiberglass 17-foot Hermann catboat in 1968 in his Long Island shop. Eventually, several more small companies would also enter the field. By the year 2000, there were at least a half-dozen builders offering fiberglass catboats of varying sizes and designs.

A century after the classic golden age of the wooden catboat had begun to fade, a promising new era had clearly arrived. Carl Beetle and Breck Marshall led the way.

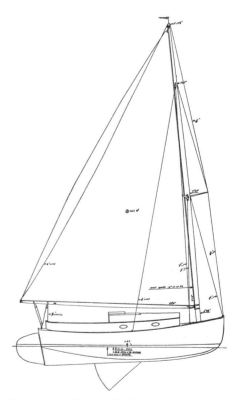

Designed by Ernest Arnold in Rhode Island, Haidee's *lines and sail plan were published in* Yachting *in April 1944. The boat was a fast sailer and her design would ultimately be modified by Breck Marshall to become the famous Sanderling. Marshall also converted the marconi rig to gaff.*

CHAPTER EIGHT

DAYSAILERS

—•◆•—

"We headed home in that smoky southwester. From Cuttyhunk that day to New Bedford, a distance of about 12 miles, we made it in an hour and a half."
—LEO TELESMANICK ON CRUISING IN A
BEETLE CAT IN THE 1930S

FOR A SAILOR seeking a fun boat that is stable, traditional in appearance, quick to get under way or put to bed, it would be hard to imagine a more suitable craft than a half-decked catboat. There is a long record of such boats. Photographs taken over a century ago reveal that previous generations of sailors understood the simple virtues of an open catboat. Here was a roomy cockpit surrounded by a gracefully steam-bent coaming and an ample, well-rigged sail providing entertaining performance in the lightest of winds. Today's rather wide variety of catboat daysailers means that those now in the market for such a boat have plenty to choose from. There are no fewer than four 12-footers, several 14-footers, and a pair of 15-footers as well. It is possible that a new 16-foot and 18-foot model will appear in the not-too-distant future.

Horace S. Crosby is leaning against the mast of the half-decked daysailer on a calm summer day at Osterville (circa 1885). The child's model boat appears to be a replica of Horace's catboat, and one wonders how well they got this model to sail. Beside the catboat is a Barnegat Bay sneakbox.

Such choice begs the inevitable question, "Which is best?" But the fact is that all the boats in this category have something to offer. All have been built for a long enough period that their various functions have been pretty well honed. Often, selection may be biased toward which builder is closest, or what boat is popular in local fleets. It's nice to have something unique, but if you want to race in a given fleet, you're best off buying the same boat. If you have the chance, certainly talk to other owners and take the boats that interest you for a test sail. Does the sail go up and come down without snags? If not, can the builder suggest why? Is the outboard arrangement really functional in terms of raising the motor out of the water? This can be a concern on some of these small boats. Have the gaff jaws or masts been subject to breakage and, if so, how has the builder responded? Generally speaking, in the niche market that is small boat building, builders can be counted on to make things right. One nice thing about a simple boat, of course, is that there is a lot less to go wrong than on bigger, more complex models. What follows is an alphabetical listing of models currently in production. In most cases it includes input from several owners of each boat.

Arey's Pond 14

The Arey's Pond 14 is about as yachty a daysailer as they come, and the option list includes everything from different levels and varieties of wood trim to wood-shell blocks. There's even a strip-planked version available for those who want a wooden boat and are willing to make the investment. The standard AP 14 is an attractive boat, however, with teak coamings, rails and floorboards, and wooden spars. Those spars were reported to be an attraction by several owners, although one expressed a wish for a hinged mast.

According to Merv Hammatt, who originally developed this boat at Arey's Pond in 1971, it is a fiberglass version of an Edson Schock wooden hull similar to the Stur-Dee Cat. In fact, the hulls of these boats are within four inches of each other in length and are identical in beam and draft. The most obvious difference is the rig. The AP 14 has a gaff rig. When the first boat was built for its Orleans owner, the price was about $2,000. After some 31 years, the price has increased accordingly.

Freeboard is low, making the boat easy to enter and leave, but owners report it contributes to a rather wet ride as the breeze increases. But this is typical of most daysailers of this size. That low freeboard at the bow means the mast originally had less support than was desirable. Improved support was gained by making the mast eight-sided at the partners where it can be very securely located with the wedges. The hull is unusual in this market, for it is molded of foam-cored fiberglass, which together with foam flotation inside the cockpit seats, gives it level-flotation ability. Owners report the AP 14 is an easy boat to paddle should the wind die, a particular advantage since there was little appetite for either the idea of using an outboard or for the outboard's mounting bracket, of which three alternatives are offered as options.

The AP 14 is positioned at the upper end of the market for 14-foot catboats. The option list is long and the quality is high, features that seem to attract buyers looking for a traditional half-decked boat that they plan to keep for a long time. AP 14 owners are an enthusiastic bunch. Said one of them: "I just love it. I have even slept aboard." A Cape Cod owner, retired, reported that he spent hundreds of hours aboard his AP 14 and, other than a problem with the gaff jaws that was resolved to his satisfaction, he enjoyed every one of them.

Arey's Pond 14

Builder: Arey's Pond Boat Yard, South Orleans, MA

Length: 14'

Beam: 7'

Draft: 10"/38"

Weight: 700 lbs.

Sail Area: 145 sq. ft.

(See Chapter 11 for a photograph of this boat.)

Arey's Pond Kitten

With a displacement of just 400 pounds, and lightweight spruce spars, the AP Kitten represents an easily managed, trailerable little catboat capable of skimming along in less than a foot of water. Although its lines, length, and beam are comparable to those dimensions of a Beetle, this is not a replica. The Kitten has a larger sail and a foot greater draft with the centerboard all the way down. The Kitten's construction and array of options are comparable to the AP 14's.

Arey's Pond Kitten

Builder: Arey's Pond Boat Yard, South Orleans, MA

Length: 12' 6"

Beam: 6'

Draft: 9"/36"

Weight: 400 lbs.

Sail Area: 119 sq. ft.

Barnstable Catboat

Although there are other 12-foot catboats available, the Barnstable Catboat is the only one that is a faithful replica of the original Beetle Cat itself. It owes its existence to the brief flirtation with boatbuilding of a retired executive who considered going into the business of building and selling fiberglass Beetle replicas in the early '80s. "He bought a new boat from Leo Telesmanick and made the molds from that," said Peter Eastman of Howard Boatworks. "But when he decided not to make a business of it, Bunny Howard bought the molds."

The Barnstable Catboat is as faithful a replica as one is ever likely to find of a Beetle, capturing the little boat's shape and proportions exactly and even managing to reproduce the canvas texture of the deck. The boats are ballasted so that they weigh the same as a wooden model with which they may race in most yacht club events but not in the premier regatta on each year's calendar, the New England Beetle Cat Regatta at which the Leo Telesmanick trophy is awarded.

Eastman, who himself owns a bright yellow Beetle built in 1962 for Waldo Howland, believes that the market for the Barnstable Catboat is quite distinct from that for the Beetle. "There's a big philosophical difference," he said, "and 90 percent of those who buy our boats never had a Beetle Cat. Relatively few seem attracted to the Barnstable Catboat because of its reduced cost or maintenance." The latter is generally estimated to be between $600 and $1,200 annually for a wooden Beetle Cat if done by a yard.

Barnstable Catboat

Builder: Howard Boatworks, Barnstable, MA

Length: 12' 4"

Beam: 6'

Draft: 8"

Weight: Approx. 450 lbs.

Sail Area: Approx. 100 sq. ft.

(See Chapter 11 for a photograph of this boat's cockpit.)

Beetle Cat

Of all the various small boat designs to emerge during the '20s, only one was destined to achieve really long-term success, a success that few boats of any type have ever enjoyed. This was a catboat designed in New Bedford in 1921 by Carl Beetle and his father, John. The Beetles positioned the "New Bedford Catboat," boat as a "club catboat" and suggested to the New Bedford Yacht Club that it be the basis for a club fleet. According to historian Llewellyn Howland III, however, the club rejected the idea and chose instead the Wee Scot, a 15-footer with a full keel that drew 3 1/2 feet. In the often rough local waters, the Wee Scot soon became known as the "Buzzard's Bay submarine." The little catboat, meanwhile, proved itself practical, able, and charming. It attracted so much attention that its production grew into a viable family business. Now known as the Beetle Cat, the $300 boat became a staple at yacht clubs as a trainer and one-design racer, a status it still enjoys today.

The business of building the boats remained within the Beetle family until after World War Two when Carl, believing himself to be looking to the

Sometime in the 1930s, these Beetles search for a breeze.

future rather than the past, sold the rights and tooling to Waldo Howland, head of the Concordia Company in South Dartmouth. As things worked out, Carl Beetle's new fiberglass catboat never attracted much of a following but Howland found a buyer for every Beetle that could be built. Today, more than 80 years after that first Beetle Cat was launched, the boats still add a colorful touch to harbors all around Cape Cod and can be found in many other spots as well. It's a record unlikely to be matched by any boat, let alone a 12' 4" x 6' catboat, but it's another example of how just how well adapted a catboat is for the sort of sailing that so many people do. Of the Beetle Cat, and its fiberglass cousins, one might say that no single boat offers such a combination of roominess, stability, beachability, and practicality in terms of transport, storage, and maintenance — not to mention a salty, traditional look. But the fact is that, for many, a daysailing or "half-decked" catboat can be the boat of a lifetime. Today, new Beetle Cats are still popular, perhaps the last wooden "production" boat of traditional plank-on-frame construction in America.

Wenaumet Kitten

plank-on-frame method. It's a comparatively large 13 1/2-foot boat, as its displacement indicates, and the cockpit is fitted with seven-foot benches beneath which is flotation. With its comparatively narrow beam and marconi rig, the Kitten is known as a good performer.

Beetle Cat

Builder: Beetle Inc., South Dartmouth, MA

Length: 12' 4"

Beam: 6'

Draft: 8"

Weight: Approx. 450 lbs.

Sail Area: Approx. 100 sq. ft.

Wenaument Kitten

Designed by Reuben Bigelow in 1901, the Kitten is still built to order in Bourne in the traditional

---

Wenaumet Kitten

Builder: R. Bigelow & Co., Bourne, MA

Length: 13 1/2'

Beam: 6'

Draft: 17"

Weight: 900 lbs.

Sail Area: 121 sq. ft.

Cape Dory Handy Cat

Back in the late 1960s, on the eve of a decade-long sailing boom, Merle Hallett, the proprietor of a boatyard in Falmouth Foreside, Maine, chanced upon an old wooden catboat hull lying in a field. Hallet was intrigued enough by the boat's shape to purchase the hull, change some of its lines, and turn the result into a plug for a fiberglass version. That was how the first Handy Cat, named for Hallett's boatyard — Handy Boat Service — came into being. Hallett molded the first hull in 1967, an attractive-looking boat with a rather hollow bow section, modest sheer, and a graceful transom. As things developed, this was the only Handy Cat that Hallett built. In 1970, he received a good offer from Cape Dory Yachts to build the little vessel under license.

The Handy Cat served as an interesting counterpoint to Cape Dory's Alberg-designed, full-keel sailboats, and the company built the boat for years during which it was frequently displayed at boat shows. With its wooden spars, a generous amount of teak, and bronze fittings, the Handy Cat made an attractive appearance and eventually garnered a loyal following.

The Handy Cat's wood and "traditional details" were cited by owners as a primary appeal. One of those who responded to the survey had bought his boat new and was still sailing it 29 years later. His biggest complaint was that the boat is not self-bailing and exhibits too much weather helm, although he admitted that he never reefed the sail. Another long-time owner reported high overall satisfaction. His primary changes were to add a gaff bridle and new bronze blocks throughout the boat. As always, there are few, if any, production boats with really adequate rigging.

When Cape Dory ceased operation, the molds for this boat were sold, but it appears unlikely that it will be built in the foreseeable future.

Handy Cat

Length: 14'

Beam: 6' 8"

Draft: 12"/4' 6"

Weight: 750 lbs.

Sail Area: Approx. 141 sq. ft.

Com-Pac Picnic Cat

Designer Clark Mills clearly had function rather than tradition foremost in mind when developing this boat, and the Picnic Cat is quite unlike today's other available daysailers. But then, Com-Pac Yachts is located in Florida, not New England. The Picnic Cat's tubby hull has a deep cockpit that is dominated by the centerboard trunk. This is a wood-clad, stainless steel subassembly that houses a stainless steel centerboard. The proportions of the boat are also different from those of the other catboats discussed here. That's because the 9 1/2-foot cockpit extends almost to the mast and the beam is just slightly narrower than one might expect. Contributing to the boat's unique appearance are its fiberglass coaming and a deck molding that projects over the hull. A permanent boom gallows and hinged mast are engineered to speed setup and takedown time. A fixed outboard bracket is standard equipment. The boom, which must clear the gallows, looks comparatively high on this boat, but headroom beneath it is doubtless improved.

According to the builder, Picnic Cat buyers tend to be older sailors who place the most value on the boat's appearance, and the convenience of its easily set-up rig. One owner echoed this, reporting the ease of setup and seating capacity as chief attractions. He rated his boat as a 3 out of 5 overall and reported hull blemishes that required repair, and a centerboard trunk leak. He also planned to rework the mainsheet arrangement and was seeking ways to improve the raising and lowering of the sail. That said, owners reported the sheer convenience of this boat remains a compelling purchase motivation.

Com-Pac Picnic Cat

Builder: Hutchins Co. Inc., Clearwater, FL

Length: 14'

Beam: 6' 6"

Draft: 6" / 38"

Weight: 500 lbs.

Sail Area: 109 sq. ft.

Compass Classic Cat

The lines of the Compass Classic Cat were developed by Merv Hammatt in 1996 after he found that customers, intrigued by his 12-foot Rainbow, reported that they would prefer a larger boat with more comfortable seats. The hull is a solid layup of glass. The deck molding has flotation on its underside so the boat will float on an even keel if swamped. Despite its comparatively short mast, the Classic Cat is equipped with a shroud on each side, necessary, according to the builder to support the 4" x 4" Douglas fir mast, a readily available size of timber that contributes to the boat's affordability. So, one assumes, does the absence of stern cleats, although these may be ordered as an extra, if they are required. Hammatt has found a ready

market for the Classic Cat in people who appreciate its combination of value and traditional appearance. "This is definitely a niche market," he noted. "But the catboat has a mystique and even those who don't really know what one is think our boat is neat. The web site gets hits from all over, from Texas to Canada." Hammatt reported that demand for used models has remained strong, contributing further to the value aspect of the boat.

Compass Classic Cat

Builder: Compass Classic Yachts Inc., South Orleans, MA

Length: 14' 2"

Beam: 7'

Draft: 10"

Weight: 600 lbs.

Sail Area: 130 sq. ft.

Compass Classic Cat

Compass Rainbow

This 12 1/2-footer is based on the lines taken from a Beetle Cat, although builder Merv Hammatt said he was not interested in creating a true replica. For example, unlike the cedar floorboards of the Barnstable Cat that make it so evocative of a wooden Beetle, the Rainbow has a fiberglass cockpit liner. Between the liner and hull is foam flotation, and the liner itself has seat areas molded in. More than 50 of these boats have been sold to date, with most owners using them as a "get in and go" knockabout and as a training boat for their kids.

Compass Rainbow

Compass Rainbow

Builder: Compass Classic Yachts Inc., South Orleans, MA

Length: 12' 6"

Beam: 6'

Draft: 5"/24"

Weight: 450 lbs.

Sail Area: 100 sq. ft.

Marshall Sandpiper

The Sandpiper might be the smallest of the Marshall lineup, but it's about the biggest half-decked catboat you'll find. It's a foot-and-a-half longer than the 14-footers and, more to the point, offers about one third more displacement, 200 pounds of which is ballast. The boat draws another half-foot, although whether a 16-inch draft is a meaningful disadvantage versus 10 inches is something of an individual consideration. The Sandpiper's size, displacement, and freeboard may be of interest to those who sail on more exposed bodies of water and seek the driest boat possible when the wind and chop picks up. A cuddy model is available. It provides additional dry stowage space and somewhat greater protection from spray at some reduction in seating room and the aesthetic loss of the half-decked model's beautifully curved and grained cockpit coaming. This 15 1/2- footer is probably as much catboat as is readily trailerable for most people, and the addition of an optional tabernacle mast was a worthwhile innovation for regularly trailered boats. Particularly in a boat that may well be sailed without an outboard, the location of the stern cleats — out of the direct line of the traveler and further protected from the mainsheet by the coaming — is one of several nice touches.

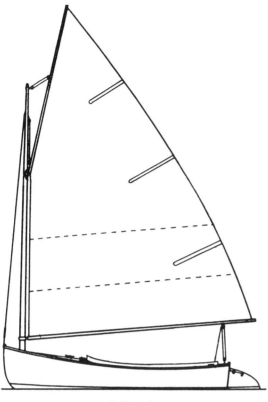

Marshall Sandpiper

Marshall Sandpiper

Builder: Marshall Marine, South Dartmouth, MA
Length: 15' 6"
Beam: 7' 1"
Draft: 16" / 3'9"
Weight: 1050 lbs.
Sail Area: 166 sq. ft.

Menger Daysailer

The Menger "Daysailer" is based on the design and molds created by Peter Legnos during the mid-1970s as the "Mystic River Cat." With its rather flat sheerline, a seven-foot beam carried well aft, and decidedly low freeboard (but with a flatter bottom), the boat is reminiscent of the so-called skimming dish of the 19th century. This boat promises exciting performance in a nice breeze and smooth water. But, while attractive, the low-sided hull will do little to protect crew from spray. A cuddy version is available for those to whom this is a concern and, for further protection, an optional dodger is also available for that model. In addition to the cuddy option, Menger also modified the boat's sailplan, developed a new gaff saddle, added wooden spars, and designed a kickup rudder. This boat is equipped with a forward mooring cleat, aft cleats, and halyard cleats, all of them cast of bronze. A tabernacle mast is a useful option for those who will regularly trailer the boat.

Menger Daysailer

Builder: Menger Boatworks, Amityville, NY
Length: 15'
Beam: 7'
Draft: 7" / 3'6"
Weight: 600 lbs.
Sail Area: 145 sq. ft.

Menger Daysailer

Stur-Dee Cat

The Stur-Dee Cat is a faithful replica of a design originally published by Edson Schock that he named *Hortense*. Like so many naval architects that set themselves to the task of creating a "modern" version of the catboat, Schock designed the boat with a marconi rig. This has been retained on the Stur-Dee Cat, but the sail, at 130 sq. ft., is 15 feet larger than the original's. Although the rig might not be what some expect in terms of traditional appearance, it offers the benefit of extraordinary simplicity. With just a single halyard and a mainsheet, this boat is quickly rigged and easily gotten under way. That tall spar also has some advantages in very light air, and helps make the Stur-Dee good at ghosting along in the slightest zephyrs. The Stur-Dee also has the little cuddy cabin of Schock's original. In this case, the cuddy is a rather gracefully integrated feature that looks as if it was always intended to be there, rather than like a later addition. I've gotten wet enough sailing these boats to know that the cuddy is of modest help in keeping you dry when the breeze and seas increase. Stur-Dee Boat has been building this daysailer since the late 1970s and owners enjoy its relatively comfortable cockpit and how quickly the boat can be gotten under way and put to bed. Stur-Dee Cat owners like their boats and seem to get a great deal of use from them.

Stur-Dee Cat

Summary

In terms of sheer sailing fun with a minimum of fussing with equipment and rigging, it would be hard to surpass any of the daysailing catboats now available. Going sailing in such a boat involves little more than stepping aboard, removing the sail cover, hoisting the sail, and departing. For trailer sailors, the simplicity of such boats is likewise an attraction. The old saying that the simpler a boat is, the more it gets used, might have been created to apply to a half-decked catboat. Those surveyed during research for this chapter expressed uniform delight with their boats and sail them a lot.

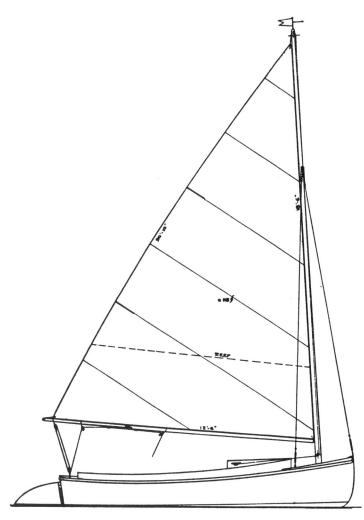

Edson Schock's Hortense *was an appealing design for wood construction that has been successfully adapted to several fiberglass versions, including the Stur-Dee Cat.*

Stur-Dee Cat

Builder: Stur-Dee Boat Co., Tiverton, RI

Length: 14' 4"

Beam: 7'

Weight: 680 lbs.

Draft: 10" / 3'6"

Sail Area: 130 sq. ft.

These Marshall catboats are rafted up at Cuttyhunk.

CHAPTER NINE

FIBERGLASS CRUISING
CATBOATS

———— ·•·•· ————

*"The catboat is a national type and should be more popular among yachtsmen, as it is suitable for the type
of sailing most of us do. . . . In fact, the Cape cat is suitable for any type of cruising, except off-shore."*
—HOWARD I. CHAPELLE, *Yachting,* November 1932

IN THE MID-1880S, to demonstrate what was possible for a small boat and determined skipper, designer C. P. Kunhardt undertook a single-handed voyage from Port Morris, New York, to Beaufort, North Carolina, and back. As one of the most outspoken of the cutter cranks and a ceaseless critic of centerboard yachts, Kunhardt made a most contradictory choice of boat for his journey. His 20-foot *Coot* was a Great South Bay-type catboat with low freeboard and a summer cabin that Kunhardt covered over with staving for better protection from the weather. Kunhardt must have been a most capable sailor for the *Coot* was a less than ideal craft for such a passage, and Kunhardt advised others not to do what he had done.

A Cape Cod-style catboat with higher freeboard and a permanent cabin would have been better suited to Kunhardt's cruise than *Coot.* That's precisely the sort of boat sailed by Henry Plummer on his celebrated trip from New

England to Florida in 1912. His *Mascot* was a counter-stern model with a proper-sized centerboard, and self-bailing cockpit. Despite an odd, horizontal steering wheel, which must have had the advantage of shielding the mainsheet from a more exposed wheel's spokes, *Mascot* was pronounced by Plummer to be "as safe and able a little ship as a man could want to go to sea in." *Mascot's* voyage, made with the aid of a power dory that served as tender and pushboat, involved courage, stamina, some apparent foolhardiness, shipwreck, and recovery. It has been an inspiration to every small boat sailor who has ever read it.

Catboats like Plummer's, generally 24 feet long or longer, gave their owners the opportunity to freely roam much of the East Coast. As the years passed, however, all these boats changed hands and their care was not necessarily expert. More and more catboats succumbed to poor maintenance, to the fatal maiming of insensitive modification and, eventually, to old age. It is safe to speculate that, in the absence of fiberglass, the resurgence of interest in catboats would never have happened. But the introduction of the Marshall Sanderling in 1963 offered buyers the traditional charm and roominess that was always a chief attraction of the catboat, and combined it with the benefits of fiberglass and outstanding performance. Two years later, the Marshall 22 greatly expanded the possibilities of the fiberglass catboat as a modest cruiser. Both these boats have made some impressive voyages.

Departing from Kittery, Maine, Lance Gunderson sailed his Marshall 18 to Florida and back and, although he suffered a broken mast and several misadventures, Gunderson demonstrated what could be accomplished in such a boat given the enthusiasm, will, and seamanship. Marshall 22s have also cruised from New England to Florida, not to mention the voyage of the late John Church, who sailed his 22 from Cape Cod to Labrador. In the years since Breck Marshall introduced his pioneering catboats, a variety of other cabin models have been offered. While several companies that once built these boats are no longer in business, the boats themselves continue on, and an apparently steady demand remains for fiberglass cabin catboats that are now 25 or 30 years old.

As with the half-decked models now available, a number of questions routinely arise about these catboats. Unlike the daysailers, which, perhaps, have more similarities than differences, there are more clear-cut distinctions to be found among the larger models. Time and again, questions are posed regarding which boat to select and why. But, in the almost complete absence of a critical boating press, prospective purchasers of sailboats, whether new or used, have few places to turn for answers. Customer satisfaction surveys, so com-

mon for other high-ticket items, are rare in most segments of the marine industry.

In response to this long-standing situation, Internet forums have provided a modest outlet for information, some of which is valuable, while some is based entirely on limited experience or misinformation. Owners' associations are among the best sources of information — when they exist. What follows is an overview of a variety of catboats based in all cases on feedback from several owners, interviews and, in some cases, personal experience. The boats are listed in alphabetical order.

America

Introduced in 1972, the America presented a salty, attractive appearance that was enhanced by a colorful sail with an American flag-like insignia. Although the marketing literature for the boat was not detailed, it was likewise attractive, having a color rendering of the boat on one side and drawings on the other that showed its layout. Good looks, the nice marketing piece, and display at boat shows accounted for a fair number of sales.

When introduced, the boat was marketed as the Herreshoff America built by the Nowak and Williams Company in Barrington, Rhode Island. The arrangement was for Halsey Herreshoff to do the basic design with the understanding that there would be certain features necessary to meet the expectations of potential customers. Stan Nowak and Bruce Williams were responsible for production and for running the business. Hulls were molded by a subcontractor with Nowak and Williams doing the finishing. The best record of how the boat came to be exists in a brief article written by Catboat Association member Bob Alling after visiting with Stan Nowak at the company's facility in 1972. Bob wrote: "Several old Herreshoff half models were examined, and one

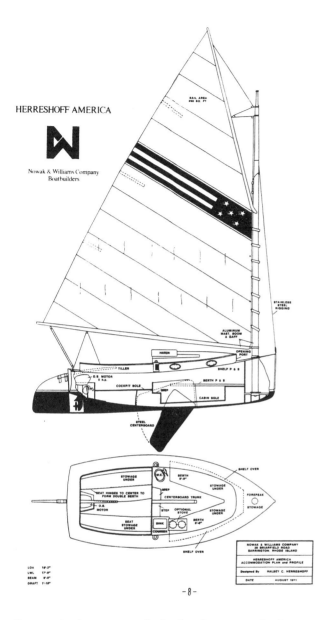

HERRESHOFF AMERICA

Nowak & Williams Company
Boatbuilders

NOWAK & WILLIAMS COMPANY
28 BRIARFIELD ROAD
BARRINGTON, RHODE ISLAND

HERRESHOFF AMERICA
ACCOMMODATION PLAN and PROFILE

Designed By   HALSEY C. HERRESHOFF
DATE   AUGUST 1971

LOA   18'-2"
LWL   17'-9"
BEAM   8'-0"
DRAFT 1'-10"

-8-

from which a particularly fast boat was built was selected as the basis of the design. Keeping most of the underwater shape as is, some alterations were made in sheer, freeboard and deck layout to conform to the dictates of what was pretty close to a full-scale modern market survey."

The blending of market surveys with a 19th-century half model for a catboat to come up with a modern version poses inevitable conflict, and this was reflected in the America. The two most obvious "modern" features of the America are its outboard motor well and its centerboard configu-

ration. The well did away with the need to mount an outboard on an unsightly bracket on the transom, a location also perfectly suited to snagging the mainsheet should one be less than constantly vigilant. The downside of the well was the cutout required in the bottom which, together with the motor's skeg and propeller, combined to hamper performance. In addition, exhaust fumes could be trapped in the well and stall the motor, requiring that the well's hatch remain open at times.

It is also clear that an effort was made to have a centerboard trunk that intruded minimally into the cockpit. In fact, the trunk ends with the cabin doors and no protrusion is needed above the cockpit sole. The board itself was a high-aspect ratio type, rather more like a daggerboard than a traditional, rectangular centerboard, and thus was comparatively small in area. It was also made of steel and so required a winch for operation and, over the long term, would require maintenance. Inside its cabin, the America offered the usual layout of berths running along each side of the hull, with the head mounted at the port bulkhead aft, opposite the sink. The molding for the berths was rather high making for uncomfortably limited sitting headroom.

When Nowak and Williams ceased operation, the molds for the America were acquired in 1977 by a new builder called Squadron Yachts. A change was made to the outboard well to reduce or eliminate the problem of the motor stalling because of fumes. The interior molding was revised so the berths were lowered dramatically, affording much more comfortable headroom. But the berths also became quite narrow. The America as built by Squadron Yachts also had an improved, thicker hull layup to increase the boat's durability.

Eventually, Squadron Yachts sold the America's molds to Nauset Marine on Cape Cod. Merv

Hammatt, who built one of the few boats produced there, and certainly the last, recalls that a change was made to the centerboard and trunk. "We built one America [dubbed America II] with a full-size centerboard," he said. "We actually modified the mold to do so. The trunk split the companionway. The board was rectangular. We also filled in the outboard well and added a new molded skeg. That boat was a 100 percent improvement."

Today, the America still shows up regularly in Boats for Sale listings. Several owners responded to questions about their experiences. One, who owned a Squadron Yachts-built version, reported the boat was in good shape although the wooden cockpit seats had warped. He added that the main sheet tended to snag on the stern cleats and stern light, rather negating the advantage of the motor well which, he and others reported, presents a problem in terms of installing and removing the motor. On a scale of 1 – 5 for overall satisfaction, he rated the boat a 3. Another owner reported that, having given up on the motor well, he wanted to mount an outboard bracket on the transom, but found the fiberglass to be overly thin and also that the deck was coming loose in that area. Another boat, an early Nowak and Williams model, was reported to still be in good condition and rated overall at 3. Among the respondents was one man who had bought his America new in 1981. He rated his boat highly for quality.

In general, the America seems to appeal most to new sailors or first-time catboat buyers who find one for sale conveniently close by and no other brand with which to compare it. Although the boat does not compare favorably to others in its size range in terms of speed and some other functional areas, this is not necessarily deemed a disadvantage by those who buy them.

America

Length: 18' 2"

Beam: 8'

Draft: 1' 10"

Sail Area: 260 sq. ft.

Arey's Pond 16

This handsome little boat offers modest accommodations in its cuddy cabin, affording some privacy and the opportunity for an occasional overnight stay. A number of strip-planked examples have been built even though the fiberglass version is more popular. See the previous chapter's comments on the AP Kitten and AP 14 for more detail about the company's construction approach.

Arey's Pond 16

Builder: Arey's Pond Boat Yard, South Orleans, MA

Length: 16' 6"

Beam: 7' 11"

Draft: 14"/4' 6"

Weight: 1,800 pounds

Sail Area: 200 sq. ft.

Atlantic City Cat

Designed by naval architect David Martin and built in New Jersey by Mark-O-Custom Boats, the Atlantic City Cat was introduced in 1979. A primary goal was to produce a roomy boat with standing headroom. For anyone accustomed to a typical 18- to 22-foot fiberglass catboat, going below in the AC was, and probably remains, something of a shock. With the cabin's over six-foot headroom, one can walk around down there. The centerboard trunk, which several owners reported

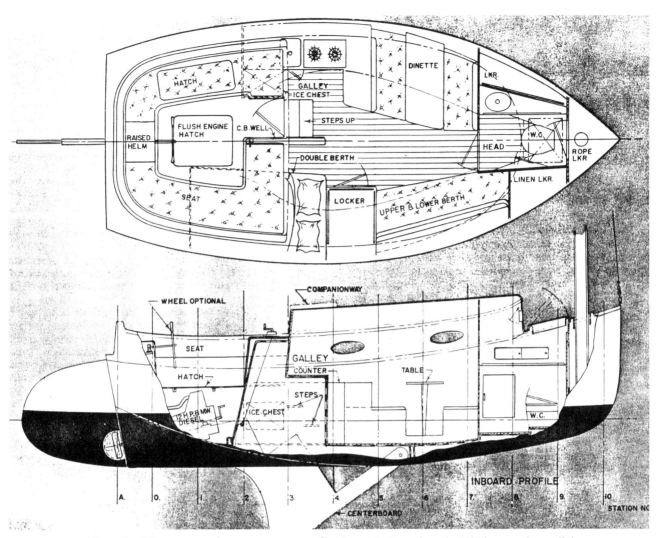

Atlantic City 24 — in terms of interior roominess in a fiberglass production catboat, the AC24 has yet to be equalled.

they had capped in order to stop water from splashing in, is compact. It houses a steel board with less area than would normally be expected, but this meant that the trunk was also comparatively small and required relatively little space in the cockpit and alongside the companionway steps. There's also a reasonable head compartment. Upper and lower berths are located on the starboard side.

The interior was finished with a liner and plenty of wood. In the cockpit, seating wrapped around an engine hatch beneath which resided a single-cylinder 12-horsepower BMW diesel, perhaps not the best choice in terms of ready availability of parts or service. More power would not have hurt, either, given the boat's weight and windage. The Yanmar 3GM is a popular, and much more appropriate, replacement engine.

With an 8,000-pound displacement, the AC24 had ballast that, alone, weighed as much as the typical 18-foot catboat — 2,200 pounds. It was not, however, comparably rigged. The AC24's sail, at 471 square feet, is just 36 square feet larger than a Menger 23's, but the latter boat's displacement is 1,500 pounds less. Still, a more appropriately sized sail would probably have been well beyond the interests of those who bought the boat when new, or who own them today. There were several reports of the gaff jaws binding when raising the sail.

The high topsides of this boat create a lot of windage. That contributes to a lot of movement when anchored and can make maneuvering in close quarters a challenge. One owner suggested that a bow thruster would be an improvement. Another noted that, even with the board (which probably lacks enough area) down, maneuverability in tight quarters is poor.

In all, this is a modestly rigged catboat that offers exceptional accommodations. One owner of both an Atlantic City Cat and Atlantic City Kitty called them the "Cadillacs of modern catboats." The AC Cat is a boat that would appeal to powerboat-oriented customers who wanted to try sailing, or to sailors whose primary desire was an interior with most of the comforts of home, shoal draft, and decent performance, rather than windward ability or boat speed. In fact, of all the fiberglass catboats built, the Atlantic City Cat probably offered the most practicality in terms of serious cruising potential, and some of these boats have ranged comparatively widely.

Atlantic City Cat Boat

Length: 24'

Length of waterline: 22'

Beam: 11'

Draft: 2'

Displacement: 8,000 lbs.

Sail Area: 471 sq. ft.

Atlantic City Kitty

Introduced in 1982, this smaller version of the Atlantic City Cat carried a list price of $16,900, slightly over half the price of the larger boat. Its high freeboard permitted comparatively good headroom, a bit over five feet, and the head was enclosed at the forward end of the cabin. It was originally powered by the same 12-hp BMW engine as the larger model, and this engine was probably appropriate in terms of output for the Kitty.

Several of those who responded to the survey reported that they were neophyte sailors attracted to the boat because of its combination of stability and roominess. "Good and steady," wrote one. Ventilation was reported as good, although owners seem to have added various vents. The inboard engine was also an attraction. Those responding to the survey reported that the original BMW had been replaced in all cases.

Ratings of construction quality ranged from 5 to 3. One owner reported that his boat had required a new bottom. Another reported a toe rail sprung from the deck and discovered the rail was not through-bolted, something that would complicate the repair. Unlike the Cat, the Kitty has an underhung rudder, and the through-bolts holding the rudder support can, when tightened as much as needed, lead to leaks, a "design defect" according to one experienced owner. Those considering a purchase of one of these boats, which may be available at a comparatively attractive price, should include the cost of a capable surveyor as part of the budget.

Powering into a head sea results in some leaks from the centerboard trunk. The board itself is a different configuration from the larger model's, although it may still be comparatively small. None of the owners was particularly happy with the rig-

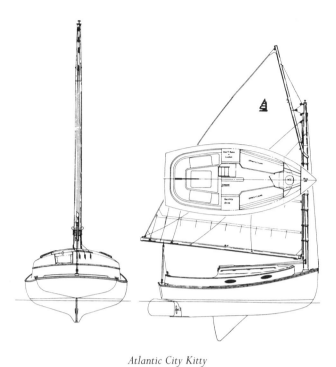

Atlantic City Kitty

ging on their boats. Some reported problems lowering the sail, and one had rigged a downhaul. Another had rerigged the mainsheet. Bigger and better blocks, some repositioned, for all running rigging, are also worth consideration.

Atlantic City Kitty

Length: 21' 3"
Length of waterline: 17' 10"
Beam: 9' 6"
Draft: 2'
Displacement: 5,300 lbs.
Sail Area: 350 sq. ft.

Most rated sailing qualities as a 3 out of 5. By way of comparison, the waterline of a Marshall 22 is one inch longer than the Kitty's length overall, and the latter's waterline is several feet shorter than the Marshall's. The Marshall has some 360 pounds more displacement but 38 square feet of additional

sail and less windage thanks to its lower profile. Clearly, the two boats are fundamentally different in approach and appeal. One Kitty owner reported, however, that he really wanted a Marshall 22, but the Kitty's price was within his budget.

Cape Cod Cat

In 1971, having seen demand for his Wittholz-designed boat drop off, Ted Hermann made an arrangement with the Cape Cod Shipbuilding Company in Wareham, Massachusetts, which was interested in adding a catboat to its lineup. Cape Cod made some changes to Hermann's molds and upgraded the boat's hardware, changing, for example, from rectangular aluminum ports to oval bronze ports. Only the gaff rig version is offered with earlier models having an aluminum mast and spruce spars, but later boats having all-aluminum spars.

Perhaps the biggest change Cape Cod made to the boat was the option of a new "keel" version. In this case, the keel is a lead molding affixed to the bottom of the boat, increasing draft a few inches but doing away with the centerboard trunk altogether. As with most such things, there are pluses and minuses. In addition to opening up room in the cabin, the keel model sails surprisingly well although windward performance is reduced. Still, the boat's bottom is full and there is a sizable skeg, important design features that make it possible for the additional three inches of "keel" to make this model practical. A decided advantage is that the centerboard models suffer splashing up through the slot, which a short-lived rubber gasket does nothing to stop. Most owners wind up making a removable cap to plug the slot when the board is lowered, an issue that should be addressed by the builder. Of course, having a centerboard adds overall flexibility whether when sailing to windward or, even, downwind, when the board can be lowered if necessary to damp the boat's tendency to roll.

How does the boat compare to the Marshall 18? Most consider as an advantage the three built-in lazarettes of the molded cockpit. In addition, although the Cape Cod Cat is a foot shorter than the Marshall, its cabin is comparable in size and amenities. At least one owner has added a swing-up extension to one or another berth to compensate for the limited shoulder room beneath the shelves that run above the berths, something that would improve many of the boats in this size range. The Cape Cod Cat has more deadrise (a rounder bottom) than the Marshall and is initially a more tender boat. It is not quite as fast, either. The boat is, however, surprisingly able in a seaway. The Cape Cod Cat most definitely should be reefed early to help maintain balance or it quickly becomes heavy

on the tiller and develops a very strong weather helm. Owners reported problems with lowering the sail, and some had rigged downhauls.

As is typical, the mainsheet needs care to avoid snagging the outboard. In risky conditions, it is wise to leave the motor down, and a cover that shields the motor and its tiller is also worth adding. Of course, this is not a problem with inboard-powered boats. Boats without inboard power benefit from having the propeller aperture filled in.

Owners rated construction quality as a 4 or 5 despite some problems. One noted delamination of plywood inside the cockpit lazarettes. This is worth inspecting when evaluating a used boat. So is the fiberglass mast collar in the deck. It should be checked for any cracks that could let water below even with a mast boot installed. If there is a crack, a professional repair may be required. Cabin ventilation was rated as poor by all owners.

Cape Cod Cat — designed by Charles Wittholz, this boat was originally produced by Ted Hermann's Boatshop. A variety of detail changes were made when Cape Cod Shipbuilding, which built the example shown here, acquired the molds.

Today, the Cape Cod Cat remains available although it has never been very actively marketed by a builder that focuses more on its one-design models. Still, for those looking for something a bit different in a daysailer/overnighter, and particularly those seeking a boat designed for the practical installation of an inboard, it may be attractive.

Cape Cod Cat

Builder: Cape Cod Shipbuilding, Wareham, MA
Length: 17'
Beam: 7' 11"
Draft: 20" centerboard/23" keel
Displacement: 2200 pounds
Sail Area: 250 sq. ft.

Com-Pac Sun Cat

The Sun Cat was designed and built by Clark Mills in 1965, and the prototype was strip-planked. It was followed by some 50 fiberglass versions before Mills sold the design in 1979. The Sun Cat has the gaff rig and general appearance of a traditional catboat, but closer examination reveals it is more of a contemporary interpretation rather than an effort at recreating such a boat. To those who will be attracted to the Sun Cat, this is probably a selling point. Beneath the water, the hull has a shallow keel in which a steel, high-aspect ratio centerboard is housed. The hull lacks the wide beam of a traditional catboat hull. It is, for example, eight inches narrower that the Arey's Pond 16 1/2 footer, not to mention being 300 pounds lighter. An aluminum kick-up spade rudder is used. Topside, a bridge deck divides the cabin from the cockpit, and the mainsheet traveler is located on the bridge deck, well away from the

Sun Cat

outboard. The builder reports that dealers requested a mid-boom sheeting arrangement, which tends to much reduce the chance of the sheet to foul on an outboard and also can improve sail shape because the end of the boom has less tendency to rise.

The boat's cabin is attractively finished. Opening oval ports and an available solar vent together with the sliding hatch promise reasonable ventilation. On deck, the two dominant features include the folding mast and boom gallows, both designed to make it as easy as possible to trailer the boat.

The rather high boom offers added headroom and makes a bimini possible.

Sun Cat

Builder: Hutchins Co. Inc., Clearwater, FL
Length: 17' 4"
Beam: 7' 3"
Draft: 1' 2" / 4' 6"
Displacement: 1,500 pounds
Sail Area: 150 sq. ft.

Com-Pac Horizon Cat

Announced in the fall of 2001, the Horizon Cat is the latest incarnation of the America, which had been built by Nowak and Williams, Squadron Yachts, and Nauset Marine. Now, fundamental changes have been made to the hull, rig, hardware, and general layout, and these are so extensive that the Horizon Cat should be considered as something entirely different from its predecessors. Its key design changes include replacing the previous centerboard with a shallow keel/centerboard, and a change from the barndoor rudder to a spade-type, kick-up rudder, with wheel steering. Also gone is the infamous outboard well. Either inboard power (single-cylinder Westerbeke) or an outboard bracket may be ordered.

In common with this company's other catboat models, a tabernacle mast and boom gallows are standard equipment to make the boat more readily trailerable. Again, the boom is mounted somewhat higher on the mast than one might expect. Both the mast and boom are shorter than typical, and the boat has a comparatively small sail — 205 sq. ft. Given a 2,500-pound displacement, the sail area suggests this will be a modest performer. It should, however, require reefing less often than the 250-sq. ft, sail typical of competitive catboats in this general size range. That said, jiffy reefing pennants for both clew reef points (but not the tack) are included in the sail plan.

Two cabin-mounted winches are fitted, one to port to hoist the sail, the other to starboard to raise the mast. I'd reverse the roles to make sail handling more convenient for the majority of sailors. Halyard turning blocks are mounted directly to the mast, which should not be a problem as the sail is fitted with slides rather than mast hoops. Again, there is very little of the traditional about this boat other than its gaff. The mainsheet arrangement is also unique among catboats. It is mounted on the rear of the cockpit coaming and is double-ended, with a fiddle block and cam cleat at each end and a triple block on the boom. In theory, this looks like a practical setup that should minimize the problem of the sheet fouling on the outboard motor.

Horizon Cat

Com-Pac has addressed the long-standing issue of poor cabin ventilation with the Horizon Cat. Four screened opening ports are included and, perhaps more important, so is a hinged forward hatch. Down below, the interior appears completely different from the America and from other catboats. The keel configuration means there is no centerboard trunk. The berths extend partly under the cockpit, and a separate head compartment is located forward of bulkheads at the front of the cabin. A teak and holly sole is standard.

As a contemporary interpretation of a catboat, the Horizon Cat may well find its own niche in the market. It combines something of the look of a traditional catboat in terms of shape and rig with functional changes that may make such a boat more attractive to newer, or older sailors, most concerned with convenience and sailing ease.

Horizon Cat

Builder: Hutchins Co. Inc., Clearwater, FL
Length overall: 20'
Length of waterline: 17' 9"
Beam: 8' 4"
Draft: 26" / 5'
Displacement: 2,500 pounds
Sail Area: 205 sq. ft.

Hermann Cat

Ted Hermann's introduction to fiberglass boats came in the early 1950s when he became a dealer for Palmer Scott's Marscot line. Eventually, he began producing boats of his own, the most successful of which was a 17-foot catboat designed by naval architect Charles Wittholz. An engaging, friendly gentleman with wide experience in yacht and ship design, Wittholz always kept up his enthu-

siasm for catboats, designing a variety of hard-chine boats for amateur construction in plywood, and round-bottom models for traditional methods. Quite often, the designer received correspondence from these amateur builders expressing satisfaction with the results of their efforts.

"She exceeds all my expectations," wrote the builder of a soft-chine 18-footer, "She actually sailed circles around a 20-footer the other day." A Japanese builder of a 17-footer wrote that his boat "performs beyond my expectations. Mine is the first catboat ever seen in these islands. Its performance has been a source of much comment."

Two interesting features were typical of Wittholz boats over 15 feet in length. First, the boats were always designed with the option of inboard power, meaning the deadwood was large enough to house the right-size propeller and the hull was deep enough to house the motor. Second, there was a choice of gaff or marconi rigs. The designs were well-received. A series of 17-footer catboats was constructed by Westbrook, Connecticut, builder Russ Marston in the early '60s, and a dozen 18' 9" vee-bottom models built in Yugoslavia were commissioned by a Long Island yacht broker during the same period.

When Ted Hermann saw one of the plywood boats, he was struck by its neat appearance and its roomy cockpit. He believed such boats could have a market, and he called Wittholz to inquire about the possibility of a fiberglass version. "He was happy to hear about this," remembered Hermann. "I flew to Maryland and we made a deal for a boat according to my specifications. He asked if I wanted gaff or marconi because the position of the centerboard would depend on that. On a gaff-rig boat, the board would have to be further aft where it would run into some of the space needed for the inboard motor option." Recognizing that some sailing ability would be sacrificed on the gaff rig models, the board was positioned to make room for the motor, no matter which rig was ordered.

Ted Hermann's Boat Shop at Seaford Harbor on Long Island built the initial Hermann cat in 1966–1967. It was the first fiberglass catboat to come on the scene since the Marshall, and it was clearly a rather different proposition. "My boat had a skeg and small keel while the Marshall was more flat-bottomed," recalled Hermann. "The boat could still work to windward with the board up. We had more bilge and a molded, self-bailing cockpit, the inboard option, and the choice of rigs." According to Hermann's memory, about 100 boats were sold in a five-year period, about half of them having inboard power, the engine being a single-cylinder Palmer PW-27 turning a three-blade propeller. He believes about half were marconi rigged. The tall mast of the marconi-rigged boat required shrouds but both Hermann and Wittholz believed it probably sailed somewhat better than the more traditional gaff-rigged model.

Today, these Hermann cats, which sold for about $3,000 in 1971, offer a competitively priced choice for those seeking an affordable sailboat with modest cruising accommodations. (Wittholz sailed his own in stages from Long Island to the Chesapeake.) Like any boat of this vintage, the gel coat is likely to have suffered some crazing, but the basic structure was reported sound by those who supplied information about their boats. "Simple, well-made, and attractive," was how one owner summed up his Hermann cat. Among the most obvious areas that may need attention, if something hasn't already been done, is to make a cap for the centerboard trunk to keep water from splashing up and into the cabin.

Ted Hermann remembers 1970 as the year the "bottom fell out" of the market. At the same time,

E. L. Goodwin of Cape Cod Shipbuilding, perhaps with an eye on the popularity of the Marshall catboats, was considering building a fiberglass catboat himself. An arrangement was made to transfer the molds and building continued, on a limited basis, of the Hermann cat. Now, however, with some modification, it would be known as the Cape Cod Cat.

Hermann Cat

Length: 17'
Length of waterline: 16' 5"
Beam: 7' 11"
Draft: 20" / 5'
Displacement: 2200 pounds
Sail Area: 250 gaff / 240 marconi sq. ft.

Legnos Mystic 20

The Mystic 20, designed and built by Peter Legnos in 1974, was distinctive when it was introduced and remains so today. While all the other fiberglass boats had a barndoor rudder, the Mystic 20 has the counter stern and underhung rudder reminiscent of 19th-century catboats built as yachts. The boat's wineglass transom is undeniably pretty and remains a major attraction. The boat is comparatively fine lined. This and its eight-foot beam, narrower than tradition would dictate but legally trailerable, helps account for the Mystic 20's initial tenderness, but once it assumes a certain angle, it stiffens up considerably and can carry its sail well.

This boat was designed with inboard power in mind, for who would wish to spoil that transom with an outboard? The original Vire single-cylinder two-cycle engine was a reliable choice. Some are still in place today. Others have been replaced with a small diesel, the Yanmar probably representing the most practical choice.

The Mystic 20 has a lot of wood trim. Besides the big teak cabin hatch, doors, and rubrail, the spars were all made of spruce. All this contributes to the boat's good looks, while requiring periodic maintenance, something owners seem not to mind. In fact, of all the groups surveyed, only owners of a Mystic 20 responded en masse. They rated construction quality at either a 4 or 5. One owner had purchased his boat new 23 years ago and reported that he "would not want any other boat."

The only common problem reported by every owner was difficulty in lowering the sail, and this was generally the feature rated worst about the boat. The wooden mast hoops tend to bind. Somewhat bigger and better halyard blocks and deck-mounted blocks might be required and, if those don't help, a downhaul might be a worthwhile addition. Neither were the lazy jacks deemed adequate. Engine access was not rated highly by any of the owners.

At least some of these boats were built with a rig that was on the small side, perhaps 252 square feet. It was later increased. "Originally," said designer Legnos, "we hoped that people would take the boat without an engine. This was, of course, unrealistic. So the inboard became typical and the boat became heavier. We therefore increased the size of the sail."

Owners have increased the rig on their own. One reported increasing the sail to over 350 square feet, building a new, hollow mast six feet longer than the original, increasing the boom by four feet, and the gaff by two feet. All this increase required a one-third increase in the size of the rudder. Wheel steering was added and an additional 200 pounds of ballast was added forward to raise the boat's stern sections out of the water to reduce drag. Adjustable lazy jacks and deck-mounting of the halyard blocks accompanied the rerigging,

ensuring easy raising and lowering of the sail. This boat has recorded 6.3 mph in a 12-knot breeze.

Many years ago, I sailed aboard an engineless Mystic 20 (oarlocks were mounted on the cockpit coamings so that the boat could be rowed in a calm). My memory is of a sweet-sailing boat with a rather bright, airy cabin that offered more headroom than expected. There was wood down there, too, a sheathing of white pine that contributed much to the sense of warmth. The owner was most pleased and so, it seems, are those who own one today.

Mystic 20

Length: 20'
Length of Waterline: 18' 6"
Beam: 8'
Draft: 2' 1"/4' 3"
Displacement: 3000-plus pounds
Sail Area: originally 252 sq. ft., later 282 sq. ft. (Note: some boats were built with enlarged rigs of 320 and 350 sq. ft.)

Marshall Sanderling

The story behind this boat's development appears in an earlier chapter. The Sanderling's success is reflected in the volume of its sales over a period of years. Its sailing qualities, in terms of boat speed, have proven difficult to equal or exceed, and it has become, in certain locales, a popular one-design racer. Molding is done, as it has been for years, outside the Marshall shop, with assembly and trim handled by Marshall Marine. The hull is a sturdy layup of solid glass. The cabin top is foam-cored to reduce weight. The cockpit sole is built of 1/2-inch sheet plywood over plywood floor timbers. The plywood sole is fiberglassed. The seats are

The Marshall Sanderling is popular as a one-design racer, daysailer, and overnighter. "Classic looks, solid construction, sails beautifully," reported the happy owner of a 27-year-old model that he's refurbished to like-new appearance.

fiberglassed plywood mounted on stanchions, the latter arrangement typical of catboats of "the old days." This means that gear left under the seats is exposed. Prospective purchasers of older models are well advised to check fiberglassed wooden components for soundness.

Breck Marshall once wrote, with tongue in cheek, of his costly experience with installing an inboard engine in the Sanderling, a boat originally intended only for use with an outboard auxiliary. Today, the boat may be ordered with an inboard, an obviously personal decision that must balance performance loss versus convenience gain. The owner of one such boat noted it was difficult to access the propeller shaft seal and the raw water impeller. Owners of inboard-powered Sanderlings rated sailing qualities at 3 out of 5 and one said that "lack

of speed" was the thing they liked least about the boat. Again, the tradeoff is a personal choice.

The Sanderling interior is plainly finished but functional, considering the boat's size. Ventilation was judged inadequate, suggesting that a small hatch and vents are much-needed additions. Owners noted generally low maintenance as a plus, although the owner of a 1990 model reported with some surprise that he had to rebed leaking portlights and running lights. The need to rebed leaking ports was reported by others whose boats were eight years old or older. Lowering the sail was an issue for most owners, whether they had purchased the boat new or used. Several owners reported they had upgraded blocks for halyards and the mainsheet, as well. In the end, the Sanderling's sleek but traditional good looks, basic sturdiness, shallow draft, and performance reputation are among its highest attractions. It's worth noting that the Sanderling's popularity has contributed to good resale value and, assuming the boat is well maintained, it should represent a reasonable investment.

Marshall Sanderling

Builder: Marshall Marine, South Dartmouth, MA
Length: 18' 2"
Beam: 8' 6"
Draft: 19"/4' 4"
Displacement: 2,200 lbs.
Sail Area: 253 sq. ft.

Marshall 22

For many, the Marshall 22 has long represented the ultimate in catboats. Handsome looks and a proven reputation for seaworthiness and performance have always made this scaled-up version of the Sanderling popular. What's more, the earliest boats to be molded are still sailing. Some may have had their share of upgrading and repair along the way, as one might expect, but the basic soundness of the hull and deck molding seems to have been amply demonstrated.

This is a boat that has been offered in three slightly different configurations. The original 1965 version was built with no fundamental change until 1976. At that time, Breck Marshall slightly altered the mold to give a somewhat finer entry and to add more tumblehome to the stern. Later, in the early '80s, a new all-fiberglass cockpit was designed that featured molded seats with lockers beneath them. The early model's open interior gave way to one with a bulkhead behind which the head is mounted. Prospective buyers of a used Marshall 22 need

to be aware that they are looking at a boat with all the systems of any inboard, cruising auxiliary. That means a diesel engine (which most greatly prefer to the gasoline engine models) and drive system, fuel tank, batteries, and electrical system. There's also a galley that will be equipped with one sort of stove or another, a water tank, a galley sink and, probably, a marine head. If the latter is not equipped with a holding tank, the boat will need to be upgraded if it is to be legal. The builder's solution to the holding tank question, a specially molded nine-gallon fiberglass tank located beneath the aft-most starboard lazarette, is probably the most sensible arrangement.

Given the Marshall 22's level of equipment, prospective buyers are well-advised to have a boat under consideration surveyed, just as they would any boat that involves its complexity and expense. While the basic structure is typically very sturdy, there are several things to look at. These include checking the fuel tank for leaks; checking the cabin bulkhead trim in the cockpit for leaks; checking the molded scupper areas where they meet the centerboard trunk for leaks; the soundness of plywood in bulkheads; the condition of the engine hatch insulation (which should be mechanically fastened rather than simply glued to the hatch); and inspecting the centerboard pennant for wear. The latter is always worth checking on any centerboard boat. The mast should be inspected for possible corrosion in the area of the gooseneck, although boats built after 1978 have insulating material between the mast and gooseneck to reduce potential electrolysis.

Owners report high overall satisfaction with this boat, rating it a 4 or 5 in terms of quality. The owner of an older boat was more complimentary about the woodwork in his cabin than was the owner of a six-year-old model. Weak points cited included cabin ventilation, and the owner of a 1995 model noted, as one part of this, the "primitive" hatch. In fact, it is removable but not hinged, an obvious disadvantage. A support can be made to hold the hatch open but a better original equipment solution is warranted. One additional ventilation recommendation involves replacing the solar power mini vent that is an option with a larger model that runs day and night.

More than one owner complained that the topping lift required too much effort, something that could be improved by the addition of tackle to give greater mechanical advantage. This might even make it possible to locate the lift further forward on the boom where it won't foul the end of the gaff. The mainsheet arrangement of two double blocks, one with a becket, invites a fouled sheet as soon as tension on the sheet is released. The stern light that protrudes beneath the traveler and the stern cleats are not entirely protected from the sheet either.

Despite areas in which it can be improved, the Marshall 22 remains the boat of choice for many catboat enthusiasts. It has proven to be a reasonably accommodating little cruiser. The addition of the optional dodger makes the boat seem a good deal bigger than it is, and provides excellent protection when necessary. As long as the sail is reefed in good time — essential for any catboat — the Marshall 22 is capable of providing entertaining coastal cruising during which its shallow draft can be used to advantage. That draft also means it can sometimes find a place for the night away from the more crowded parts of an anchorage.

When cruising, the boat offers much the same performance as a 24- to 27- foot cruising sloop with an inboard engine. The two-cylinder Yanmar diesel typically installed burns about a quarter gallon to a third of a gallon per hour. When fitted

Anchored at Nashawena in the Elizabeth Islands, this Marshall 22 has a functional awning that permits the crew to take best advantage of the boat's big cockpit.

with a 13" x 10" three-blade propeller that permits it to reach its rated rpm, this engine will capably power the boat against a headwind and head sea or a strong adverse current.

Marshall 22 owners say that, given the same circumstances, they would buy their boat again. What's more, the always steady demand means this is a boat that represents a reasonably sound investment when resale time comes.

Marshall 22

Builder: Marshall Marine, South Dartmouth, MA
Length: 22' 2"
LWL: 21' 4"
Beam: 10' 2"
Draft: 2'/5' 5"
Displacement: 5,660 lbs.
Sail Area: 388 sq. ft.

Menger 19

Although he designed many types of boats, naval architect Fred Goeller always maintained an enthusiasm for catboats, and he published a variety of designs and construction articles in *The Rudder* as early as 1911. This boat traces its ancestry to a wooden daysailer, one of several such boats that Goeller created. When developed for production in fiberglass, this particular design expanded from its original 15 or 16 feet to 17 feet, and gained some additional freeboard. The original molds for the boat were lost in a fire, after which the design was slightly revised to arrive at the current 19-foot length.

While traditional in appearance, the Menger 19 is innovative in its construction and details. The cockpit is a fiberglass molding that has a 1/4" plywood stiffening core completely encapsulated by mat and roving on both sides. Inside, the cabin has a nicely finished appearance thanks to the use of bonded liners in the cabin top and under the side decks, and varnished pine staving around the cabin sides. The boat's molds were built in Menger's own shop, which also does the actual molding. In fact, there are 30 molds involved in the production of this boat including those for the custom diesel fuel tank (tested to 5 psi), and even for the electrical panel. Owners, whether they had purchased their boat new or used, rated quality as a 5, the best.

Among the 19's noteworthy features is its amply sized propeller aperture. The 19 was designed with inboard power in mind and the great majority of new boats are sold with diesel power. The big aperture means that a properly sized two-blade propeller can be fitted and lined up with the skeg to minimize drag when sailing. Boats to be equipped with outboards have the aperture filled so that a smooth after-hull/skeg

The Menger 19 — a nicely finished boat designed for an inboard engine.

area is produced. Menger has also engineered an innovative outboard well with doors that close around the motor leg to minimize drag and keep exhaust smoke from backing up and possibly choking the engine.

The boat's mainsheet arrangement has also been adapted to improve function. The traveler is mounted atop the coaming. Whether or not this unusual arrangement was really necessary, the sheet itself runs through fiddle blocks resulting in generally smooth operation free of fouling. "We tried," said Bill Menger, "to keep the sheet away from everything." The tiller is arranged to come over the coaming, rather than through a slot in the transom, increasing space in the cockpit.

Menger pioneered mast tabernacles for catboats, and this feature alone was cited by owners as an important factor in their purchase decision. Relatively easy trailering and launching were noted as important advantages. One owner noted that the mast hoops bind on the tabernacle, making lowering the sail a bit of a problem. Another reported that jiffy reef lines can snag deck cleats, suggesting a better method of rigging the reef lines may be needed.

In general, Menger 19 owners seem primarily interested in a well-constructed, well-engineered boat that offers maximum comfort (the optional opening forward hatch is recommended for improved ventilation) and convenience. The boat, with its comparatively roomy cabin with good sitting headroom and hideaway galley, and its cockpit replete with molded-in, roomy lazarettes, earns it high praise from owners. A useful owner's manual accompanies each boat.

Menger 19

Builder: Menger Boatworks, Amityville, NY
Length: 19'
LWL: 18' 5"
Beam: 8 feet
Draft: 1' 10"/4' 6"
Displacement: 2,900 lbs.
Sail Area: 270 sq. ft.

Menger 23

Currently the only catboat in production to offer standing headroom and an enclosed head, this boat is based on revised versions of molds originally made for the Americat 22 in 1970 by George Benedict on Long Island. Benedict used as the basis for the Americat a 1927 design by naval architect Francis Sweisguth. The original boat had been developed for a client in Pelham Manor,

New York, and was built by William Haff, who built a number of catboats at his New Rochelle yard during his career. This 22-footer, with a 37-foot mast and 490-sq.-ft. sail, proved, like most of Sweisguth's catboats, to be a fast sailer. In fact, two more were built.

Although generally comparable in length and beam to a Marshall 22, the Menger 23 weighs in with a displacement of 6,500 pounds, about 15 percent more than the 22. It has slightly greater sail area to power that additional weight.

The hull's lines remain, according to Bill Menger, essentially those of the Americat and, thus, of Francis Sweisguth's original design, but several important changes were made above the waterline. "We changed the sheer," said Menger, "because the Americat really had a reverse sheer due to how they had to build the mold. And we made new a new deck mold, revised the cabin coamings, and raised the cockpit seats enough so you could see over the cabin. The helmsman seat, in particular, affords a good view." Underneath the helmsman seat is a big lazarette, one of several places that afford good storage.

Owners reported high satisfaction with overall quality of the boat and hardware. One noted that he'd had to replace the hatchway fasteners and tighten the hot and cold water lines to stop them from leaking under pressure. The hatch itself is adorned with a pair of small grab rails, the aesthetics of which are, perhaps, in the eye of a specific beholder.

Although the cabin accommodations are clearly important to buyers of the boat, purchasers also reported what they considered to be excellent performance under both sail and power. One claimed that his boat has recorded a steady 6 1/2 - 7 knots in a breeze heavy enough to require double reefs. He has found the boat's balance to be

The Menger 23 offers standing headroom and an enclosed head.

together with the optional louvered doors, gave adequate ventilation. That same owner found the bimini top needed to be lower to avoid being rubbed on by the boom, and its stitching lasted only 18 months before requiring repair.

The Menger 23's roominess, enclosed head, and spacious cockpit with rather high backrests, give it special appeal to sailors, including older sailors, moving down from bigger boats. More than one reported selling a boat over 30 feet in length before deciding to order a 23.

Menger 23

Builder: Menger Boatworks, Amityville, NY
Length: 23'
LWL: 22' 6"
Beam: 10'
Draft: 2' 6"/5' 6"
Displacement: 6,500 lbs.
Sail Area: 435 sq. ft.

Molly Cat

Among those who responded to the owner's survey that was the basis for much of the information in this chapter, were some who sail their boats on the West Coast, including an owner on windy San Francisco Bay. These would not impress one as being ideal waters for a typical catboat, and this demonstrates that the catboat's

excellent, although it is at its best when the fuel and water tanks are nearly full. The propeller aperture is sized and shaped to permit any likely propeller. Under power, with its standard two-blade prop, the boat can cruise, according to the builder, at 6.4 knots at 2,300 rpm. Only one of those surveyed had an objection to the 23. As much as he appreciated the boat's roominess, he believed the higher cabin sides contributed to excessive wandering at anchor or on a mooring. He also found the boat to be more tender than anticipated.

According to Bill Menger, a goal was to present an open, airy appearance when looking below through the cabin doors, which are offset to starboard. Although the 23's cabin layout is not traditional, neither the builder nor the owners who responded had any complaints, and Menger is willing to entertain customer's ideas about changes. One owner reported that he was glad he had specified a larger forward hatch than the 10-inch model normally offered. The larger hatch, appeal sometimes results in boats showing up in places where they are not ideally suited. The Molly Cat was built for a time, beginning in 1988, by the Fernandes Boatworks in Richmond, California. The design was an effort to adapt a traditional-looking catboat to the winds and seas of San Francisco Bay.

As the boat's specifications indicate, the chief differences between it and a typical catboat of its size include its small rig, higher displacement, and narrower beam. It also had a bridge deck. The boat was built with a 7/16" thick cored hull, and cored coaming, and deck moldings. It had a raked transom, underhung rudder, and was designed to accept a Yanmar 1GM diesel. No owners of this boat participated in the survey. However, for those who sail in an area where its design features are appropriate, it might well be worth a look.

Molly Cat

Length overall: 17 feet
Length of waterline: 16' 1"
Draft: 2' 2"/4 feet
Displacement: 3,000 lbs.
Ballast: 1,000 lbs of lead
Sail area: 200 sq. ft. (225 sq. ft. optional)

Whither the Fiberglass Catboat?

Although Breck Marshall got as far as making the molds for a 26-foot catboat, no builder has yet gone into production with a boat comparable to what was, a century ago, the heart of the market for a cruising catboat. Those models, the 24 - 26 footers, built by the Crosbys and others, were big enough to offer practical cabins and small enough so that, in that era, at least, they were deemed capable of being sailed single-handed.

Rather often, in the yachting periodicals of a past era, one finds references to boats of this sort regularly completing impressive coastal pasages from New England to Virginia, or from Boston to downeast Maine. A 26' 9" Daniel Crosby-built model, for example, had sleeping accommodations for four people, a head, galley, and cabin with five feet of headroom. A Lathrop two-cycle engine produced speeds of six to seven miles per hour.

Today, using modern materials, a catboat like Daniel Crosby's could be built with a flat cabin sole, enclosed head, and roomy cabin with more than adequate headroom. While its rig would, and should, be large, the lighter weight of modern materials and the improved performance of synthetic sailcloth compared to cotton would certainly suggest that the sail area would be less than it was in the old days. Properly rigged according to traditional methods, such a boat would be an entirely practical cruiser that would represent a logical top end of the market, a segment that remains unserved.

A few catboats of this general size have, in fact, been built, but they've all been wooden. The best include Fenwick Williams's 25-footer and Charles Wittholz's 25-foot Prudence design. Others have been built as well, but their sailing qualities have not always been all that might be desired. Is the market there for a traditional, gaff-rigged, fiberglass cruising catboat? We may never know. The fact is, however, that if the fiberglass pioneers had listened to naysayers, there would not be hundreds of fiberglass catboats sailing today. It is also true that the market for gaff-rigged, fiberglass catboats has remained reasonably solid for a long period of years, times that have seen the arrival and departure of most major production boat builders. Clearly, there is a niche here.

The only fiberglass boat to offer the look of a traditional catboat combined with a truly roomy cabin was the Nonsuch. Its similarity to a Cape Cod catboat ended, however, with its general topsides appearance. Below the waterline, the Nonsuch was a modern, fin keel design. Its rig, although technically a cat rig, was a modern interpretation based on a wishbone with a jib-headed sail. The genius of the rig is that it combined reasonable simplicity and an absence of standing rigging with easy handling. About 1,000 of these popular boats, ranging in size from 22 to 36 feet were built before the company went out of business. Today, Nonsuch owners have an active class association that supports a boat that appeals to those who seek a good-performing cruising vessel combining surprising simplicity of rig and good sailing qualities with exceptional roominess. The majority of the popular 30-footers, however, have a five-foot keel; even the "shoal" keel model draws 3' 11". "What I'd really like," said one of those who took part in the owner survey for this chapter, "is a centerboard Nonsuch."

The Alerion Cat is another modern interpretation. This 19-footer weighs some 400 pounds less than a Marshall 18 yet carries a slightly larger, jib-headed sail. It combines an easily handled rig with a contemporary hull form and the latest in fiberglass technology. It's a simple boat, but its improved speed comes at the expense of an entirely different aura, appearance, and cabin amenities than the traditional variety. For its intended market, this is doubtless acceptable.

Summary

Perhaps the biggest single improvement that can be made to today's fiberglass catboats is to upgrade and improve their rigging. The largest and best ball-bearing blocks are desirable, and every-thing possible should be done to reduce potential binding on mast hoops that can make the sail difficult to lower. Deck-mounted halyard and topping lift blocks merit serious consideration. So does anything that can lessen the chance for a mainsheet to foul on itself or the boat. Cabin ventilation is the other area of uniform weakness. Some builders do more in this regard than others.

Today, the prospective buyer of a fiberglass catboat equipped with a cabin and at least the basics needed to advance the boat from daysailer and overnighter to a modest cruiser, has a wealth of choices. Each boat, whether currently still in production or long out of production, occupies one niche or another. Some offer more comfort at the expense of sailing qualities while others offer just the opposite. The most popular models manage to strike a compromise. In the end, it is up to individuals to determine which boat comes closest to meeting their specific needs.

Business was good for the skipper of this Nantucket party boat, for there are at least 16 passengers aboard for an afternoon outing.

CHAPTER TEN

THE ENDURING CATBOAT

—•◆•—

"Although the Piscator *was only about 24 feet long, she was nearly half as wide as she was long and as Coridon would say: 'By golly, sir, she is roomy and shallow, comfortable and handy and you can't beat that combination."*

—L. FRANCIS HERRESHOFF, *The Compleat Cruiser,* 1956

MANY YEARS AGO, just before the beginning of World War One, the journalist Winfield Thompson paused to reflect on the peculiar but undeniable attraction that catboats still held for many sailors. By 1914, Thompson, like others, had seriously begun to question whether the coming of the gasoline engine might actually cause people to forget how to sail. In fact, it meant that many would never learn to sail in the first place, but sailing remained a popular activity and, despite the many alternatives, catboats continued to attract a small but devoted following. The appeal was, even to Thompson, a bit mysterious.

"Whatever there may be in catboat sailing that charms men and holds them more loyally through life than any other sort of boat sailing, I know not," he wrote. But then he noted that responses to his catboat articles had come from places as distant as South Africa and Alaska. The readers asked for more information and said they were "praying

that I stray not from the path of the catboat man, but continue to write of things I knew about."

The charm of the catboat has continued right down to the present day. The late Captain Adrian Lane of Noank, Connecticut, who had commanded an ice breaker, Mystic Seaport's schooner *Brilliant,* and the Woods Hole research vessel *Atlantis,* fell under the catboat's spell himself. He became the owner (together with Edward Bowditch Watson) of the Crosby catboat *Dolphin.* "I think," he said once, "that maybe it's the snugness of the cabin. The cabin of a catboat gives you a wonderful sense of security." Even the old *Dolphin*'s leaks didn't dim his affection.

Today, a new generation of sailors has been attracted to the boats, whether because of their snug cabins, wholesome looks, essential simplicity, or the indefinable but very real connection with something valuable about past life and traditions that the catboat represents. It is these enthusiasts who have been central to the preservation of the remaining wooden catboats, and also to the building of new boats, whether in wood or fiberglass. An idea of the variety of these catboats, and of the loyalty and perseverance of their owners, is presented here.

An Unusual Daysailer

Born in Middletown, Connecticut, in 1900, Winthrop Warner grew up with boats on the Connecticut River and managed to spend a long career, after studying naval architecture at MIT, in the field that he so loved. Among Warner's many designs for both power and sail boats were a number of catboats. These included models as diverse as a 24-foot keel model with six feet of headroom and

Bob Cat: 17' 5" x 16' 7" x 7' 8". Draft: 19"/4'. Displacement: 2,980 lbs. Sail area: 175 sq. ft.

an enclosed head, and a most interesting daysailer design that Warner named Bob Cat. Mr. Warner himself was intrigued enough with Bob Cat that he made the boat a stock plans offering. In fact, most anyone with an eye for boats would recognize Bob Cat as worth a close look and, for a period during the 1980s, a builder in New York even attempted to establish a business based on building and selling a cold-molded version of the boat.

The conversion drawings for adapting Bob Cat's traditional construction to cold-molded were made by Duncan Stewart. A highly skilled loftsman who had worked for many years at Newport News Shipbuilding, Stewart was widely recognized as an artist at his trade and, at about the time he was finishing the Bob Cat project, he became involved in lofting the Jamestown replica ships *Discovery* and *Godspeed*. How many cold-molded Bob Cats were produced (at a 1980 price of some $12,000) is not known. Perhaps a half-dozen were commissioned, and the one shown here may have been the very last. It was delivered not as a completed boat but as a cold-molded hull — built of five layers of 1/8-inch western red cedar — to Mark Harper who, over a three-year period of nights and weekends, finished the boat.

"The builder had started the boat for an owner who was then transferred overseas," remembers Mark of the project's beginning. "So he sold me the empty hull, which probably saved me at least a third of the time it would have taken if I'd tried to build the boat from scratch. I had the spars made by Randolph, who did a superb job, and got wooden mast hoops from Lowell."

As an experienced designer's modern rendition of a daysailing catboat, Bob Cat offers considerable food for thought. Perhaps the most noteworthy aspects of her specifications are her comparatively heavy displacement (2,980 lbs.) and her comparatively modest sail plan (175 sq. ft.). Mark does not know the weight of his boat, although he presumes her to be overbuilt. Bob Cat's specifications promise less speed than good balance and easy single-handing. In fact, according to Mark, the boat has "barely any weather helm at all. I carry a couple hundred pounds of trimming ballast because the boat is sensitive to weight, but it's only when sailing downwind that there's any weather helm. It happens, as well, to be very responsive and stable. We've never taken any water aboard. She's just as fast with a reef in as without if the breeze picks up. What's been a surprise is how well the boat goes to windward."

The one dimension that Warner made less than traditional (other than the modest sail plan) was Bob Cat's beam, which is 7' 8". Nominally, a catboat of this length would have had several inches more beam. Still, the boat has a very roomy cockpit, comfortable for four and able to accommodate six, and her relative narrowness probably contributes to the responsiveness that Mark refers to. What's more, this boat has a good-sized centerboard, enabling a skipper not only to proceed smartly to windward, but offering sensitive adjustment on all points of sail. "Just a little trimming has good effect," says Mark. Worthy of note is that the board itself is lightly ballasted so it stays where it's put, and the centerboard trunk is neatly capped to eliminate splashing.

Bob Cat offers a lot of storage space. Her sliding hatch on the cuddy cabin is reminiscent of some 19th-century half-decked catboats, and the cuddy offers a sizable storage capacity. What's more, there is additional space beneath the cockpit seats.

Mark sails this boat in the shallow waters of New Jersey's coastal bays where, he says, she draws favorable comments "even from power-boaters." As the boat is regularly trailered and

The Bob Cat's modest sail plan is evident here.

must make her way out through crowded marina slips, a five-horsepower outboard can be mounted on the rudder. When the boat is left in the water, a boom tent keeps water out of the cockpit and the sun off the varnish. "I add a couple coats of varnish every few years," says Mark. "That's pretty modest maintenance for a wooden boat."

To Copy a Crosby

Adrian Offinger, who was in his 80s when this was written, and still working hard on his Connecticut farm, had been a catboat sailor since he was a boy. His father owned a catboat built in the late 1800s and Adrian learned to sail and cruise on this boat. As an adult, he and his brother owned another catboat, which supplied good fun until it was lost in the hurricane of 1938. Then, in 1952, Adrian decided it was time to have a boat of his own. He drove to a variety of yacht clubs and boat yards looking at a variety of vessels until he inspected a 36-foot yawl that, he still remembers, "had a cockpit the size of a bath tub." After that, he refocused on catboats and went to see a Wilton Crosby-built boat that then was for sale and moored at the Edgewood Yacht Club in Rhode Island. He bought the boat, named *Elizabeth,* and sailed her down to his home port at Westport, Connecticut, with his uncle and a friend as crew.

This boat was a 25-footer that had been built in 1920 and was still equipped with a two-cylinder, two-cycle, Lathrop engine with make-and-break ignition. Although *Elizabeth* had, as Adrian said, "some age on her," she was a remarkable performer. Her 550 sq. ft. sail had four sets of reef points and drove the boat so well that she distanced herself in the few Catboat Association races that Adrian entered. He remembers "leading the fleet until I rounded a mark the wrong way."

Still, the boat needed work. He eventually replaced the Lathrop with a four-cylinder, raw water-cooled Palmer, and the wooden mast with an aluminum one made from a utility pole. But *Elizabeth* was clearly going to need extensive repairs. Offinger had the forward eight feet of the garboards replaced and was looking at more work when he decided he'd be better off replicating *Elizabeth* rather than rebuilding her.

"In 1970, I asked Edson Schock to come and take her lines," Adrian said. "So he came down with a transit and I met him at the train station and he did the job."

In addition to reproducing the boat's lines, Schock added a few construction drawings. Soon afterward, however, he was able to more fully engineer the boat when, quite unexpectedly, Wilton Crosby, Jr., presented Adrian Offinger with a sheet of drawings — dated 1920 — from the company files. With these as reference, Schock completed his construction plan for the boat in January 1971, and Offinger took the drawings to several boat yards for quotes. Roy Wallace, whose yard, Newbert and

Wallace, was located in Thomaston, Maine, got the job. There the boat was heavily constructed of oak frames, cypress planks, and bronze fasteners. The specifications make interesting reading and are reproduced below.

Cathy Ann (now *Surprise*)

Length on deck: 25 feet
Length of waterline: 24 feet
Beam: 11' 2"
Draft: 30" board up
Frames: White oak, 2" x 2" on 12" centers
Planking: 1" cypress
Floors: 2" white oak at every frame
Fasteners: Bronze
Centerboard: Fiberglass (16 plies with white oak shoe)
Mast (step to truck): 34 feet
Mast diameter at partners: 8 3/4"
Boom: 34 feet
Gaff: 21' 3"
Sail area: 555 sq. ft. (Foot: 29' 2", Luff 16' 11", Leech 38' 11", Head 18' 6")
Engine: Yanmar 3GM turning 17" x 12" two blade bronze wheel (under-propped)
(See Chapter 11 for photos.)

Offinger found his new boat, which he named *Cathy Ann,* to be a generally faithful rendition of *Elizabeth* but without her many serious problems. An unexpected difference, however, involved the height of the cockpit seats. While both the Crosby and Schock drawings showed the seats should be 14 1/2 inches above the cockpit sole, *Cathy Ann's* seats were about two inches higher. This made room beneath them for gas tanks but reduced the height of the cockpit coamings accordingly, something Offinger says he learned to live with. As for the old *Elizabeth,* she was sold to a new owner who planned to restore the vessel, but the plans did not work out.

Today, *Cathy Ann,* is named *Surprise* and is owned by Catboat Association members Jon and Roxane Agne, who are steadily working away at the modest structural, cosmetic, and detail work needed to really finish the boat. "Lowering the cockpit seats is on the list and will be fairly easy to do," reports Jon. "We'll also be recaulking the garboards and the centerboard trunk."

This catboat is very nicely rigged. All the halyard blocks are mounted to the deck and twin topping lifts are fitted, each with an intermediate block to reduce effort, so that the boom can be raised, as necessary, when under sail without disturbing the sail's shape. The boom is fitted with the traditional bronze eye screws to which the sail is attached, and the gaff has the traditional jackstay as a stiffener along its underside. Twin gaff bridles are fitted. The dimensions of the spars are such that the boat's current sail doesn't reach the end of either the boom or gaff, suggesting their dimensions, which could be original in specification, date to the time of cotton sails.

Raising *Surprise*'s sail is rather easily accomplished, as is lowering it. The mainsheet is rigged with two single blocks on the boom and one on the traveler, a system that provides plenty of advantage without any nuisance fouling. The big wooden stern cleats are mounted well ahead of the traveler and are protected by the cockpit coaming.

Briefly sailing *Surprise* on the upper reaches of the New Meadows River near Brunswick, Maine, in a light but steady breeze revealed a very nicely balanced boat. At the times the breeze increased, the boat moved ahead with authority and recalled Adrian's remarks about performance relative to

other models. Jon would like someday to sail the boat to Cape Cod to participate in a catboat event there, and is methodically working toward that time, experimenting with ballast — *Surprise* now carries about 1,100 pounds of lead — and making plans for a new sail. The boat is, as her owner suggests, "a work in progress," but, when complete, will be a credible replica of a Wilton Crosby catboat that recalls a wholly different era in American sailing, and the spirit of a different time.

Tabby's Tale

In August 2001, the antique boat show normally held in Boston was moved up the North Shore to Salem's Hawthorne Cove Marina. A nice variety of boats turned out, both power and sail, and one of them was the 18-foot catboat *Tabby.* When she made the trip from her home port in Hingham to Salem, *Tabby* was 54 years old and going strong. But things could have been different. *Tabby*'s tale is one of endurance, of the undeniable attraction that catboats of her design exert, and of the great perseverance and creativity of the man who bought *Tabby* in 1978 and still owns her. His name is Phil Carling.

"She had a decent survey," Phil remembers of the boat when he acquired her. "But during the 1980s, she lost all her iron fasteners. The decks began badly leaking and the rubrails became a bit 'mobile.'"

Planning to replace the deck canvas and rubrails, Phil removed the rubrails and, as is almost always the case with such projects, discovered that he was just scratching the surface of *Tabby*'s ills. The top of the sheer plank was rotten, which was why the rubrail fasteners no longer held any too well. He then found the main deck beam was gone and so was the breast hook and part of the stem. This prompted him to take the cabin apart to look for more problems. He found

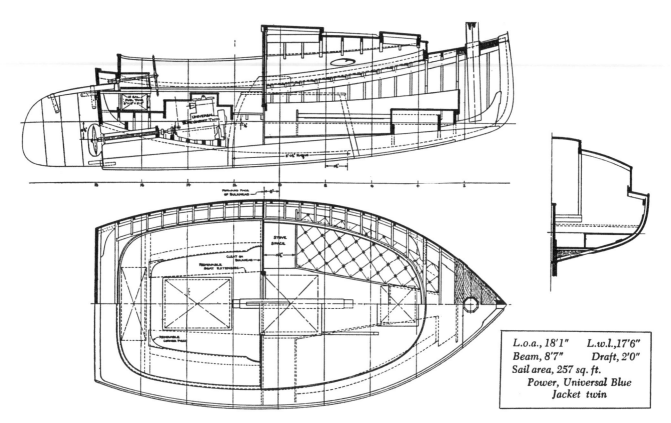

L.o.a., 18'1"   L.w.l.,17'6"
Beam, 8'7"   Draft, 2'0"
Sail area, 257 sq. ft.
Power, Universal Blue
Jacket twin

The drawings for FenwickWilliams's updated 18-footer were published in Yachting *in June 1949.The plans show wheel steering and a Universal Blue Jacket twin.*

every frame on both sides of the boat was broken. In short, with the removal of his boat's rubrails, Carling found himself embarked upon a project that would ultimately consume five years of nights and weekends and cost more than four times the boat's purchase price.

Perhaps, if *Tabby* had been the product of an unknown designer and a forgotten builder, she might have simply been broken up, as has happened so often. But she was from the drawing board of a man renowned for his catboats, and had been superbly put together by an accomplished builder for a man with a lifetime of catboat experience. It's hard not to love a Fenwick Williams 18-footer!

Tabby was built in 1947 by Seth Persson in Saybrook, Connecticut. She was commissioned by John Killam Murphy, who had known Williams

during the years they worked together in John Alden's Boston office where Murphy was a yacht broker. At the end of World War Two, however, Murphy was serving in the Coast Guard and looking ahead to peacetime and a new boat. In a brief commentary published in *Yachting* in 1949, Mr. Murphy described how he felt about *Tabby* after two years of owning the boat. "She is so small and easy to get under way and to put to bed that I do much afternoon sailing, yet her accommodations are adequate and comfortable for my wife and me for our Long Island Sound cruising."

If one assumes that *Tabby* was merely the same 18-foot design that Fenwick first published in 1931, one would be wrong. Among other things, John Killam Murphy wanted the earlier boat's squared-off cabin and cockpit coamings to be rounded. He also wanted an inboard engine, in

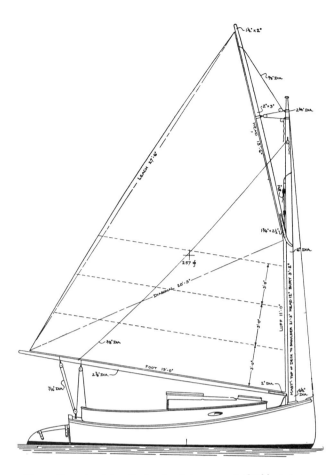

The profile and sailplan display the obvious appeal of Tabby's *design.*

larger cockpit was equipped with pull-out seat extensions. Wrote Murphy: "The extension cockpit seats, with stock air mattresses and a tent awning, provide satisfactory sleeping quarters for the parents while the children find good accommodations in the cabin."

Tabby's board-up draft of two feet was four inches less than the first Williams 18-footer. However, the general hull shape appears identical and so does the manner in which the keel protrudes several inches below the garboard planks. Together with the boat's ample skeg, this permits some progress to windward even with the board raised. Finally, *Tabby*'s sail was nine square feet larger than the earlier model's, no doubt an effort to maintain similar performance despite the drag of the propeller.

The fact that Williams redrew the design to accommodate all these modifications resulted in problems for him with his employer. When Alden's office manager learned of the project, she sent the designer a letter reminding him that he was forbidden to work under his own name while employed by the company. The result was that Williams had to hand on the modest fee he received for the design drawings to Alden's, and John Killam Murphy's Fenwick Williams 18-foot catboat became John Alden plan number 383.

Phil Carling approached the restoration of his boat with an open mind about both methods and materials. His basic approach was to use epoxy as an adhesive in the lamination of different parts. "I tried a lot of experiments," he says of the early days of the project. "I learned, for example, that you can laminate oak if you use thin enough strips." With *Tabby*'s hull shape maintained by turnbuckles and rigging, Carling began the slow task of laminating in place the needed new frames, which he made of oak strips 1/8" – 1/4" thick. In

this case, a Universal Blue Jacket twin. But the changes were in fact, more extensive than these requirements might suggest. *Tabby* had an inch more beam than the earlier boat — 8' 7" vs. 8' 6"— but, more important, carried the beam further aft to a broader transom. The gaff angle was increased to give a higher peak and improved windward ability. The rudder was significantly enlarged to improve mechanical advantage, and the centerboard was lengthened to improve overall balance. Wheel steering replaced the earlier tiller. The cabin top was given a slight crown to add a couple of inches of headroom and a hatch was added at the forward end of the cabin to improve ventilation. The ratio of cockpit to cabin was increased slightly on *Tabby,* and the slightly a few places where he was not concerned about moisture, he laminated frames of cherry, which he found beautiful to work with. He also laminated a new main deck beam.

Inspection of the boat's cedar planking revealed it to be in excellent condition. "The exception," remembered Carling, "was the sheer strake. The top was rotted because of the leaking canvas deck covering. I removed the bad part and laminated on strips necessary to bring the strake up to its original height." Much of the planking below the waterline was refastened with walnut trunnels that Carling made to replace the original iron nails. "Beneath the waterline under the cockpit, I drilled half-inch holes through the planking and the original oak frames and drove in the trunnels I'd made. It was a successful method."

In the cockpit itself, Carling decided not to keep the pull-out berth extensions that John Killam Murphy had found so important. Instead, he redid the cockpit benches to follow the curve of the coaming, much like the seats of the earlier 18-foot model.

The one job that Carling decided not to undertake on his own was repair of the deadwood. "Where the shaft log was bored, there was a lot of deterioration and leaks," he said. "I had the boat trucked to a yard in Maine and they put in a new deadwood, new engine beds, and a new Yanmar 1GM diesel. They also put in new garboards."

Having seen first-hand the damage that can be caused by old, leaking canvas on a cabin top and deck, Carling used Dynel fabric and epoxy resin when he recovered *Tabby*'s cabin top and decks. The Dynel has held up very well, and Carling puts only a thin wash of paint on it each season. Spring commissioning is now a relatively enjoyable task that usually involves two coats of paint on the hull and cabin sides. "The boat probably takes about 20 hours of work to keep it up," he said. "And a lot of that goes into maintaining the brightwork."

Like virtually every Fenwick Williams 18-foot catboat, the renewed *Tabby* has demonstrated herself to be an entertaining and able little boat capable of going as far as an owner wishes to sail her. When *Tabby* was new, Fenwick Williams occasionally accompanied his old friend John Killam Murphy on Long Island Sound cruises. Other 18-footers have cruised rather widely on the East Coast, from Maine to the Chesapeake. Carling has sailed *Tabby* as far as Newport and thinks nothing of the trip from Boston to the North Shore. Given this design's staunch looks and proven abilities, it's no wonder that the Fenwick Williams's 18-footer, Alden plan 383, continues to attract would-be owners and builders.

Still Sailing After All These Years

Forty or 50 years ago, during the early days of fiberglass boat construction, it was commonly asked — "How long will she last?" Most everyone involved with the then new material believed it would last a long time, but there was no way of putting an absolute number to it. Now, decades after the first fiberglass hulls were molded, answers to the longevity question are still coming in. One testimonial to fiberglass durability is the very first Marshall 22. *Grayling,* ex-*Grimalkin,* built in 1965, was entering her 37th year when this was written.

"I can remember," says Bill Coleman, who became only the boat's third owner when he bought her in 1975, "that the question of fiberglass longevity came up when I went to buy insurance. I had some trouble at first because they said they didn't know how long fiberglass would last."

In fact, the boat not only remains sound today but has never even been painted. "She still has the original gel coat," says Bill, "and when the boat is polished in the spring, it looks brand new."

Precisely how much different the hull laminates of the boat are from subsequent versions is unknown, and Marshall Marine reports that the laminate schedule on the production 22 has never changed. The fact is that most of the 22s from the early years still seem to be in commission. Coleman believes, however, that the boat may have been overbuilt simply because she was the first of the genre and Breck Marshall would have chosen to err of the safe side. "I don't think they really knew just how much glass they were putting in this boat," said Bill, "but it's three-quarters-inch thick in places. The boat does seem to have a rather different feel as it goes through the water than the others I've sailed."

One of the specifications that certainly has changed is the rig. The sail is approximately 410 square feet, significantly larger than the 388 square feet that became the standard size. According to Marshall Marine's John Garfield, the very largest sail tried was 440 square feet, which was "too big." Because *Grayling*'s boom extends an additional foot beyond a typical Marshall 22's, the

Stoutly built in 1965, the first Marshall 22 is still sailing.

spring ritual of putting on the big sail requires clambering into a dinghy or tying up alongside a dock to rig the foot outhaul. The owner also rigs a permanent pennant for the first reef point. "One reef is all that's needed," he says, again suggesting a comparatively heavy boat.

How much work has been done in terms of modifying and updating this catboat? Probably, about what one might expect. "I replaced all the wiring," says Bill, "and I had Marshall Marine put in their holding tank system. I also replaced the alcohol stove with a propane model. The propane bottle is a small one that is mounted under the cockpit seat on the port side." Not surprisingly, the original Atomic Four gasoline engine, which itself had been replaced by a newer block, is now gone, and with it the boat's original exhaust system.

"The original exhaust was not good," said Bill. "It was below the waterline and could siphon water into the engine when starting. We replaced this with a Volvo marine-type exhaust. But the gasoline engine was never really satisfactory and, in 1998, I took the boat to Marshall and they installed a two-cylinder Yanmar. A new fuel tank was installed aft of the ice box on the port side."

Perhaps the boat's most unfortunate mishap involved the shearing of the centerboard pin while the boat lay at her mooring. Although *Grayling* didn't sink, the water level in the cabin nearly rose to the top of the bunks and filled the engine well. Coleman replaced the original centerboard pin, which had been made of a brass rod, with a stainless pin on which threads were cut to mount a manganese bronze nut. A leather washer between the nut and centerboard trunk made for a watertight seal. Production Marshall 22s have an improved centerboard pin.

Grayling has benefited from some modest but useful changes to her rigging. The halyard and topping lift blocks are mounted on a welded-on bracket at the gooseneck that moves them outboard of the mast to improve the raising and lowering of the sail. Two Harken double ball-bearing blocks are used for the mainsheet, but the top block is equipped with a ratchet that, when engaged, slows the block and helps control the rate at which the sheet pays out in a jibe. The sheet itself is long enough to permit the boom to be eased to 90 degrees, more than the standard-length sheet.

Down below, this Marshall 22 retains her original cabin layout. There are vee-berths forward with a filler piece that makes a large, comfortable bed. Next aft on the port side is a hanging locker, followed by the galley with its sink and stove. To starboard is a quarter berth. The toilet is installed beneath the starboard cabin step, which is hinged, and this installation is, according to Bill, surprisingly functional. In fact, the cabin has proven more than adequate for the occasional week-long cruise that Bill and his wife Roslyn embark upon from their Stage Harbor mooring. They've sailed the boat to Nantucket, Martha's Vineyard, Cuttyhunk, and Mystic, and once spent 17 days aboard. "Time aboard is ultimately governed," noted Bill, "by how long you want to sustain the 'catboat crouch.'"

"First Place for *Grayling*"

By all accounts, catboat racing along Boston's North Shore was a vibrant sport from 1904 until the time that World War One put a serious damper on such activities. Boats traveled from one harbor to the next, from Quincy and Hull to Marblehead and on to Cape Ann, sometimes making a race even of the trip itself. After a race, the crews were often joined by wives and friends who had arrived by train to view the spectacle and to spend some time afloat themselves. A photograph of the C. C. Hanley–built *Iris* taken in 1908 shows no fewer than eight couples aboard. The women are dressed in skirts, blouses, and hats, the men in their yacht club uniforms. Such was D-Class catboat racing in the years before the Great War.

That the races continued for well over a decade, and apparently attracted from eight to 15 or more boats, gives a pretty good indication of the ongoing enthusiasm that owners held for their vessels. Writing in *The Rudder* in 1908, Winfield Thompson noted: "Some could afford to go into a more expensive class, others could not; but all are in the cat class from choice, and therein lies its strength. They love the type of boat they represent."

The enthusiasm even survived World War One, and at least a half-dozen of the D-Class catboats raced on into the 1920s. Inevitably, of course, the number of boats dwindled. Years later, people might remember the day that one or another of the old catboats sailed off to New Jersey or "somewhere up around New York," never to be heard from again. The same thing happened with the racing fleets in Buzzards Bay and Narragansett Bay until, with the passing of years and then decades, the D-Class catboats and all their siblings faded away. Finally, sometime in the fall or winter of 1982, the very last example quietly sank in her slip on Long Island. She was raised, and then dragged unceremoniously across the parking lot at the Cedarhurst Yacht Club to await her fate.

"They had put a block of styrofoam under each bilge to hold her up, and left her lying there on the ground," remembers Doug Goldhirsch of his first sight of the boat. "That's how I found her."

It was an important "finding" for both man and boat. Goldhirsch, then a student of naval architecture at the Webb Institute, had gone to see the boat on a whim after noting an ad in *WoodenBoat* magazine. The boat's name was *Grayling.* "Somehow," he said, "*Grayling* set my mind in motion and helped me solidify a dream to own a classic old boat and go places with her. I left that parking lot trying to figure out how I could justify buying this boat."

Thus began a story of one man's involvement with a very special boat that is still unfolding some 20 years after their first meeting. As D-Class catboats go, *Grayling,* at 22 feet in length, was the smallest allowed by the rules of the Cape Catboat Association. But her history, as best it can be traced, is similar to that of many fine 19th-century catboats, for it appears to have its beginning in the heart and home of one of those immensely wealthy men whose patronage was so important to the creation of many fine yachts. In this case, the man may have been J. P. Morgan himself. The boat — believed to have been built by Wilton Crosby in 1898 — was named after a species of freshwater fish, *Grayling.* It was a name that Morgan would use on other boats as well.

Although the specific details of Mr. Morgan's apparent ownership have either been lost or remain currently beyond reach, it appears that he kept the boat far longer than he did most others. The catboat *Grayling* was sold, apparently in 1913, when Mr. Morgan purchased a New York 50 that he called by the same name. The catboat was purchased by a Hull, Massachusetts, schoolteacher named Clarence V. Nickerson who would become her devoted caretaker for some three decades.

It was under Mr. Nickerson's ownership that *Grayling* became a steady entrant in the D-Class races, which were regularly reported by the *Quincy Daily Ledger.* Goldhirsch researched the results of a number of races in 1914 and 1915, which indicate that *Grayling* was at her best in light air. That was the sort of wind that greeted the racers on a late August weekend in 1914. The headline on Monday, August 24th, read: "First Place for *Grayling* — Had Big Lead Over the Class D Fleet."

Grayling was sold shortly before or after Clarence Nickerson's return from World War Two. In his research on the boat, Goldhirsch learned that a subsequent owner on Great South Bay was a distant relative of his. The boat then began passing through the hands of some five more owners, some of whom were more successful than others at keeping her going. One of them was responsible, probably sometime between the mid-'40s and mid-'50s, for moving the mast to its current location, which is about three feet behind the stem. That's far enough so that the boat would no longer meet the old Association requirement: "The forward side of the mast shall not be more than one (1) foot aft of the forward end of the waterline." Goldhirsch believes the mast was moved either to

Here is Grayling *as she appeared during her D-Class years.*

reduce stress on the bow section of the boat or because it became too slender after repeated wear and refinishing.

After he purchased *Grayling,* Doug Goldhirsch had the boat trucked to the Webb Institute where a more thorough assessment could be made of just what her restoration would entail. Out came the interior joiner work and ceiling, the cockpit, and the off-center centerboard trunk that had been installed sometime after the original slot in the keel had been plugged. "It was evident that this boat needed to be reframed," Goldhirsch remembered. "Most of the frames were very rotten and many had already been sistered." He began reframing the boat and continued until the day that he decided to open up the old centerboard slot and better inspect the keel. He found bad news. "It was on a hot August day," he says, "that I discovered that this old keel was not in suitable condition to be used as the backbone of a rebuilt *Grayling.*"

It was not until the next summer, the summer of 1983, at a boat yard in Mattituck, New York, that the real work began on bringing back the 85-year-old catboat. The old keel was removed and a new keel, sternpost, deadwood, and the forward portion of the stem were fashioned from white oak. Floor timbers and a new centerboard trunk followed. The process would continue as Goldhirsch's budget and time permitted. Many of the original bottom planks — 10 and even 12 inches wide — were still in good condition and could be reused. The garboards needed to be replaced, however, but the forwardmost six feet of these planks presented a major challenge because of the extreme twist involved. They were finally made up of three 1/4-inch- 3/8-inch thick layers. In many places where the gaps between planks was too wide to permit caulking, a spline was glued in to close the seam. An expert caulker

named Don Taub was now hired to recaulk the boat, which had by then been out of the water for several years. Goldhirsch spent dawn-to-dusk weekends painting and varnishing and then, finally, on a misty June morning in 1987, *Grayling* was ready to be relaunched.

"We expected lots of leaking," Goldhirsch said, "because the boat had been dried out for so many years. But despite Don's comment that his caulking work was unconditionally guaranteed — until the boat went in the water — *Grayling* was tight as a drum from the very first."

That winter, a single-cylinder Yanmar diesel was installed off-center beneath a newly built self-bailing cockpit. New fuel and water tanks were made, but *Grayling*'s original rack-and-pinion steering gear remained. Bit by bit, during 1988, all the many details attendant to a project such as this one were completed. New bilge stringers were put in and a sheer clamp replaced. A new mast partner and mast step were built, and then an ash ceiling was installed in the cabin along with a small galley, a table on the centerboard trunk, and lighting (part of a new electrical system). A head was mounted beneath the portside companionway step.

In 1989, Goldhirsch began spending weekends aboard his new, century-old Crosby catboat. He began to learn the boat's sailing abilities, which proved to be formidable and, once Goldhirsch learned the importance of reefing *Grayling*'s 470-square-foot sail, he became ever more comfortable in taking longer cruises in the boat. He sailed from Long Island to New England, eventually reaching Osterville itself, and he learned that the boat is seaworthy, safe, and surprisingly fast for a 22-footer. What's in *Grayling*'s future? Long impressed with the photos of 19th-century racing catboats equipped with jibs and even spinnakers, Goldhirsch has begun experimenting with both.

Here is Grayling *as she looked in the late fall of 2001.*

What's more, he has begun efforts to try to determine the dimension of the boat's original boom and mast. There's a chance, as the special relationship between *Grayling* and Goldhirsch continues, that a new mast may be built and the bow remodeled so that the spar can be placed in the original location. Should that happen, the last 19th-century racing catboat still afloat would look almost exactly as she did on that long-ago day when she was first launched at Osterville. What a sight it would be!

Saving *Genevieve*

The fact that so many old wooden catboats are still afloat is testimony to their inherent appeal together with the skill and sheer determination of those who, at various times in the boats' lives, emerged to give them what was needed.

How close did *Genevieve* come to being lost to time and the sickness of her old iron fastenings? "She probably should have been burnt," says Bob Luckraft of the boat on the cover of this book. Instead, she became a seaworthy boat again, and is still sailing her native waters not far from the Osterville shop where Herbert and Andrew Crosby built her in 1927.

In the 63 years before Bob Luckraft bought this boat in 1990, she passed through rather fewer hands than one might guess. Built for a Cotuit family that named her *Skippy,* the boat remained with her original owners until the late 1960s. She did not remain in her original condition, however. The hurricane of 1938 broke *Skippy*'s mast and, although a new mast was built, it was not installed. Instead, her centerboard was removed and she was used as a launch.

In 1962, *Skippy* was sold and renamed *Do-Me.* The new owner got the new but unused mast and the old centerboard, which had served for years as a divider in a goat shed. The gaff, boom, and hardware were original. "I did quite a lot of work on her," Charles De Walt recalled. "My wife and I loved her." Mr. De Walt installed a 25-horsepower Palmer P60 to replace the elderly 1930 Universal. He built a new rudder, a stainless steel-lined icebox, a new main hatch, installed a forward hatch, and he fiberglassed the decks. In 1967, Mr. De Walt sold the boat to just her third owner, and she spent three years on the Connecticut River at Middletown, which is where Bob Reddington purchased her in the spring of 1970.

An early spring cruise brought the boat to Bay Head, New Jersey. There, at Beaton's Boat Yard, Bob began a major reconstruction project in preparation for a planned cruise to Mystic,

Connecticut, for the annual meeting of the Catboat Association in 1975. The hull was stripped and refastened with bronze screws. Wherever an old iron fastening left its tell-tale rusty streak, it was removed, a task that accounted for the majority, but not all, of the old nails. The garboard planks were reset and caulked. Numerous frames were sistered and new floorboards, king plank, decks, and a variety of other parts were renewed. The Palmer engine, based on an International Harvester block, was shipped to the nearest dealer, where the needed work was performed by a man who had spent much of his working life devoted to exactly the same model.

By the winter of 1975, the old Crosby was in good enough condition that Bob felt confident in undertaking the trip. He described what became an alarming sail from Shark River Inlet to the East River in a 20-knot winter wind gusting to 27 knots. A problem developed with the reefed sail, which was slowly but steadily threatening to tear out its reef points. This problem was compounded when a line trailing astern in an effort to slow the boat, which at times was exceeding 10 knots in big seas, became fouled in both the propeller and centerboard trunk. That was bad news. Writing his thoughts of the trip, Bob noted: "We are being tossed about so violently that the boat is like a kernel of corn in a giant popcorn machine. The ocean does everything except turn us turtle." Years later, he would remember that the 25-degree temperature they experienced at day's end "seemed like the tropics."

Do-Me and her crew eventually made it safely to Mystic and back, and Bob kept the boat for several more years until selling her to Arthur Bloomer in Chatham, Massachusetts. Arthur, whose father, grandfather, and great- grandfather had all fished out of catboats, named the boat *Genevieve* after his

mother. He continued the effort to keep after her many needs. "I had an old boat carpenter to help," he said. "I once told him that when he stopped working, I'd have to sell the boat. It was, for me, a losing battle. When the carpenter passed away, it was time to sell *Genevieve*."

The man who bought her, in 1990, was Bob Luckraft. "I had a 1910 Charles Crosby-built 20-footer," says Bob, "but the centerboard had been removed and there was concrete ballast in the bilge that was a potential problem for the wood. I also wanted a larger boat."

At the time that Bob Luckraft bought *Genevieve*, he believed he was purchasing a boat in need of extensive upgrading. But when he began seriously poking around inside *Genevieve*'s roomy hull in the late fall of 1990, he got some bad surprises. What he could see of the boat's frames had looked good, but when he removed some planks, he learned that just the opposite was true. "The frames were gutted," he remembers, "grooved from being burned by the old iron fasteners. What's more, the boat had been kept by the steel fish pier in Chatham with steel fishing boats nearby often with their engines running, so further electrolysis was at work."

Luckraft sat for several hours staring at his boat's frames and confronting the true nature of the work ahead of him. Still, he had grown up with wooden boats and admits to enjoying working on them as much as sailing them. Gradually, he formed a plan for a two-year rebuild. He began by replacing every frame from the stem to behind the centerboard trunk. He did this three or four frames at a time to assist in keeping the hull's shape. The frames were laminated, each 11/16" x 2" layer steamed and put into place inside the hull. After the new frame layers dried, they were removed, glued together with epoxy, and installed permanently. The hull's original clamp was never removed.

"During the waiting days, I would begin work on another bank of frames in another section of the boat," Bob said. "This way, workdays were full. I worked a minimum of one-week stints as it took too long to set up my workshop. Getting a rhythm going is the key."

He kept what he could of the old cypress and cedar planking, epoxying 1/2" bungs into the old fastener holes. The rest of the planks, including the sheer strake and the one beneath it were replaced. He built a new cabin top and covered it with Dynel fabric. The opening for the forward hatch, which was not original to the boat, was not built into the new cabin. Neither were handrails, which were not usually found on catboats. Instead, the halyards and topping lift serve as handholds. The new decks were covered with Xynol, the texture of which somewhat resembles canvas. He built new cabin sides from 18-inch wide oak planks and added a hanging locker down below.

In the cockpit, a new sole was installed. The vertical staving that is a signature feature of Crosby boats was replaced with mahogany staving with the same bead and width as the original. He built a new rudder of mahogany and bronze. He built a new mast of red spruce, which quickly rotted and was replaced by a 34-foot aluminum spar left over from Breck Marshall's aborted project to build a 26-foot catboat. But the mast is cleverly faux painted and looks, even close up, quite like wood.

The result of all this is a boat that has retained the shape and proportions of the original launched by the Crosbys so many years ago. In fact, Luckraft was able to retain the boat's original oak keel and stem, and the transom. "I believe," he said, "that I have kept her soul alive."

Genevieve has a deep and spacious cockpit, a comfortable cabin, and is properly rigged with deck-mounted halyard blocks so that raising and lowering the 536 sq.-ft. sail is easily done. Reefing pennants together with a good topping lift minimize the effort of reducing sail. She's a good sailer, too, and her seaworthiness has been proven time and again. As it happens, under her previous owner, she also became something of a tourist attraction. During the years Arthur Bloomer owned the boat and docked her at the Chatham fish pier, *Genevieve* became a focal point for tourists who, by the thousands, snapped her picture. But there was another photograph that was destined to be seen by the general public. Today, in his file on the boat, Bob Luckraft still has a copy of a tourism brochure published years ago by the state of Massachusetts. It includes the famous Chatham pier and the famous catboat. The fact that *Genevieve* was not painted in anything like the traditional colors used by the Crosbys, or any other catboat builder, doesn't seem to have counted against her.

"Well," said Bob Reddington, remembering the conditions of sale at the time that he sold the boat to Arthur Bloomer, "I had wooded the hull and primed it and was getting ready to paint it the traditional white. But then Arthur called and told me what color he wanted. So I went ahead and did it."

That is how *Genevieve,* perhaps the most photographed single Cape Cod catboat ever built, came to spend an important time of her life with a hull painted dark green.

CHAPTER ELEVEN

THE TIMELESS ALLURE OF THE CAPE COD CATBOAT

On a tranquil early autumn day in Maine, the 25-foot catboat Surprise *slips easily through calm waters.*

"Catboats with Committee Boat" by James E. Buttersworth. This 8" x 12" oil painting is important for its comparatively early depiction of the type of catboat used for racing in the New York area, probably between the late 1860s and mid-1870s. The vertical stem, very long rudder, and the shape of the committee boat's transom all suggest a rather early generation of New York-area catboats. The painting is in the collection of the Cahoon Museum of American Art in Cotuit, Massachusetts. More information can be found in Chapter Three.

Here is "catboat basin" at Nantucket circa 1900. A beautiful photograph of beautiful boats, this image shows the boats lined up and ready to take parties of summer visitors out for a sail. The graceful raking transoms and undehung rudders preferred on the island are clearly visible on the larger catboats. So is the method of rigging the mainsheet. The sheet belays to the boom and then runs to a single block on the traveler, up to a single block on the boom, and down to the cockpit.

Regarding Nantucket and its catboats, L. Francis Herreshoff wrote in The Compleat Cruiser: *"Before 1900 . . . catboats could be seen in every direction on Nantucket Sound, many sailing for pleasure or trolling for the bluefish that were then plentiful. While Nantucket may not have had as many cats as Edgartown, still there were several quite large ones here. I remember one that used to be kept down near the lighthouse that had a very striking design painted on her sail. It was the picture of a setting sun done in red and yellow and gave a Venetian effect."*

Here is the catboat Pinkletink *in the early 1960s when she was owned by John Leavens, founder of the Catboat Association. Built by Herbert F. Crosby in 1931 this 21-footer, originally named* Charlotte, *was restored in the late 1990s by Bill Sayle. John Leavens recorded for posterity every detail he could find regarding the boat's original specifications and construction. This, together with other information about* Pinkletink, *appears in Chapter Three.*

Big, beautiful, and able, Shoveller *is seen here running along in a light breeze. The 25' 2"* Shoveller *was built in Hilton, New York, by William Kaiser in 1975 according to Fenwick Williams plans. A catboat like this is just about as good as it gets when it comes to live-aboard spaciousness and seaworthiness.* Shoveller *has a 12 1/2-foot beam, displaces some 12,000 pounds, and has a 500 sq.-ft. sail. Now owned by Tom and Susan Maddigan, the strip-planked boat is powered by a Yanmar 3JH2E that produces 27 hp at 3,200 rpm. In the fall/winter of 2001, the Maddigans cruised* Shoveller *to Florida, following in the distant but still evocative wake of Henry Plummer's famous* Mascot.

Seen on these pages is Genevieve, *originally built by Herbert and Andrew Crosby in 1927 but most recently restored by Robert Luckraft, who sails and races the boat with much gusto. Surviving builder's plates, like the one shown here (a reproduction) are extremely rare.* Genevieve's *story is told in Chapter 10.*

Specifications of *Genevieve*

Length OA: 24' 9"
LWL: 24' 6"
Beam: 11' 10"
Draft: Board up/down: 2' 10"/5'
Mast length: 34'
Boom length: 26' 11"
Gaff length: 21' 6"
Sail area: 536 sq. ft.
Engine Type: Palmer - gasoline
HP: 22 with a 2:1 reduction gear
Propeller dia/pitch: 15.5" X 13"

Frames: White oak
Planking: Cypress and white cedar with mahogany garboards.
Decks: 1/2" marine plywood with Xynol cloth adhered with epoxy.
Cabin top: 1/2" marine plywood over 1/2" tongue and grove beaded mahogany covered with Dynel cloth adhered with epoxy.
Fastenings: Bronze
Spars: Faux-painted aluminum mast, spruce gaff and boom

This view of "Crosby Circle" in Osterville was photographed from Little Island, circa 1890s. From this location on North Bay, the various Crosby shops produced several thousand boats of various types, but they were best known for their catboats. Seen here are a lovely yacht-built model with overhanging stern and an elegant daysailer.

Vanity, *Oscar Pease at the wheel, sails in Osterville's West Bay in August, 1982. When this photograph was taken,* Vanity *was 54 years old but in immaculate condition thanks to the care and knowledge of her owner. This is the last photograph of* Vanity *as she originally appeared under sail during Oscar's lifetime. Offended by the increasing costs of mast stepping, Oscar simply stopped rigging the boat, and operated her solely under power. Now owned by the Martha's Vineyard Historical Society,* Vanity *has since been rebuilt and repainted. More details about* Vanity *and her owner appear in Chapter Two.*

Priming cup

Stationary electrode

Movable electrode

Removable
cylinder head

Drip-feed lubricator

JAMES W. LATHROP
MFGR. OF
Gas & Gasoline Engines
MYSTIC, CONN. U.S.A.

Muffler

Water pump

Grease cup

Flywheel

Shaft coupling

Base

Above: When Vanity was built in 1928, she was launched without a rig and
operated under the power of a two-cycle Lathrop marine engine. The Lathrop
shown here is an earlier (circa 1910) version of the model that would have
been installed in 1928 by the boat's builder, Manuel Swartz. In terms of operation and general appearance, however, the later model was similar. This
engine developed six horsepower at just 500 rpm. It was started by rocking the
heavy, cast-iron flywheel. With its low-tension, make-and-break ignition system instead of a high-tension coil and spark plug, an engine like this could
run even if soaking wet. Two-cycle, make-and-break engines could also run
equally well forward or backward, so fishermen almost never purchased an
engine equipped with a reverse gear.

Here is Surprise *sailing on the upper reaches of the New Meadows River in Maine. Built in 1971 to replicate a Wilton Crosby 25-footer launched in 1920,* Surprise *offers useful insights into both the history and impressive performance of a Crosby catboat.* Surprise *is owned by Jon and Roxane Agne. Her story appears in Chapter 10.*

Freyja was built by C. C. Hanley for George D. Follett of the Quincy Yacht Club in 1898 after Hanley had relocated to Quincy. The boat was 29 feet long and had a 10-foot beam. Freyja's superbly clean look and two forward-facing port lights, were typical of a Hanley catboat. Clearly designed with cruising in mind, Freyja has a comparatively large cabin and small cockpit. She appears to be rigged for practicality more than for racing, and her mast appears to be placed slightly farther aft of the stem than normal. A special fitting at the stem is used to mount the forestay (and the flag halyard). The stay is belayed to the mast with a special fitting, for Hanley generally disliked using a spreader, which he felt imposed unwanted stress.

Getting ready to race. One week against the New England Beetle Cat Association, being its annual regatta, the Herreshoff match championship, new to this yacht club in 2001, the race — named for the long-time builder of the boat — was sailed at Mattapoisett.

The Arey's Pond 14 is a modern, interpretation of a classic, daysailing cat-boat. The boat is available in wood or fiberglass construction.

Built of cold-molded construction to Winthrop Warner's Bob Cat design, Amelia was completed by her owner, Mark Harper, who sails the boat in New Jersey's shallow coastal bays.

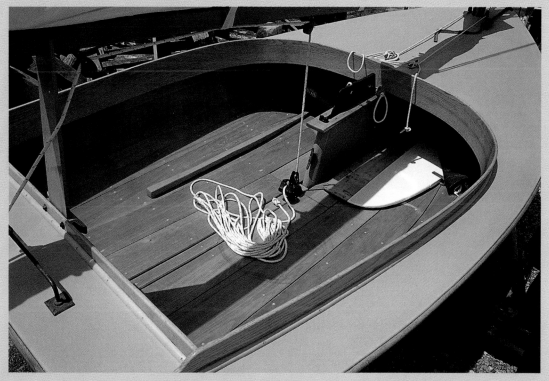

Is that wood or fiberglass? The cockpit of the Barnstable Catboat, a faithful fiberglass replica of the Beetle Cat, is cedar-sheathed.

Although best-known for his larger boats, S. S. Crocker also designed a little catboat called Dog Watch *shortly after World War Two. The original was built for a Crocker enthusiast in Hartford, Connecticut, by the Calderwood Yacht Yard in Manchester, Massachusetts. The boat was 16' x 7' 6" x 1' 8" and carried a 169 sq. ft. sail. This more recent version was equipped with a longer bowsprit than Crocker's original, and a jib.*

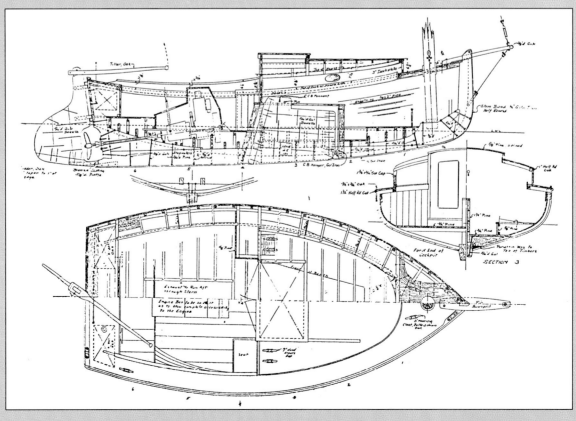

WHERE HAVE ALL THE CATBOATS GONE?

—— ·◆· ——

OF ALL THE THOUSANDS of Cape Cod catboats that were ever built, not a single one was ever preserved in its original form in a museum or elsewhere. To make an automotive analogy, this is comparable, on the one hand, to the disappearance of every factory correct Ford Model T ever built and, on the other, to the loss of every Duesenberg. From the workaday models and cruising yachts to the artworks of C. C. Hanley, no catboat has come down to us intact and as she left the builder's yard. The result has been that construction methods and materials have come perilously close to being totally lost to both historians and present-day builders. So have adequate details relating to spars, hardware, rigging, sails, engine and accessory installation, fishing gear, and paint colors. Were it not for lines drawings made at a later date from pre-existing hulls or models, there also would be rather little on paper relating to design. Some half-models, at least, remain, although giving a specific model a precise date is not always possible.

The idea of preserving for future generations a Cape Cod catboat in its original form is probably something that occurred to almost nobody who built or owned one. They were too busy working them or just sailing them. On the one occasion that an effort was made to save a Rhode Island-built boat, it didn't work out as it should have. This attempt involved the Herreshoffs and Henry Ford, whose Greenfield Village and museum were becoming, by the 1930s, a fascinat-

ing repository of Americana. Ford collected everything from kitchen stoves and automobiles to locomotives and buildings, including the Wright Brothers' bicycle shop. An authentic Cape Cod catboat would have been of enormous importance. As it happened, however, it was a Rhode Island boat that wound up on the Museum's immense parquet floor. When the Herreshoffs sent their old *Sprite* to Dearborn in 1930, she was probably in much the same condition as when she'd been built some 70 years earlier. Unfortunately, posterity's last sight of *Sprite* in original form remains a photograph of the old catboat on a truck as she was leaving Bristol. Marine preservation was not then at an advanced enough state to save the boat from insensitive treatment.

The fact is, of course, that catboats were perishable to begin with. Their wooden keels, frames, planks, floors, ceilings, centerboards, rudders, and their iron fastenings never would have had an indefinite life. What's more, the boats were always subject to accidents, not to mention the periodic need to replace rotted or damaged components. Even one such replacement could easily mask the original builder's method or the designer's intent.

Outright modification was also a threat. Sometimes, a new owner would enlarge a cabin while another might reduce it. It was not unusual for an open boat to have a small cuddy added. Installation of an engine was usually accompanied by changes to the centerboard and rig. Cockpit floors were sometimes raised so the cockpit would be self-bailing. Owners made changes to cabin interiors according to their own tastes and changing needs. Eventually, many boats bore little similarity to the form in which they had left the builder's yard.

The closest thing resembling an opportunity to enshrine an original working catboat came when Oscar Pease left *Vanity* and all her gear to the Martha's Vineyard Historical Society. There, however, the decision was made to keep the boat sailing, which meant a complete reconstruction followed by painting in colors different from those used on the boat for decades. Even *Vanity*, of course, was not the same when her owner passed away as when she was built. Many frames had been renewed, and the original Lathrop one-cylinder, two-cycle engine had been replaced decades earlier by a more modern, four-cylinder, four-cycle model. She was by any measure, however, still the real thing and the last of all her kind.

In 1969 Mystic Seaport took a different approach to the question of preserving a reasonably original catboat. Rather than rebuild the boat to a seaworthy state, the decision was made to restore a Wilton Crosby catboat named *Frances* that had been donated to the museum. This boat was painstakingly brought back to life as an indoor exhibit. As much of her original wood as possible was retained, which meant that all new oak frames were steam-bent into place but that the original and still sound 3/4" cypress planking was reused. This time, however, the planking was fastened with bronze screws rather than the original iron boat nails that had, in many cases, simply disappeared.

One of the more recent efforts at catboat preservation involved a most interesting old boat that had been built by Frederick J. Dunn in Monument Beach, Massachusetts, in 1888. Like so many builders of his era, Frederick Dunn is little known today. He was, however, highly regarded in his own time, which is why William Phinney chose to apprentice with him at his yard on Little Bay. In 1964, boatbuilder Merton

Long told John Leavens that "Dunn was a very good builder. His boats sailed well and lasted to be old. I myself had one of them named *Wild Cat* built in 1888 that went to pieces in the 1944 hurricane. She was fast in a three- or four-reef breeze and a good all-around boat."

Discovered under a rotting tarp in a field in Wareham, this particular Dunn-built catboat, originally named *Daisy* was in poor condition. Yet, her full, canoe-shaped bow, raking transom, extreme deadrise, and incredibly fine tumblehome stern sections were clearly the marks of an authentic, 19th-century catboat crafted by a man who had developed his own style. This boat was acquired by the International Yacht Restoration School (IYRS) in Newport, Rhode Island. There, a full assessment was made of what would be needed to save what was almost certainly the only surviving Dunn-built boat, and an example of just the sort of elegant craft that was a staple of Buzzards Bay yacht racing for some two decades. Close examination revealed how much Dunn's boat had been altered since he'd built her. After she was sold by her original owner in the 1930s, her centerboard was removed and the boat converted to a motor launch. Originally an open cockpit boat with a sliding hatch on the foredeck, *Daisy* — now renamed *Hester* — was modified to include a small cuddy cabin. What's more, by the time the old boat arrived in Newport, her old iron fastenings had rusted away. The pine of which she had largely been built was past saving. There was no rig. What remained, however, was the hull's intact shape, and three important photographs, one of which appears in Chapter Three.

"It all hinged on the photographs," said Clark Poston, of the IYRS. "They showed what the boat had looked like and enabled us to scale the dimensions of the spars. Throughout the project, the goal was to replace like for like." The photographs Poston referred to had been taken a century earlier by the great marine photographer Nathaniel Stebbins. That they still existed in the collection of the Society for the Preservation of New England Antiquities, together with photos of another Dunn-built catboat, made Poston's detective work considerably easier.

What remains of the original *Daisy*'s wood are some ceiling pieces and her unique hackmatack quarter knees. In some areas, such as the boat's deck construction with wide oak planks reinforcing the boat from king plank to cockpit to transom, and the sheer strakes, Dunn's original construction details were replicated. In other parts of the boat, however, Dunn's impressive techniques had been lost to modification. Perhaps the most important aspect of the whole project was simply the fact that a boat is now sailing that looks pretty much exactly like the original built over a century earlier. Although fitted with a Dacron rather than cotton sail, *Daisy* allows a later generation of enthusiasts to sail back in time and experience for themselves the qualities of an elegant boat.

One logical result of the absence of a serviceable, original catboat (or even a much-deteriorated one like *Daisy*) is the occasional effort to recreate one. But this is neither simple nor straightforward. The most recent example of such a boat was built and launched at Mystic Seaport and named after the man most responsible for the resurgence in the catboat's popularity, Breck Marshall. Although lines existed both in Chapelle and elsewhere for classic, barndoor rudder models that were definitely Crosby, the design selected for reproduction was based on a 20-foot boat from Nantucket which, as Barry Thomas noted in his book about the project, was "said to be Crosby built." (The Seaport was interested in a smaller model than those for which lines existed. In fact, *Breck Marshall* was built without rubrails because their installation inside the shop would have made the boat too wide for removal.)

The chosen boat was assumed to have been built by Charles Crosby about 1900, but its history, when explored by Townsend Hornor on behalf of the Seaport, could really be documented only beginning a half century later. Significant work involving replacement of frames and other parts had been carried out

in 1955 and a more extensive rebuild was done in the period 1976–1978. If nothing else, such work indicates the devotion occasionally bestowed on boats that, if they possessed lesser charms, would have been broken up.

As it happened, Thomas and his colleagues, while interested in the authenticity of the design, were most especially interested in trying to recreate the Crosby methods of construction. "My concern," remembered Thomas, "was duplicating the way the boat was built. I cared about construction — how the men did it."

By the time that work on the *Breck Marshall* was ready to begin, the crew at Mystic was forced to confront the reality that most details of how the Crosbys had actually built their famous catboats were lost. Using a rare "keel and setting-up plan" that had been drawn by Ralph Crosby, a Winfield Thompson article and some photos covering some basic construction techniques, and the memory of Horace Manley Crosby, Jr., who had retired in 1978 but still recalled some details of shop methods during the years 1924-1931, the *Breck Marshall* was constructed.

"I started under the impression the Crosby catboat was clunky," said Thomas. "I learned it was a marvel of engineering."

There is no telling whether the boat's rig was anything like the original. A new rig was picked from sail plans still in the files at Osterville. While the boom is mounted on a pedestal as the original's probably was, the method of attaching the sail to boom and gaff by lace line probably differs from the original method. The resulting vessel, however, used to sail parties on the Mystic River has given thousands of visitors to the Seaport some insight into what a 19th-century Crosby catboat was like. Meanwhile, the idea of actually recreating a classic, barndoor rudder Crosby catboat that is perfect in conception, construction, detail, and equipment, remains a tantalizing challenge.

PRACTICAL MATTERS

——— •◆• ———

CATBOATS CONTINUE to attract new enthusiasts, some of whom have little or no sailing experience, while others are experienced sailors but have had no exposure to catboats. This brief section is intended to answer a few of the more common questions that routinely arise regarding the boats.

Q. Is a catboat right for me?

A. Some years ago, at a seminar on catboat sailing, having listened to the many questions people posed about their boats and how best to sail them, an observer asked: "If there's so much special knowledge involved and so much new to be learned, why not just sail a sloop?" This is a valid remark. The fact is that unless a sailor sees a benefit in stepping outside the mainstream sailing world, the one presented in four-color ads in boating magazines, and at boat shows, one of the many popular modern sloops does make the most sense. Likewise, for those whose sailing involves the open ocean, a catboat should not be the boat of choice. "How well does a catboat tack in big waves when triple-reefed?" "What happens to a catboat in a knockdown?" If answers to these questions are key to a decision on a catboat, look elsewhere.

Q. Why buy a catboat?

A. Aside from their often very pleasing appearance, and their attraction as traditional boats that represent something important about the past, catboats offer several practical benefits. Their shoal draft makes it possible to access whole areas one could not otherwise explore. Their wide beam makes them among the roomiest

boats for their size available. Their minimal standing rigging, simple running rigging, and absence of winches makes them comparatively easy to rig, sail, and maintain. The existence in many locales of fleets, or at least several other catboats, ensures camaraderie, and the opportunity to take part in races and other activities.

Q. What's the topping lift for?

A. The topping lift is an important piece of rigging on a catboat. It supports the boom once it has been removed from the boom crutch and before the sail is raised or lowered. It is taken up to support the boom during reefing. It can also be used to raise the boom when, on a reach or run, the boom end is in danger of dipping into the seas. Finally, when sailing downwind, the topping lift can be used to raise the boom when the peak and throat halyard are eased to increase the sail's draft. It can also be taken up when the peak is dropped to spill wind.

Q. What should I look for when inspecting a used fiberglass catboat?

A. Everything! With that in mind, remember that the realities of boat buying often make it difficult to really inspect every piece of the boat. Has the mainsheet been replaced and, if so, is it the proper length? That's something that may neither occur to a buyer or be readily available for checking.

Unless you, or a sailmaker, can spread the sail out and check it for patches, the condition of seams, and so forth, you won't know its true condition. If you can sail the boat, and are unable to remove wrinkles along the foot and head of the sail, it's probably stretched somewhat.

If there is mildew in the cabin, the boat may have a leak in addition to needing improved ventilation.

Is the fiberglass sound? A good surveyor should be able to determine whether there are areas of delamination. Rudders and centerboards should be checked to see that water has not entered the laminate because of wear or groundings.

Check the condition of the rigging. Both throat and peak halyards are subject to wear in areas where they ride on the blocks when the sail is raised. If replacement is necessary, you may need to call the builder to get the length and diameter of the line. Although it's not traditional, braided line offers reduced stretch versus three-strand and is worth consideration.

Can the centerboard pennant be inspected for wear? If the owner hasn't regularly inspected this critical line, keep in mind that replacing it needs to be done with the boat hauled.

Was the inboard engine factory-installed? What about the fuel tank?

If the answer to either question is "No," the installation should be checked extra carefully to ensure that a professional job has been done. The fuel line should be routed in such a manner that neither a bulkhead nor anything else can pinch it. Engine cooling hoses and the exhaust system should be neatly installed and in good condition. The exhaust manifold should be, if possible, checked for clogging from scale and carbon. Older engines, particularly gasoline engines, should be checked to see that cooling performance is up to par, as passages and tight bends in system plumbing can be troublesome.

What sort of fuel filter has been installed? Factory-installed filters may be smaller than is really needed. A large Racor fuel-water separator should definitely be in the budget if the boat is not already so equipped.

Both the cutless bearing and the shaft should be checked for wear. A good mechanic can suggest whether there is reason to believe that the bearing or

shaft might require replacement. Excessive play, more than about 1/16" warrants some caution.

Q. Which is better, a two-blade or three-blade propeller?
A. There's a two-part answer to this question. Part one is personal preference. A two-blade propeller can be lined up behind the skeg when sailing and thus detract less from speed than a three-blade. Particularly for racers, that can be important. A three-blade offers especially good thrust and would normally be the choice for those who do any cruising. However, the question may be complicated by the fact that some popular boats have apertures that are on the small side. That means that it may not be possible to install the ideal diameter two-blade propeller.

Q. How fast should I run my diesel engine?
A. The answer to this question often seems to depend on the opinion of the mechanic or engine expert one talks with. A couple of points should, however, be understood. First, a diesel engine is engineered to run at its governed rpm for prolonged periods. "Governed rpm" is the speed at which fuel flow begins to automatically be reduced by the governor. It is expressly designed to prevent the engine from being damaged by over-revving. One should not hesitate to run the engine at maximum rpm or close to it.

Q. How do I know if I'm getting the best performance out of my engine?
A. By checking your tachometer and relating the engine speeds you can achieve according to the engine's performance curves. An engine's power output is graphically depicted by its performance curve charts. A glance at these charts in sales literature or a service manual will reveal how much horsepower and torque is produced at different rpm. The chart for the Yanmar 2GM shows that the engine's 16-hp output is achieved at 3,400 rpm and fuel is cut off completely at 3,600 rpm (18 hp). Peak torque is reached at about

2,400 rpm and continues to about 3,200 rpm after which it declines somewhat. Unless the engine is propped to permit reaching these speeds, or something close, it will be unable to deliver its peak performance. A propeller shop should be consulted regarding the ideal prop for a given boat. Keep in mind that a certain amount of art may be involved in addition to the theoretical side of selection.

Q. What's the purpose of the reduction gear on the engine?
A. The reduction gear reduces the speed at which the propeller turns and permits a larger diameter, more efficient propeller to be fitted. The reduction gear ratio — usually about 2.3:1 - 2.6:1 — defines the change in propeller rpm vs. engine rpm. On a 2:1 gear, at 2,000 engine rpm, the propeller rpm would be reduced to 1,000 rpm.

Q. What anchor is best?
A. There is no one answer to this question. Most sailors, as they gain experience, and anchor in different bottoms, develop a preference. Danforths and CQRs tend to predominate, with Danforth lookalikes, a Bruce, and even the occasional yachtsman style being carried. Danforths are very difficult to set in some bottoms, especially if grass is present. The holding power of each type in different bottoms varies widely. So does an anchor's ability to reset should it drag. *Practical Sailor* magazine has done several interesting anchor tests. A 22- pound Spade anchor with some 20 feet of chain is an excellent choice for a 22-foot catboat. The anchor sets quickly in various bottoms and has no moving parts. Those planning to anchor overnight and do any cruising should carry two or even three anchors of various types and weights, and have the ability to deploy at least two of them. Note that 150 feet of anchor rode, marked with tags every six feet, is not too much.

Q. What can I do to make my sail come down more readily?

A. Waxing the mast with a hard finish wax may, or may not, reduce friction enough to help matters. A common fix is to reduce the diameter of the halyards, but this results in line that is less comfortable to handle and more prone to stretch than correctly sized line. Instead, check that all blocks are in good condition. There should be no friction. If in any doubt, consider replacing blocks with ball-bearing types. If this doesn't help, check to see whether the topping lift block is exerting too much pressure on the mast hoops. If it is, relocate it from the mast to the deck or else add a large enough spacer on the mast to keep the lift from interfering. The peak and throat halyard blocks may also benefit from the same treatment. In most cases, these changes should work and eliminate the need to rig a downhaul attached to the gaff, which should be a last resort. It's also possible that simply controlling the angle at which the gaff is lowered can do much to solve the problem.

Q. What makes a good, simple winter cover?
A. There's surprisingly little in the way of published material on this topic. Assuming one doesn't pay someone to shrink-wrap the boat, either a canvas tarp or one of the blue or green poly tarps can be used. The canvas tarp, while it costs more initially, will last for years and presents a not too offensive appearance. The tarp should be wide enough to cover at least the rubrails when the ridge pole is in place.

A simple but serviceable frame can be made that consists of three 4" x 4" uprights. These include: 1) a bow upright cut at the bottom to fit the mast step and with a slot at the top to accept the ridgepole 2) a cockpit support mounted on a horizontal board to spread loads and slotted for the ridgepole 3) an upright mounted at the stern and slotted to accept the ridge pole.

The ridgepole can be made of two pieces of 2"x 4" lumber, each somewhat longer than half the boat's length. The halves are joined by bolts through overlapping plywood side plates. Finally, the slats on either side of the ridgepole can be cut from 1" x 2" or other appropriately sized lumber and joined with carpet.

Five or six slats on either side generally suffice. Carpet remnants should be used to protect coamings and grabrails against abrasion. Of course, given the budget and the inclination, a more elaborate frame and tailored cover can be fitted.

Q. What size jackstands do I need for my catboat?
A. Most 18- to 24-foot catboats will need a small jackstand suitable to a motorboat of this size or other small sailboats. Check with the maker of the jackstands you are considering, your boat hauler, or the builder.

Q. Should I spend the money for a sail cover?
A. A good sailcover protects the sail from sunlight and provides additional protection from high winds. If a functional sail cover did not come with the boat, it is usually wise to have it made locally by someone who can take measurements directly from your specific boat. This will permit accurate location of openings for halyard attachments and topping lift, and help ensure that the sail cover is long and deep enough to properly fit your rig.

Q. What's that stick I see on the rudder?
A. The rudder stick's purpose is to keep the rudder in place when the boat is moored or anchored. This reduces wear on the steering gear, pintles and gudgeons and eliminates the noise of the rudder working back and forth, which would be disturbing when staying aboard.

Q. Is it true that catboats are slow and don't go to windward very well?
A. It's hard to give a general answer to a general question, especially one that is based on hearsay. A glib answer is that one doesn't buy a comfortable sedan to race against two-seat sports cars. In real-world terms, consider the following. An effort to combine Beetle Cat racers with Herreshoff 12 1/2-footers failed to work out because the Beetles outperformed the other boat. If one compares the performance of a Marshall 18 with that of a Cape Dory Typhoon, a comparably sized keel sloop, the Marshall will be found to be the much faster boat. If a Hermann/Cape Cod Cat or Marshall were to sail against a Catalina 22, the catboats would acquit themselves well. If you left Nantucket for Hyannis in a Marshall 22 at the same time as a comparably equipped cruising sloop of 22 - 25 feet (or even larger), chances are excellent that the Marshall would reach the destination ahead of the other boat and with a dryer crew. If you sailed to a windward mark in a Marshall 22 against a J24, the J-boat would get there ahead of you.

Q. How practical is a catboat to trailer?
A. This is something for each owner to determine. The introduction of tabernacle masts has certainly made the process more practical, no matter what the size of the boat. Trailering a 12- to 15-foot catboat is comparatively straightforward. The 17- and 18-footers can also be trailered but weights of 2,200 pounds or more suggest that a rear-wheel-drive vehicle may well be desirable. Remember that trailering with a front-drive car reduces the drive-wheels' traction as weight is transferred to the rear. In all cases, a well-maintained trailer and a spare tire are prerequisites.

Q. Are catboats safe even though they don't have a keel?
A. Most sailors find catboats to be stable and forgiving. The boats' weather helm means that they tend to be forced up into the wind when carrying too much sail, a natural safety factor. Weather helm also means the boat is unlikely to sail away should one fall overboard. Also, the steps often fitted to the rudder and transom of larger boats make it relatively easy to climb back on board many models. The higher the hull, however, the more difficult this can be. Perhaps the item that requires the most watchfulness is the mainsheet on outboard-equipped boats. Vigilance is necessary whenever changing tacks. In very windy conditions, the motor can be lowered and a canvas cover installed to protect its various protruding components. Finally, catboats don't lend themselves to stanchions and lifelines like more modern boats. This may be a consideration for the less mobile.

INDEX

—◆—